INDIA

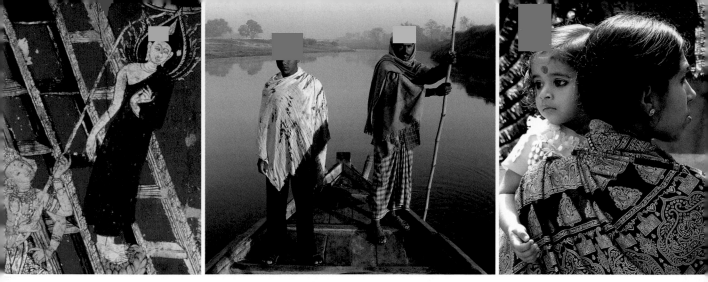

Michael Wood
INDIA

BASIC
B
BOOKS

A Member of the Perseus Books Group
New York

Introduction **6**

TAJIKISTAN

AFGHANISTAN

KĀBUL

HINDU KUSH

K2 8611m ▲ (claimed by India)

KARAKORAM RANGE

AKSAI CHIN (administered by China, claimed by India)

CHINA

Peshāwar

ISLĀMĀBĀD

Srinagar

Rāwalpindi

DEMCHOK (administered by China, claimed by India)

Chenab

Gujrānwala

Lahore

Amritsar

HIMALAYAS

Faisalābād

Multān

Quetta

Sutlej

Ludhiāna

PAKISTAN

(Much of this area is claimed by China)

Indus

Delhi

Meerut

NEPAL

Mt Everest 8850m ▲

Shikārpur

THAR DESERT

NEW DELHI

Ghāziābād

KATHMANDU

THIMPHU BHUTAN

Sukkur

Jaipur

Āgra

Yamuna

Ganges

Lucknow

Ghāghara

Guwāhāti

Brahmaputra

Hyderābād

Kanpur

Imphāl

Karāchi

Chambal

Allahābād

Vārānasi

Patna

Ganges

BANGLADESH

Bodh Gaya

Tropic of Cancer

RANN OF KACHCHH

Ahmadābād

VINDHYA RANGE

Bhopāl

Jabalpur

Rānchi

Rajshahi

DHAKA

Khulna

BURMA (MYANMAR)

Gulf of Kachchh

Rājkot

Vadodara

Indore

Narmada

INDIA

Jamshedpur

Hāora

Kolkata

Chittagong

NAYPYIDAW

Gulf of Khambāt

Sūrat

Nāshik

Nāgpur

Bhubaneshwar

Mouths of the Ganges

Arabian Sea

Kalyān

Aurangābād

DECCAN

Mumbai

Pune

Bay of Bengal

Solāpur

Hyderābād

Godāvari

Visākhapatnam

WESTERN GHATS

Hubli

Krishna

Vijayawāda

EASTERN GHATS

Andaman Islands (to India)

Malabar Coast

Bangalore

Chennai

Coromandel Coast

Andaman Sea

Mysore

TAMIL NADU

Laccadive Islands

Coimbatore

KERALA

Madurai

Palk Strait

Kochi

Jaffna

Trincomolee

Nicobar Islands (to India)

Gulf of Mannar

SRI LANKA

Negombo

Kandy

COLOMBO

Galle

INDIAN OCEAN

0   miles   400

0   km   400

Introduction

THIS BOOK HAS COME OUT of a long attachment to India – an attachment filled with deep respect and admiration, but most of all love for India and its cultures. I have made twenty or thirty journeys to the subcontinent during the last three decades, and feel that in some ways my life has become enmeshed with India. Those journeys have so often made me think what a great privilege it is to be welcomed into another culture and to spend time in it, especially one so rich and diverse and perennially illuminating. My wife and I fell in love in India and were married there; our children have Indian names. We have travelled together in India as a family, and some of our most vivid memories are associated with the children when they were young: celebrating Pongal, the spring festival in the traditional household of Tamil friends; travelling the south by local bus to visit the old shrines of the Cavery delta; or, most memorably perhaps, staying with friends in a tent in the middle of the *Kumbh Mela* of 2001, the greatest human gathering on Earth – not to mention escaping afterwards to semolina pudding and fruit cake at our favourite little Parsee hotel in Allahabad.

But this is also a book by a historian. I have been travelling the world for forty years, most of that time working as a historian, writing books and making films, nearly a hundred of them, on travel, history and adventure (sometimes, as when we followed in the steps of Alexander over the Hindu Kush, all three

OPPOSITE

The ramlilas, *the Rama play cycle at Benares, is performed over thirty days each October. Known all over north India, these folk plays reached their present form in the cultural resistance to British rule in the 19th century.*

at once). I have filmed with traditional civilizations in the Americas and Africa, in the great Old World civilizations of Iraq, Egypt, Iran and China, and have been lucky enough to see at first hand the incredible beauty, richness and diversity of human life on Earth. If there is a uniting theme in these experiences, it is the continuance of the past in our present. It is almost a truism that we live in a time when human identities – civilizations, cultures, tribes, individuals – are being erased everywhere across the globe; identities built up often over thousands of years and lost in just a few generations. When you travel you see, no less than with the environment, landscapes, climates and species, that modernity and globalization are rubbing out human differences too, the intricate web of languages, customs, music and stories that makes us who we are. We may be the last generation to see many of these things still alive. But it seems to me that nowhere on Earth can you find all human histories, from the Stone Age to the global village, still thriving, as you can in India. And that is the big story told in this book.

India became a free nation only sixty years ago, but in a real sense it has existed for thousands of years. The story of India is a tale of incredible drama, great inventions, enormous diversity, phenomenal creativity and the very biggest ideas. But it is also the history of one of the world's emerging powers. Today the population of the subcontinent as a whole – India, Pakistan and Bangladesh – is currently 1.5 billion, more than a fifth of all the world's people, and India itself will soon overtake China as the world's most populous country. India has twenty-two official languages (including English), and 400 smaller tongues and dialects: as a medieval Indian writer noted proudly, 'the people of Asia, the Mongols, the Turks and the Arabs get tongue-tied speaking our Indian languages, but we Indians can speak any language of the world as easily as a shepherd tends his sheep'. India, no doubt, has always been polylingual. It has also always been pluralist: its great regional cultures are civilizations in themselves (Tamil alone, to give one example, has a literature going back to the third century BC – richer and older than that of most western European nations). And that pluralism and diversity imbue everything from large to small. Indian society is made up of nearly 5000 castes and communities, each with its own rules, customs and stories. India gave birth to four world religions, and, along with its legendary 33 million gods, has a bewildering plethora of sects and subsects. It is also the second largest Muslim country on Earth, and the subcontinent as a whole has half of all Muslims in the world. India welcomed Christianity long before Europe embraced it, and has welcomed adherents of many other faiths, including Jews and Parsees (the Zoroastrians of Iran), as refugees from persecution.

And now, as the brief hegemony of the West is coming to an end, India, with all this amazing diversity, is rising again. Historical economists conjecture that India's GDP was the largest in the world until around 1500, when it was overtaken by China, only for both to be eclipsed in the age of the European empires when the centre of history shifted away from the landmass of Asia to the western European seaboard, transformed by the wealth of the New World. By 1900 both China and India had sunk to generating a tiny percentage of the world's wealth (in India's case, less than 3 per cent). For the first forty-five years after Independence in 1947, the Indian government followed a protectionist policy, loyal to the ideals of its founders, liberal socialists, but also Gandhians, espousing self-sufficiency, non-alignment and non-violence. Only in the last fifteen years has India followed China's lead in terms of growth. The chief factor in today's global world is sheer population, but mastery of information technology, skill in mathematics, and technical and linguistic skills are all playing their part, along with the widespread use of English as a lingua franca, and the size, spread and influence of the Indian diaspora. Leading financial analysts now predict that on present trends India's GDP will overtake that of the USA in the late 2030s. The twenty-first century, then, is seeing the history of the great ancient civilizations of Asia return to centre stage.

India's modern transformation started later than China's, and without the massive state-directed focus of that country. India also faces many problems, especially with social inequalities, rural poverty, overpopulation and environmental degradation. But India has immense advantages. It is an open society and a vibrant democracy, with formidable practical and language skills, and, as a civilization that has attempted to be pluralist and tolerant over a vast period of time, can draw on huge cultural resources from its past. The age-old life goals of Indian civilization – *artha* (worldly wealth and success), *kama* (pleasure and love), *dharma* (virtue) and *moksha* (knowledge and liberation) – are still major forces in people's lives, rich and poor, and, it seems to me, will be for the foreseeable future. Despite difficulties and setbacks, the establishment and acceptance of a dynamic working democracy has been a remarkable achievement over last sixty years: and it is a democracy that has many things to teach us all.

This book is a traveller's-eye view of the history of India, a brief and selective account of the country from the deep past to the present, highlighting some of the key moments and key themes in its story. Inevitably, it is only an introduction: the history of India is so vast, so rich and complex, that to contain even its outline in one volume is barely possible. Working there intensively over the last eighteen months has been a wonderful experience, seeing something of the latest exciting phase of India's amazing story; and on a personal level, I can only express my profound gratitude to all the people who gave us their time and their knowledge on the way. I leave the last word to the fourteenth-century Indian poet Amir Khusro: he was a Muslim, he wrote in Persian, and his ancestry was Turkic, but he counted himself the luckiest man alive to have been born in India, and to have India as his motherland.

> How exhilarating is the atmosphere of India!
> There cannot be a better teacher than the way of life of its people.
> If any foreigner comes by, he will have to ask for nothing
> Because they treat him as their own,
> Play an excellent host and win his heart,
> And show him how to smile like a flower.

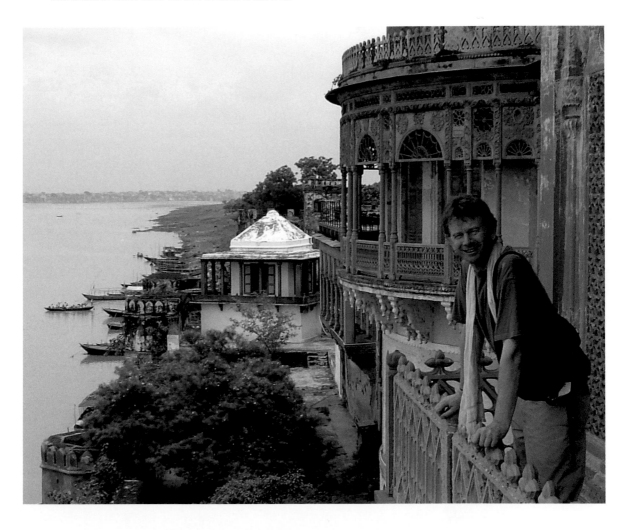

1
Origins and Identity

THE RAIN HAS STOPPED, and the canopy of palms on the steep slope behind the house is drenched and dripping; dark green fronds glisten in the last light. Outside my room I can hear the roar of the undertow and the crash of breakers along the reef at the mouth of the bay. On the beach towards the lighthouse, knots of people are strung along the edge of the water watching the sunset. The monsoon sky is clearing now, and a golden light is spreading over the Arabian Sea. I'm standing on the balcony of a lodging house on the Kerala coast near the southern tip of India. On the table are maps, guidebooks, a traveller's clutter. In the last few days we've come south down the coast from Calicut, through Cranganore and Cochin, along palm-fringed beaches under the red cliffs of Varkala, down the narrow strip between the sea and the forested foothills of the Western Ghats, the spine of India. A tourist resort like this might seem an unlikely place to begin a tale about the great migrations of the past, but this was the route taken by the first humans out of Africa perhaps 80,000 years ago: it's the first journey in Indian history.

Beachcombers

They were beachcombers, making their way barefoot down India's long, surf-beaten shores, driven as human beings always have been by chance and necessity. But also, surely, by curiosity, that most human of qualities. In only a few thousand years they skirted the Indian Ocean from the Horn of Africa to Cape Comorin on India's southern tip, and on to the Andamans, Indonesia and Australasia. Sea levels then were lower: the pale blue shelf around India that can be seen so clearly from space is the old shoreline, lost 20,000 years ago when the sea began to rise. Back then there was a land bridge to Sri Lanka, and North and South Andaman were all one island, but right around the Indian Ocean the beachcombers' modern descendants have picked up faint traces of their ancestors' passage. Even now, small pockets of aboriginal peoples still survive around its shores. Opposite the Horn of Africa, humankind's first crossing-point out of the continent, the white beaches of Yemen, strewn with crimson coral, were their first stopping places. Along this coast their campsites have yielded Middle Palaeolithic tools, similar to those from the African Middle Stone Age. Across the Persian Gulf, on the coast of Pakistan too, in one of the most inhospitable landscapes on Earth, are the Makran people, who also have a very ancient strand in their DNA. (They were probably the nomadic population described by Alexander's Greeks in the fourth century BC as ichthyophagoi, or fish eaters, the most primitive people the Greeks met on the whole of their journey.)

Continuing around the ocean shore, in the forested hills of southern India, relatively undisturbed till the modern world, are pockets of tribal peoples who may also be descended from those very first beachcombers who came out of Africa. Long before the modern breakthrough with the Human Genome Project, their cultures and their African appearance had marked them out from the people surrounding them. British district gazetteers recorded their names: the Kadar, Paniyan and Korava, the Yanadi Irula, Gadaba and Chenchu. Older than the Dravidian speakers around them, they remain distinct, self-contained, outside the caste system of Hindu India.

Over the hills in Tamil Nadu I have arranged to meet Professor Pitchappan, a geneticist from Madurai University. He's made an extraordinary discovery working among the Kallar tribal people here. He's found traces of the ancestral mitochondrial DNA and Y chromosomes from the earliest genetic heritage of India. By chance, his team tested a man called Virumandi and discovered that he carries the M130 gene from the first wave of migrations of modern humans out of Africa. To their surprise, they subsequently discovered that Virumandi's whole village has M130 – carried down by isolation, by the strictures of the caste system, and by endogamy: the Kallar practice of first cousin marriage, the oldest and most characteristic form of kin marriage in southern India.

'There were at least two early waves of migration,' Professor Pitchappan tells me. 'We think spoken language only developed later – maybe only 10,000 or 15,000 years ago. Language, of course, is not the same as ethnicity. Language is easily adopted. And the same is true with religion too. Compared with custom, kin relations and so on, it's a surface layer, just a belief system: you believe in your system, your gods, whatever you feel like. It is for this reason that I believe India has become such a cosmos of humanity with all its diversity, but still unity.'

'Is that what makes you an Indian, then?' I ask.

'Well, probably,' he laughs. 'More a human being. A human being all the more, I would say.'

Despite all the waves of history, these people have remained in isolated groups since that original long walk. It is an incredibly exciting scientific breakthrough of the last few years, to begin to pin down such deep identities. And the professor even thinks that those first beachcombers provided the basis for the genetic inheritance of the rest of us. In other words, the world was populated from here: 'If Adam came from Africa, Eve came from India.' Mother India indeed!

It was a dizzying vista at the start of a journey through Indian history. And Kerala is a great place to understand the later layers of human culture in India. Spared violence, war and mass migrations, the modern horrors of population exchanges and ethnic cleansing, people came here as peaceful immigrants or traders. Its beautiful landscape and climate, its fertility and productivity made it a desirable stopping point throughout history. Its little harbours were the landfall of Hippalos the Greek, the Chinese admiral Zheng He and Vasco da Gama, who sailed here around the Cape in 1492. And then there are the lesser people we will meet in these pages: Greek and Roman merchants in the spice trade, Muslim Arab traders from the Gulf, Chinese immigrants who left their spidery nets fringing the Kerala backwaters. You see it in the architecture too: Syrian Christian basilicas, pillared Jewish synagogues, baroque Portuguese spice warehouses, the over-grown ruins of the British and Dutch East India companies, and now the tourist havens of Varkala and Kovalam served by budget package flights into Trivandrum. All are part of the ceaseless movement and intermixing of humanity that is the story of India.

Here you see a reality that happens not through war but through peace; the waves of people, cultures and religions that all make India what it is today. India may have hundreds of languages and thousands of castes, but here in a small area you see what that means on a human scale: incredible diversity, yet unity. On that conundrum we will have more to say.

Between 3000 and 4000 years ago a new wave of migrants came into India from central Asia. Some of them moved into the south in the last millennium BC. They brought their Vedic rituals and their worship of Agni, the god of fire, but over time, the gods and rituals of the indigenous peoples were assimilated, and this was the synthesis out of which today's Indian religions emerged. They called themselves 'Aryans' (the Sanskrit word for 'noble ones'), a term much abused in modern times by Nazis and other racial fundamentalists. Although most of the immigrants intermixed, their high-caste priests, or Brahmins, practised separation, handing down the ancient rituals and taboos.

India is a land of miracles. Here in Kerala anthropologists and district officers of the nineteenth century recorded a sect of Brahmins called *nambudiri*, who regarded themselves as the purest Aryans, and whose rituals were an ancient amalgam of the Aryan religion and indigenous rites, preserved zealously over thousands of years. At that time they still performed the most elaborate of all rituals, that to the god of fire. It took twelve days, some of them continuing right through the night. The last time that this twelve-day rite took place was more than thirty years ago; but this year, at the behest of a wealthy patron, a shorter version will be performed. It is, so far as we know, the oldest surviving ritual of mankind.

ABOVE

Agni, the god of fire: the sacrificial fire and the hearth were central to the rituals of the Vedic Indians; wooden panel, south India, 17th century.

Sounds from prehistory

Huge crowds jostle for a glimpse as fires send sparks high into the night sky. There are two specially built enclosures with altars, covered by rattan roofs. The biggest contains a large brick altar constructed in the shape of a bird with spread wings. Among a dozen officiating priests – young and old, fathers and sons – the chief priest sits on a black antelope skin, his head covered. He and his wife (here, unlike in mainstream Hinduism, women play a role), along with the other priests, may not leave the enclosure for the duration of the ritual. There are blood sacrifices, milk offerings to the Asvins (the divine boy twins who ride the winds), and a sacred

ABOVE AND BELOW

Rites to Agni, the god of fire. An ancient endogamous clan, the nambudiri *Brahmins are famous for their meticulous performance of some of humanity's oldest rituals; one of which, it has been speculated, may go back before human speech. Top left: teaching the mantras to the next generation. Top right: the performance takes place. Bottom: the huts are destroyed at the end in an act of purification.*

drink called *soma* is consumed, which is pressed from a mountain plant. For thousands of years these Brahminical rituals have been zealously guarded and never shared with the outside world; and this is especially true of the mantras. These magical formulas can take days to recite, only Brahmins can utter them, and they have been passed down orally from father to son, with exact accuracy, over a vast period of time.

Mantras still exist in many societies. They have spread in historical times from India to China, Tibet, the Far East and Indonesia. They are a part of the archaic past of mankind, but no culture has assigned more importance to them than that of India. They work on the emotions, the physiology and the nervous system; along with yoga, they are a way of achieving a heightened mental and physical state. Representations of figures on seals from the Bronze Age show men sitting in a yogic posture: it is probably one of the oldest obsessions of Indian culture.

Westerners were first able to get close to these practices and record them at a performance in 1975. But when they sat down to analyse them, to unpick their mystery, scholars were perplexed. During parts of the ritual there was no communication through ordinary language. The patterns of sounds that were recited – patterns that took years to learn and days to recite – clearly followed elaborate rules, but they had no meaning. In fact, meaning was something on which the Brahmins could offer no light. This was 'what was handed down'. The doing was all. What could be the purpose? How had they developed?

Two important ideas from other forms of human creativity can perhaps help us to approach this problem. The first is music: another way of organizing sounds into an experience to create emotion. For music also has no meaning in itself; in other words, it is not capable of expressing anything. The second is ritual, which also need have no meaning. Hence, meaning need not have been important in the early roots of religion. It was only later in human history, through sacred texts and stories, that humans tried to give a rational explanation, a system, for their most archaic practices.

When experts analysed recordings of the mantras they were mystified. The patterns had no analogue in human culture. Not even music in the end was helpful, although mantras do have refrains, cycles and triplets. The breakthrough was only made possible by the development of computer technology. Patterns of mantras from the twelve-day Agni ritual recorded in 1975 were put on to a computer, and computer analysis showed that the nearest analogue of these sound sequences was birdsong. An astonishing conclusion might follow: the possibility that the performance of such patterns of sounds is older than human language, a remnant of a pre-linguistic stage when sound was used in a purely syntactical or ritual manner. *Homo sapiens*, it is now suspected, developed speech only in the last 50,000 years, since the migration from Africa, and perhaps much more recently. But we know from the animal kingdom that there was ritual before there was speech – when sound and gesture are combined in 'ritual' behaviour. If so, the combination of ritual with pre-speech sounds perhaps takes us to the dawn of humanity, the beginning of ritual and religion and science.

At the end of the great ritual, the two specially constructed houses are set alight and crumple into their own flames. Red fire licks up the bamboo scaffolding,

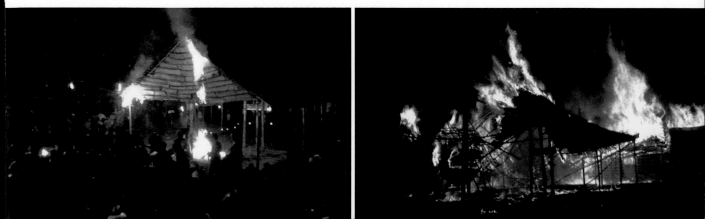

consuming the thatch and flaring into the night sky. Swirling showers of sparks fly as the structures crash down, firelight catching dark fronds of palm forest. At the start of our journey, then, it's clear that India may be leaping ahead in the global economy, predicted to overtake the United States in the 2030s, but here is a modern state in the twenty-first century that has preserved habits from its deepest past, and from that of humanity as a whole. It is nothing less than a laboratory of the human race.

The long, slow rise of humanity

The story of early humanity is still to be written, but with the new genetic discoveries, dramatic changes in our view of the human past are being made even as I write. What we can say is that over the first tens of thousands of years we are dealing with tiny numbers of people – the hunter-gatherers circling the fringes of the subcontinent and moving up river valleys to avoid the arid, fissured massif of the Deccan that dominates India's geography. The gene pool was replenished by several later migrations. The world that emerged in the Middle Stone Age already had many language families. The population of India at that time had a hard existence. Excavations at Mahada have turned up the skeletons of one community of hunter-gatherers; they were almost all around twenty years old, one was around thirty, none was over forty. Their material life, though, is depicted with brilliant vivacity on Late Middle Stone Age paintings in the caves at Bhimbetka, which show the communal animal hunts, the killings and propitiatory ceremonies of these hunter-gatherers.

Of the early gods we know little, but looking at the dancing deity at Bhimbetka with his bangles and trident, one can't help but recall the image of the dancing Shiva seen on pilgrim posters today. The mother goddess too, with her full figure and 'eyes like fish', represents an ancient and irrepressible current in the Indian imagination, which has never been forsaken in the face of the monotheisms of Islam and Christianity, nor by the Westernization of modern times. What is certain too is that the symbols of procreative power – the stone lingam and yoni (male and female principles) – that are found in the worship of Shiva come out of the deep past. Not so long ago, when archaeologists excavated a shrine near Allahabad, south of the Ganges valley, a broken yoni stone from around 14,000 years ago was instantly recognized by today's villagers. These aspects of the indigenous culture of India are part of the givenness of the deep past, which is shared by all Indians, whatever their ancestry, language or religion.

My beginning is necessarily impressionistic. The passage of time is vast, and there are hundreds of generations about which, as yet, little is known and much is still to be discovered. The tale of the hunter-gatherers is the tale of the long, slow

BELOW

The oldest religion? Terracotta of the mother goddess from Mohenjo-Daro from c.2000 BC with an elaborate headdress. Similar figures are found in the Indus valley from the 7th millennium BC.

rise of humanity, the gradual, imperceptible tracing of India's early languages, beliefs, ritual traditions and gods. A period of tens of thousands of years has left its legacy in the indigenous peoples who still live all over the subcontinent. But then, starting in western Asia about 10,000 years ago, the first signs of settled cultures emerged in villages with agriculture, trade, metalworking and handicrafts. Whether changes in the monsoon regime helped bring this about is not yet clear, though it is suspected that climate change and a much wetter annual cycle helped bring migrants into the subcontinent from the west. In the culture of this time, on the edge of the Afghan plateau around 7000 BC, are the seeds of Indian civilization. And among the most important archaeological discoveries of the last hundred years was the breakthrough made out in the wilds of Baluchistan.

Baluchi dawn

The road from the Indus at Sukkur heads northwest towards Quetta and the Afghan border up the Bolan river. This is an ancient travel route between Iran and India, used by migrants for thousands of years. It is more ancient, so the archaeology suggests, than the Khyber Pass. You go through Jacobabad, now the site of a fortified US base for the war in Afghanistan. Founded by a British general, John

BELOW

The river Indus, which gave India its name. Rising near Mount Kailash in Tibet, it was encountered by Indo–Aryans below Khyber. The root of the name in Persian Hind means 'boundary stream'.

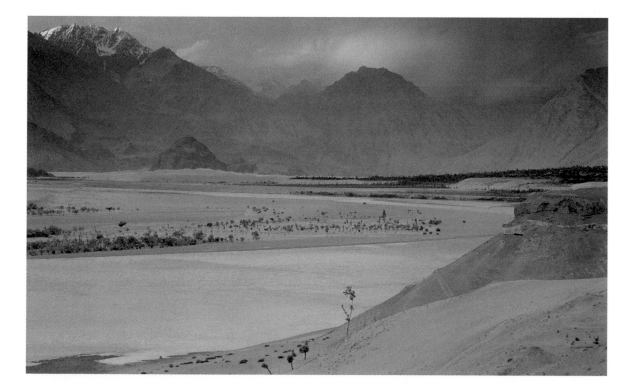

Jacob, in 1847, it was famously the hottest place in India – nearly 54°C (130°F) in June before the monsoons hit. From here the route leads more than 90 miles into the hills, where it meets the Bolan river snaking across the Kachi plain. This is still a world where you see nomads in their black tents on spring migration, their camels and mules loaded with tent cloths, matting and cooking pots. Women trail behind on foot, their dresses splashes of bright red and orange against the monochrome desert. Up into the hills for summer, down into the plain for winter: it's a scene from prehistory, the old routine of transhumant humanity.

The site lies above the road, on a low hill below the entrance to the Bolan Pass – a little, mild climatic zone free of the winter snow that blankets the plateau. The site spreads along the Bolan river, where the water comes down steel blue and cold across a gravel bed a couple of hundred yards wide. A century ago the river changed course, cutting through the site and exposing a cliff-like cross-section of cultural deposits. The first examination thirty years ago brought mind-boggling results. Charcoal from one of the early levels gave a carbon date of the sixth millennium BC, and there were 30 feet more debris underneath it! To their amazement, the French team realized they had a site going back to before 7000 BC, not just centuries, but millennia earlier than anything yet known in the subcontinent. One of the biggest surprises was the scale of the place. The site at Mehrgarh extended 1 mile along the river, nearly 750 acres in all. One place remained where the mud-brick walls, 100 yards long and 10 feet thick, still stood to a height of seventeen courses. One of the precious gifts of archaeology is that from so far back in the human past it can reveal such intimate details of the life lived. Seldom on Earth can one so closely inspect the dwellings of such distant ancestors. The packed, rectangular houses were roofed with cut branches, and walled with wattle reed and mud, just as houses are still made in these hills today. The people of Mehrgarh made beautiful pottery patterned with geometric lines and given a lustrous burnished sheen like polished walnut. There were numerous handmade terracotta figurines, female figures, some holding a child. The people here domesticated goats, sheep, cattle and water-buffalo, though not the horse. From the sixth millennium BC cattle were the cornerstone of their economy, but the river valley also teemed with gazelle, spotted deer, blackbuck and wild sheep, the Indian elephant and the rhino. Their chief crops were barley and wheat. From the rampart of mountains on the western horizon, tipped with snow in the spring, the waters of the Bolan river flowed down into the plain and on to the Indus, providing a secure environment in which to sustain human life; and, incredibly, human life lasted in this one small place for over 4000 years.

The Mehrgarh excavation proved that there was settled, continuous occupation in the Indus region dating back to approximately 7000 BC, 4000 years before the flowering of India's first cities. During this same period agricultural communities were forming across the ancient Near East, from Anatolia through Palestine to Iran. Looking at it now, it is extraordinary to think that as late as the 1970s there was no evidence of agriculture in India much before 3000 BC, underlining what a revolution these new finds have brought about. And this was not only a farming economy; there was craft specialization, including steatite cutting and long-distance trade in turquoise and lapis. In the fifth millennium BC builders at Mehrgarh used the long plano-convex brick found later in Indus cities, and cotton was already cultivated as a mainstay of India, as it is to this day.

These new discoveries show beyond doubt that the rise of civilization in the Indus was an Indian phenomenon; it did not, as was previously believed, arise from the diffusion of cultural ideas from Iraq. Indeed, there are recognizable traits in today's culture going back to the Mehrgarh world.

Mehrgarh (and twenty villages like it are now known) was already long lived when changes arrived around 4500 BC, perhaps with the arrival of new migrants from the Iranian plateau. These were possibly, as we shall see, speakers of an early form of the Dravidian languages still spoken widely over southern and eastern India. During the last period of its life (3500–2500 BC), Mehrgarh was part of a wider cultural zone extending into Iran, whose people used stamp seals in terracotta, constructed a large, brick-platform monumental complex, made figurines of the mother goddess with pendulous breasts and fantastical headdresses, and bore some similarity to the brilliant culture then thriving in Iraq. Then, in 2500 BC, the place was abandoned to be replaced by a new settlement, Naushero, 5 miles away, with massive brick fortifications and impressive buildings, including what may be a temple. This settlement would last all the way into what we call the Harappan age – the age of cities and writing.

So at last archaeologists have been able to trace Indian civilization to one of its roots. The root went back to 7000 BC, and it was indigenous. Until then hunter-gatherers had lived all over the subcontinent, as they still do, though now being squeezed out by post-Independence nation states. In these villages of Baluchistan direct continuities can be traced with the world of historical times, when, in the third millennium BC, huge cities arose, with writing, architecture and long-distance commerce, heralding the birth of Indian civilization.

The discovery of Harappa

On Pakistan's N5 national highway in the Punjab, the 'land of the five rivers'. The sun sets in a ball of fire over Sahiwal as headlights sweep the rainy highway. 'Take a rest – speed kills' says the big billboard. Huge red banners strung across the lanes proclaim the new act for the protection of women: women's rights are the next big battle in a country caught between its Islamic heritage and its burgeoning modernity. Huge new motorway service stations stand like palaces in great, glistening pools of light, and sprawling industrial towns dot the road from Lahore to Multan. This is the new Pakistan, where dramatic modernization has occurred in the ten years since I last came this way. Pakistan is now the sixth most populous country in the world. It was divided from India in 1947 by nationalism and religion, but it is still a part of the subcontinent, still an inheritor of Indian civilization.

It is dark by the time we pass Sahiwal and leave the main road. We cross a huge irrigation canal as wide as a river, the air suddenly cold now, then on to a deserted country road, the occasional bus rattling past, horn blaring. We are now on a much more ancient road. This is the old main highway between Lahore and Multan, the artery of the Punjab for thousands of years, right back to when the Punjab was the heartland of Indian civilization. Along this stretch of the plain the mounds of ruined ancient cities are as abundant as they are in Iraq. Then the road sign appears in Urdu and English: Harappa.

Our headlights momentarily light up a ruined Mughal caravanserai and a mud fort. A bunch of sleepy camels chews patiently. This was the road taken by a British deserter, James Lewis, aka Charles Masson, the first outsider to describe Harappa. On his way south one night in 1828 he camped at dusk and saw 3 miles of walls along undulating wooded mounds by an old bed of the river Ravi. Amid thick 'jangal' – the tangled forest of rakh trees that once covered all this part of the Punjab – he noticed ancient pipal trees, which were sacred in the old Hindu religion. Masson saw that dominating the site, was 'a ruinous brick castle … an irregular rocky height crowned with the remains of buildings', walls and towers still 'remarkably high, though long deserted, that exhibit the ravages of time and decay'. What he had found was a ruined medieval city in the last stage of its life, built on a great, ancient mound 50–60 feet high, with a core of giant brick defences, berms and revetments, huge ruinous bastions like the mud-brick *qalats* (fortified villages) still to be seen in Afghanistan and the Khyber region. The last major construction on the site had been a Sikh fort in the eighteenth century. Making his way up on to the mound, Masson inspected an abandoned brick mosque of the Mughal period, with pointed windows. The city had largely died out when the Ravi moved its bed in the Middle Ages. But Masson heard another story from his local guides – the legend of 'a great city that was destroyed by a particular visitation of Providence, brought down by the lust and crimes of the Sovereign'. What he could not know was that the city in fact went back over 5000 years.

Finally, we reach the site. The dig hut is in a grove of trees, nestling under a giant banyan. Muffled figures come out and help to unload our gear. The joint

US–Pakistani archaeology team are not here at the moment, and the site custodian has let us take over the bedroom, with its three bedsteads. Wisps of pale mist curl across the garden on to the veranda, and Tanweer, the expedition cook, has swathed himself in a blanket against the cool, dank night air. In the kitchen we wolf down some rice, vegetables and daal, and hot black tea. Hassan, the archaeologist in charge of the site, has stayed to greet us and comes over in a quilted jacket, hands stuffed into his pockets: 'Welcome to Harappa!'

We make the dormitory as comfy as possible, stacking the camera gear and unrolling our sleeping-bags, while we try to swat the mosquitoes. Masson was plagued with them in 1828, 'swarms of tiny antagonists' he called them, to the point where he got up in the middle of the night and rode 12 miles to Chichawatna, abandoning his camp after his tantalizing first glimpse of Harappa. A pity, because he never had time to sketch it and leave us one of the excellent drawings he did of other lost sites in the Indus region and Afghanistan. Less than thirty years later what Masson saw was destroyed by British railway contractors, who were laying the track from Multan to Lahore, spreading the tentacles of empire. Finding a ready supply of burnt bricks, they demolished the citadel, quarrying the bricks for ballast for hundreds of miles of track. From the debris they retrieved fine pottery and strange seals, which eventually came into the hands of the head of the newly formed Indian Archaeological Survey, General Alexander Cunningham. On the seals Cunningham saw an unknown system of writing. Although he could not have known it then, they came from a lost civilization. This would only be revealed in the 1920s. Then, in just a few years, the history of Indian civilization would be entirely rewritten. As the British archaeologist John Marshall wrote:

ABOVE

A miniature red sandstone torso from c. 2000 BC: a rare piece of figural sculpture from the Indus civilization.

> Not often has it been given to archaeologists, as it was given to Schliemann at Tiryns and Mycenae, or to Stein in the deserts of Turkestan, to light upon the remains of a forgotten civilization. It looks, however, at the moment, as if we were on the threshold of such a discovery in the plains of the Indus …

The excavations developed slowly, initially on a small scale. Eventually, under the ground at Harappa, untouched by the railway contractors, the huge brick

LEFT

Harappa today. Its enormous medieval walls and ancient revetments were quarried by Victorian railway contractors. All that remained was, as here, below the surface of the ground.

*Seals from the Indus,
tiny masterpieces of
glyptic art. Top: an
Indian hump-backed
bull with huge dewlaps.
Bottom: a 'unicorn'
standing in front of an
altar. The unknown
system of writing may
be an early relative of
the Dravidian languages
spoken in south India.*

revetments of a fortified citadel would be uncovered, and on the west side, where the railway contractors had left off their depredations, a cutting through the citadel wall would expose a canyon of bricks, still solid, 50 feet deep. It was immediately apparent that the place had been a great city on the scale of the urban centres of the Near East. The finds at Harappa, and at Mohenjo-Daro in Sind in late 1923, took place in the same period of eighteen months or so that saw Leonard Woolley excavate the tombs of Ur in Iraq, and, of course, Howard Carter's discovery of the tomb of Tutankhamun. Although the finds at Harappa were less spectacular in terms of artefacts, the significance of the dig went way beyond either.

The discoveries here and at Mohenjo-Daro represented the beginning of the history of the Indian subcontinent, taking its cities back to 3000 BC – before the Pyramids of Giza. Until the dig at Harappa, it had been widely believed in Europe that civilization in India was a foreign import, that it was the creation of the classical civilizations of the Mediterranean, and the Judaeo-Christian tradition of the Near East, with a little help from their ancient predecessors in Egypt and Babylon. The Indian Brahmin priests, however, had long asserted that their own civilization went back thousands of years. Their tradition of the great war in the epic poem the *Mahabharata* took it back 5000 years, while their traditional genealogies, the ancient texts known as Puranas, contained king lists that, if taken literally, would take Indian chronology back to the Bronze Age. In the eighteenth century some Western thinkers had been prepared to take these ideas at face value and to seek connections (however misguided they might seem now) with ancient Egypt and the Bible. But the colonial orientalist project tended in the main to dismiss Hindu thought as superstition and fetishism, a more 'primitive' stage of culture, which needed to be emancipated by the science, reason and religion of the West. No one believed that an indigenous Indian civilization could go back far before the classical civilizations of the Mediterranean. Back in 1924, though, Marshall could have had no idea how far back Harappa might go, just that it was 'older than anything known in India', and (with uncanny intuition) that it must be indigenous, and 'as distinctive of the region as that of the Pharaohs was distinctive of the Nile'. My mind whirling, I closed his account and finally fell asleep with a last feeble swat at the descendants of Masson's mosquitoes.

A little after 5 a.m. Tanweer wakes us with hot water and black coffee under the huge banyan behind the house, which stands like a massive, aged sentinel from a time when this region was still India. The first mauve light brings shapes out of the mist and reveals a white dusting over the salt-encrusted landscape. Cheered by the coffee, we walk out on to the site, past spoil heaps and the stumps of walls, with burnt bricks littered everywhere. We watch the sun rise from the top of the site surrounded by feathered trees, all that remains of Harappa's rakh forest. The atmosphere is still and ghostly white. Long plumes of pale smoke rise from brick kilns, whose spindly chimneys can be seen a few miles off, spreading flat across the fields to the west along the horizon. Brick was the great building medium of the Harappan civilization, and in the Punjab for thousands of years. The brick kilns must have been working overtime back then when these giant cities were built by thousands of workers, who created huge brick-foundation platforms and giant berms and bunds to fight the unremitting floods. From our vantage point, we look over the old bed of the Ravi, which once flowed under the city walls, and we can hear the village rising, ox-carts beginning to trundle down the banks of the irrigation ditches as the muezzin calls the faithful to prayer.

The joint Pakistani and US team is currently engaged in a new dig. Rolling back the frontiers of knowledge still further, it is now possible to trace the links with the earlier Baluchi sites excavated by the French in Mehrgahr, and to put the Indus cities in the context of a 10,000-year history of civilization in the subcontinent. Mark Kenoyer, the American on the team, is a remarkable man. Born in India, he speaks four native languages fluently, and it is his experience of the life lived rather than of books read that informs his insights into the continuities of Indian civilization. I had caught up with him in the UK before our journey, and he told me:

> Even in today's Harappa you can see the legacy of the Indus cities reflected in the layout of houses and settlements, and in the traditional arts and crafts, which still use the old techniques. We have even found little clay toys that are identical to the ones made in the Punjab until today. These are the living links between the people of the Indus cities and the later population of Pakistan and India.

Mohenjo-Daro: the mound of the dead

About 150 miles below Harappa the rivers of the Punjab join to become the Indus, from which the name India (*Hind* in Persian) is derived. The sensational finds in the early 1920s showed that, like the Nile and the Euphrates, the Indus river valley was home to a great early civilization. The Indus, like the other Himalayan rivers, is swollen by the spring snow melt, and above all by the summer monsoon. Before the modern construction of barrages, a million tons of silt a day were carried past to be deposited on the riverbed or at the delta mouth. This led to a progressive aggregation of the plain, which has pushed the mouth 70 miles into the Arabian Sea since the time of Alexander the Great. Sometimes the huge weight of silt forces the river to break its banks and find another course. A famous passage in the writings of Strabo about Alexander's expedition describes how they saw 'a deserted zone which contained more than a hundred towns with all the villages dependent on them. The Indus having quit its bed, had moved across to another bed on its left bank, a deeper one, and poured into it like a cataract. No longer irrigated, the region formerly inundated on its right bank, whose bed it had left, now found itself high and dry above the level of the annual floods.'

After the initial discoveries at Harappa, Marshall and his Indian colleagues now looked for an untouched site in this southern region of the Indus and in 1923 they chose a promising site 400 miles to the south in the arid plains of Sind. Here was a vast ruin still crowned by a Buddhist stupa of the Kushan period, the time of the Romans in the West. Mohenjo-Daro, the 'mound of the dead', lay on a ridge in the floodplain known to locals as 'the Island'. Although the ridge is now deeply buried by the annual flooding that covered the plain even in Indus times, it must have been much more prominent during the prehistoric period, with the early city standing on a massive artificial platform high above the plain and entirely surrounded by water during periods of flood. Despite the ravages of time, and of floods that had cut a great swathe across the site, it was still huge, by far the largest of the Indus cities, extending over 1 square mile, with widespread mounds and outlying suburbs.

On the mound whole sectors of housing had survived in good condition, with deep, brick-lined wells, and latrines at the end of every block, which were connected to sewers large enough to walk in. Everything was planned with strange regularity: 'Anyone walking through it for the first time,' said John Marshall, 'might

fancy himself surrounded by the ruins of some present-day working town in Lancashire.' The most imposing part of Mohenjo-Daro was the Great Bath, which was in the citadel. It is a finely built, brick-lined bathing tank 40 feet long, with a large building on the side variously interpreted as a temple, or even some kind of 'college'. Not unnaturally, the excavator, Rakhhaldas Banerji, suspected some connection with later ritual bathing tanks in Indian temples. The citadel is an impressive construction built on a high mound of dirt, with an artificial brick platform that it is estimated would have taken 10,000 workers about thirteen months to create. This upper city rises from the floodplain, covering an area about 600 x 1200 feet. An ancient brick bund or flood barrier 4 miles to the east diverted the main flow of the Indus away from the city.

In its heyday, Mohenjo-Daro would have dominated the riverine trade networks moving from the coast to the northern Indus plain, as well as the trade routes leading to the passes in the Bolan valley to the west. One of today's excavators of Mohenjo-Daro,

Michael Janssen, thinks the empire must have been linked by boat. 'Life in Mohenjo-Daro was semi-amphibious. For four to five months of the year the plain of Sind was a vast sheet of water. The cities were linked by river, and there must have been a revolution in boat transport to create what looks like a gigantic network; this may also help to explain the homogenization of the material culture.' Close to Mohenjo-Daro, on the Indus at Sukkur, you can still see these kinds of boat – great wooden vessels with ornate sterns some 80–90 feet long, carved wood deck-houses, and huge sails – just as depicted on Indus seals. Flat-bottomed, to cope with a wide, shallow river, strong current and frequent winds, they are a living continuity with the Bronze Age.

If you could have glimpsed it from the air, Mohenjo-Daro in its heyday would have been a vast, irregular hexagon, the suburbs protected by enormous brick embankments against the river inundations. The main part of the city was a warren of houses, overlooked by the citadel with its fine buildings. Imagine the burning Sindhi summers, with cotton awnings stretched over sun-baked courtyards and streets, just as one can see today; or the chill winters, with domestic wood fires sending myriad streamers of smoke lifting over the rooftops and swirling in spindrifts across ink-black monsoon skies, while carved boats with great cotton sails leave the jetties and head downriver towards the Gulf, with their cargoes of precious wood, elephant ivory, cotton and lapis lazuli.

ABOVE

Traditional boats on the Indus with their carved stern house and huge rudder are depicted on Indus seals. They carried goods up and down the Indus until very recently. But this ancient way of life is almost gone now. This picture was taken in 1996.

The Indus civilization

So a picture emerged with dramatic swiftness in the 1920s of the earliest civilization of India. It was bigger in area than Egypt and Mesopotamia or any other ancient civilization. We now know there were over 2000 major settlements, extending as far as the Oxus river in northern Afghanistan, some of which were big, planned cities on the Near Eastern model. Most of its mounds remain unexplored, including several huge ones near Harappa. Using data from Alexander's day, the Greek geographer Strabo, writing in the first century AD, said the Punjab had 5000 large settlements that deserved the Greek name *polis* (city). The old riverbeds here are still lined with great city mounds; and the dried-up Ghaggar-Hakra bed has 1500 prehistoric sites, some, like the untouched mound of Ganwerianwala, the same size as Mohenjo-Daro and Harappa. Not only were they vast, they were also populous. The size of the civilization is estimated at anywhere between 2 million and 5 million people, although no one knows for certain, and is surely a pointer to the fact that with nearly 1.5 billion people today, the Indian subcontinent is the most populous place on Earth, and it no doubt was in ancient world.

But who were the rulers? The archaeologists think that there are several perplexing clues. Mohenjo-Daro bears all the signs of a city that was willed into existence by some powerful person or group of people; a 'founder city', like, say, Alexandria. The streets were straight, laid out on a north–south and east–west grid. The houses of brick on top of stone foundations seem to have been built to standard designs. Nearly all of them were connected to a city-wide drainage system, and each block had one or more water wells, but there are no great tombs as we find in, say, Egypt, Iraq or China, and no great palatial buildings. Yet although there is no material evidence for rulers, all around is indirect testimony to some kind of powerful, centrally directed organizing influence. Who oversaw foreign commerce by sea and regulated the system of weights? Who established the uniform sign system in the script? How to explain the apparently common religion, uniform pottery and coherent Indus style of artefacts over a period of 700 years, spanning nearly thirty generations? 'We have the strange situation of a complex ancient society without the ostentations of ideology or evidence of a focused leadership, like a king or

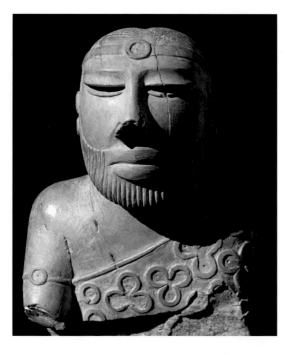

queen,' says Mark Kenoyer. 'There's no real model in history for a civilization like this one.'

Strangest of all for the archaeologists is that they found no evidence of war and conflict. In Egypt and Mesopotamia war was the great occupation of Bronze Age rulers. In inscriptions and images on stelas, art and sculpture, war is the central theme. Here that is not the case. And did the ancient Greeks not say of Indians that they never waged aggressive war beyond India out of their own deep-rooted cultural aversion and 'their respect for justice'? Certainly they had fortified cities, but there are no images of war on the thousands of Indus seals, and no depiction of warfare, captive-taking or killing.

'Is it possible,' asks Mark Kenoyer, 'that in the long, gradual evolution of over 4000 years of local cultures before the age of cities, they worked out how to organize their settlements, interact with other communities, what to do with surpluses, how to pass on knowledge and how to resolve conflict? It's an intriguing idea that early India was different from other civilizations. The answer to that is that we don't know.'

Although the later history of India was often incredibly violent, it is clear that the idea of non-violence runs very deep in Indian thought, from the Buddha, the Jains, the Ashokan edicts and the Gupta kings through to Mahatma Gandhi, and it may not have been new in the fifth century BC. Jain culture in particular has very archaic features, and derives from the zone of the Indus civilization in Gujarat. But if anything like that were true, it would be unique in the violent history of humanity.

Why did the civilization collapse?

Towards 1800 BC, after 700 years of apparent stability, the Indus civilization collapsed and its cities were abandoned. Its disappearance, apparently leaving little trace, poses another big question: what led to its downfall? There have been many suggestions, including, as we shall see, outside invasion. But experts are now increasingly looking at climate change as a chief factor. In London I went to see Sanjiv Gupta, an expert in geology and hydrography at Imperial College. Sanjiv deals in aeons of geological time, in which a mere 4000 years is as yesterday. The level of analysis now possible in his field is staggering; for example, he can take grains of sand from a riverbed and tell us where they came from. At present he is looking at one of the most controversial questions in early Indian history – the possible existence of a great river system east of the Indus that dried up in the Bronze Age and that some identify with the legendary lost sacred river, the Saraswati. He is still formulating the questions he will ask when he can take an expedition on the ground.

On the screen in Sanjiv's office are satellite images of Rajasthan, different colours denoting sand-dunes, vegetation and the presence of water. He explains:

> The Punjab has many lost watercourses. Here rivers change course quite dramatically, and most of the big rivers have shifted by several miles, even in the last two or three thousand years. But the big question at the moment is whether there really *was* a lost river. Local oral traditions were noticed by the British in the nineteenth century, and several gazetteers pick up this idea of a lost river. The explorer Aurel Stein, searching for sites connected with Alexander the Great in the 1930s, took horses down the Beas, where he came upon a vast depression, up to 2 or 3 miles across. Now look at what we see with the satellite photos …

On the computer screen a montage joins three landsat images, and a dark, snaking line appears, stretching from northeast to southwest across the Rajasthani desert.

> Look at the dark line winding across Rajasthan before it loses itself in the sand-dunes of the Thar desert. There's definitely something there, though we need to go on the ground to confirm it. There are no habitation sites there today, but now look at this. We've computerized the main Bronze Age sites using information from Indian and Pakistani archaeologists, and data from surface surveys on both sides of the border. The Pakistani team tracked 1500 sites through the desert of Cholistan, and they all seem to map out a feature that connects with ours.

On the screen, a line of orange dots appears, clustering alongside the dark, snaking feature, all of them representing settlements from the Harappan civilization in its last phase, when we know the big cities, such as Harappa and Mohenjo-Daro, were still functioning. The feature seems to extend for over 90 miles of the Thar desert, from Rajasthan across the Pakistan border.

> We can go in and focus on individual places. Let's take one site. This one, 120 miles southeast of Harappa, is Kalibangan, excavated by Indian archaeologists in the 1970s. It's a major Harappan-period city and stands right on the dried-up bed you saw on the satellite imagery. Clearly, this once held water. In the Bronze Age Kalibangan was on a river, or a major seasonal source of water, and was an important centre of population. Now obviously, you couldn't have had all these sites

where there was no water, and the reason for their existence is the river whose drying up we can date pretty closely. So what happened to the people? Now look at this.

On the screen appears a new set of data: a series of green dots flashes up, spreading across from the area of the lost river to the plain of the river Ganges and the Jumna. The number of sites along the Indus has now declined, and they vanish altogether from the area of the presumed lost river; but many more have now appeared in the Ganges–Jumna doab (the tract of land lying between the two rivers). It looks like a massive shift of settlement and population.

'These green dots are the sites that were occupied after the end of the Indus cities. Those cities died out over a century or two around 1800 BC, including all the sites along the lost river; then these sites developed, moving eastwards into the upper Ganges and Jumna valleys, becoming the centre of the next phase of Indian civilization – indeed, right up until today.'

'So did they move due to environmental collapse or climate change?' I ask.

'Maybe there was a change in the monsoon regime,' says Sanjiv, 'but it certainly looks as if the amount of water on the Ghaggar-Hakra diminished, and that helped prompt the movement of people eastwards. It looks like it, but the only way to be sure is to go and examine the geology and sediment. To get accurate dating we have to get out on the ground.'

Clues from the lost river

Early British administrators were eye-witnesses to the last phase of these changes. The Thar district gazetteer of 1919 describes two absolutely distinct worlds: to the west were the rich alluvial plains of the Indus; to the east, sandy desert. The old gazetteers also give crucial information about the apparent lost river revealed on Sanjiv's landsat images. The lower course is called the Nara, which empties into the Rann of Kutch and joins up with the line on the satellite images. But the gazetteers also prove that it is not exactly true to say that all the water dried up. The course of the Nara flooded annually, and a century ago a district officer reported 'a carpet of evergreen grass with a dense tamarisk, kandi and babul jungle interspersed with large deep lakes running miles into sandhills, and having a perennial stream of water running through the valleys'. In the times of seasonal inundations this was almost all water. Of these lakes the greatest was the Maakhi Dhand, the haunt of outlaws and robbers who defied British forces in the 1890s. These lakes disappeared after the introduction of British irrigation works, but the description perhaps gives us an idea of what conditions might have been like here in the Bronze Age. Remarkably, this may find an echo in Indian myth. The earliest Sanskrit poetry, composed in the period after the Indus cities, mentions a big river that joined the sea east of the Indus; later legend says this river disappeared, but today it is still remembered as a goddess in the hierophany of Indian sacred rivers. Her name is Saraswati, 'river of lakes'.

So the lost river was real – an important centre of civilization during the Bronze Age. Perhaps it was never one great flowing stream like the rivers of the Punjab, but a series of lakes and channels subject to seasonal floods and periodic contractions throughout history. When sections dried up, or the flow diminished, large tracts of land dried up, and cities and settlements died. The mapping of literally thousands of sites of the Harappan civilization, and the population movement into the Ganges valley at the end of the Bronze Age, strongly suggest that the Indus civilization declined because of the abandonment of the cities, caused by environmental change that led to the shift of the lower courses of the Indus and the Punjab rivers, and the drying up of the Ghaggar-Hakra.

Now let's put the evidence together for the end of India's first great civilization. There were many causes of its decline, but modern archaeology suggests big changes occurred after some 700 years of stability in the Indus world. Mohenjo-Daro was badly flooded several times between 1900 and 1700 BC; the grand buildings on the citadel were subdivided into small houses and workshops; the great bath was built over. At Dholavira ordinary people moved into the public buildings. At Harappa there was overcrowding on the high mound; the drains were no longer cleared; the streets became clogged with rubbish, including dead animals, and were abandoned. There is also evidence for violence. Skeletons at Mohenjo-Daro were left in the streets; at Harappa reburials of disarticulated skeletons killed by violence suggest that the city had entered a time of uncertainty, as do the hoards of ornaments and jewels buried by their owners who never returned. At Lothal the harbour installations were burnt down; trade fell apart and long-distance commerce vanished altogether: evidence from Mesopotamia too suggests that trade with the Indus region dried up. And, of course, the written script ceased to be used, suggesting that the elite's structures of power had broken down. Although a population remained in the Indus valley, many were leaving the area and farming new lands on the Jumna and Ganges rivers. It was the end of a great era, but a long, slow decline rather than a cataclysm.

So the world of the Indus cities collapsed, and a sub-Indus culture emerged, mixing with new elements. But was the fall of cities accompanied by the arrival of newcomers, migrants or invaders? The question of newcomers is one of the biggest issues in Indian history today, massively controversial in recent years, with heavily politicized debates about Indian identity. The next phase of the story centres on one plain and incontrovertible fact: the speakers of the languages spoken across northern India to Bengal, languages that are first traceable after the end of the cities, are closely related to the family of languages across Eurasia known as Indo-European. Everyone agrees on this, but its significance is now bitterly contested. Many aspects of the argument are still shrouded in mystery, and there are many places this tale could begin, but one is Calcutta in the days of the East India Company.

The coming of the Aryans

In 1786 a British judge in Calcutta, Sir William Jones, made an extraordinary discovery. A Welshman and a brilliant linguist, who knew Greek, Latin and Persian (the last of these essential for a judge and administrator in Mughal India), Jones's great desire had been to learn Sanskrit, the language of the ancient Hindu texts and laws. Eventually, a Brahmin offered to teach him, and as he worked his way through the Sanskrit texts, he was fascinated to see close linguistic resemblances with Latin, Greek and modern Western languages. Some were obvious: for example, 'father', *pater* in Greek and Latin, is *pitar* in Sanskrit; likewise 'mother', *meter*, is *matar* in Sanskrit. Some links are intriguingly precise: the crucial word for 'horse' (*asva* in Sanskrit) is the same in Lithuanian, far away on the shores of the Baltic Sea. How could this have come about?

Jones announced his discovery in a lecture to the newly formed Asiatic Society of Bengal on 2 February 1786:

> The Sanskrit language, whatever be its antiquity, is of a wonderful
> structure; more perfect than the Greek, more copious than the Latin,
> and more exquisitely refined than either, yet bearing to both of them
> a stronger affinity, both in the roots of verbs, and in the forms of
> grammar, than could possibly have been produced by accident; so
> strong indeed, that no philologer could examine them all three without
> believing them to have sprung from some common source, which,
> perhaps, no longer exists.

Jones was not, in fact, the first to see the connection. From the sixteenth century earlier visitors, such as the English Jesuit Thomas Stevens, had seen the similarities of Sanskrit to Latin and Greek. What Jones did was to use this as evidence that the languages had a common root. He first speculated that India itself was the mother country, but he later came to believe that the language had come from outside – that Sanskrit was not indigenous to India, but had migrated into the subcontinent. Out of that idea in the nineteenth century came the theory of the coming of the Aryans.

This word is used by the early Sanskrit speakers, the Rig-Vedic people, to describe themselves; it means 'noble ones', and comes from the same linguistic root as the names Eire and Iran – 'the land of the Aryans'. But the whole question of the Aryans is now massively controversial in India, leading to the rewriting of school history books under a Hindu nationalist government after 1997.

Many Indian scholars and polemicists have gone back to the earlier idea that the Aryans were indigenous to India, that the Indo-European languages spread from India westwards into Europe, and hence that the Indus civilization was Aryan and Sanskritic, and the earliest and most sacred texts of the Aryans, the hymns of the Rig-Veda, describe the world of Mohenjo-Daro and Harappa. It is now claimed by some that the Aryan hypothesis is nothing but a form of orientalism created by the British to justify their rule (even though the theory was actually created by Germans). The question is very complex, but there is one thing on which all competent linguists agree: Jones was right – the languages *are* connected; and the time depth of the 'family tree' of the Indo-European languages precludes the idea of India as the place of origin. The Sanskrit language must have originated outside India. But how far back? And from where? Was it brought by invaders or travellers, by elites or mass migration?

This is now one of the hottest arguments in modern India, where the battle over history that began under the British in the nineteenth century is now at the heart of politics and education because it bears on central questions of identity. Even DNA evidence has been brought into play, though elites rarely leave much of a mark: it would be hard, for example, to find the British in the DNA of India, despite their tremendous influence on the language and culture. Language, in short, does not necessarily bear on ethnicity. As so often happens, it is all a matter of how to interpret evidence. The answers are likely to involve a combination of textual history, archaeology and linguistics, maybe genetics too. But all the arguments go back to the oldest Indian sacred text – a text composed in the second millennium BC, and, incredibly, transmitted orally from then until the Middle Ages, passed from teacher to pupil, as it still is in the traditional Vedic schools.

The Rig-Veda: the first text of Indian history

'Here we are, bundle 14!' says Professor Biswas, beaming as she unties the packet of manuscripts. Bespectacled, hair in a bun, wearing a light brown sari, she lightens her scholarly gravitas with a delightful smile.

The library catalogue lists this as the oldest manuscript of the Rig-Veda; it's written on paper, and the dating in the scribal colophon is the

Samvat year 1418, which is 1362 in the Western calendar. 'Appearance very old' it says. So here's a written text from what you would call the Middle Ages, coming at the end of a long period of oral transmission. The composition of the hymns in the Rig-Veda may be spread over several centuries, but the oldest may be from the middle of the second millennium BC, maybe even earlier. Quite an idea, isn't it?

We are in the reading room of the Asiatic Society in Calcutta. Tremendous claps of thunder cause the roof to shudder, and monsoon torrents falling out of an ink-black sky are pouring off the eaves. A plaque on the wall commemorates the founding of the society by Jones. Up the grand, neo-classical staircase are busts and paintings of the great British figures who opened up the study of India during the eighteenth century and who, in the age of independent India, are still admired for their role in reconstructing Indian history. The society is still a major research institute, with a great collection of manuscripts, and around us there are many scholars working away at tables under the gaze of worthies from an earlier age. The professor warms to her story:

> The Rig-Veda comprises about a thousand hymns. They were sung by families of bardic priests in praise of gods and kings. The kings ride chariots or wagons, fight battles, take forts, and drink the sacred *soma*, which is seen as a kind of elixir of the gods. The gods themselves are not in the main the deities you see today: they represent natural forces – rain, wind, fire and thunder – very like the Greek gods. In fact, William Jones wrote home asking his friends to imagine India as a Greece where Apollo and Zeus were still worshipped, and the sacred books were known only to the priestly class. The texts you see were secret: they were and are passed down only in Brahmin families. For more than 2000 years they were transmitted orally. It was maybe only in the Middle Ages that the first texts were written down on palm leaf, and later, like this one, on paper. Almost miraculous, isn't it?

Professor Biswas is right: it's an extraordinary idea. You might expect textual corruption over such a vast time, but the Rig-Veda has been amazingly well preserved considering that the earliest manuscripts are medieval. All the manuscripts are faithful to one orally transmitted version, the master version of the priestly families who had conserved it orally: and that written version is extremely faithful to the original Bronze Age compositions. Over the generations the families took elaborate steps to make sure it was transmitted correctly, even when parts were no longer understood. Today it still has the same wording, whether in Kashmir, Orissa or Tamil Nadu; a more faithful transmission, then, than of some of the Greek and Roman classics. During the twentieth century the growing reliance on written texts at Vedic schools means that purely oral transmission has probably now died out, and the text taught today derives from written versions. Nonetheless, listening to a present-day recitation is rather like hearing a tape recording of what was first composed between 3000 and 4000 years ago.

Understanding the Rig-Veda, though, is another matter. It is a collection of notoriously riddling and difficult texts, full of inscrutable allusions, in very archaic language. The majority are hymns of praise and supplication addressed to the gods; many sing the delights of *soma*, the sacred drink; there are also battle songs that celebrate the crushing of enemies, and verses giving thanks in response to the gifts of chieftains (a well-known genre in Anglo-Saxon and Old Norse poetry too). As for the date, it's impossible to be exact, but one very important clue was unearthed in the 1920s. In the text of a treaty from the kingdom of Mitanni in northern Syria, datable to around 1380 BC, the names of the rulers, to scholars' great surprise, could be read perfectly as Sanskrit. The treaty also lists the Vedic gods Indra, Mitra and Varuna, in the very order in which they appear in a formulaic phrase in the Rig-Veda. The text also invokes the Nasdatya or Asvins, the heavenly twins who are very important in Vedic poems. Another Mitanni text, on chariots and horse training, written in the Indo-European language used by the rulers of Mitanni, is so close to Sanskrit in its numerals and technical terms that it is hard to imagine the languages of the Mitanni and the Aryans had been separated for very long. The mysterious Mitanni rulers were probably a warrior elite who came into northern Syria around 1700 BC and ruled what is now the area of Kurdistan. Their texts strongly suggest the early Rig-Vedic hymns came from a similar time, that is, not long before *c.*1400 BC. Further clues back this up. The Rig-Veda hymns describe a bronze-using world (iron first appears in India around 1200 BC); their authors seem unaware of great cities, such as Mohenjo-Daro, and know only of ruins whose people have fled, 'driven away by Agni, the god of fire'. All this combines to suggest that the bulk of hymns were composed after the Indus civilization. This gives us a triangulation: the composition of the hymns perhaps spreads over a few centuries, beginning around 1500 BC, though possibly a little earlier.

The home of the Aryans

The Khyber Pass, above Peshawar, in the Northwest Frontier of Pakistan. The road twists up into bare brown mountains, past rocky outcrops painted with the regimental honours of British army units who fought grim wars out here in Queen

Victoria's day. From the hilll overlooking the Afghan border at Torkham we can see queues of container lorries on the road between Pakistan and Kabul. Even up to the 1970s, these would still have been immense *kafilas* (camel caravans), 5 miles long, snaking down the pass twice a week – the drivers with their central Asian and Mongol faces, long plaited hair, gold teeth and brightly coloured clothes, and sporting old guns and daggers, children on their backs, their dogs as big as donkeys. The caravans brought kilims and bukhari rugs, jewels and precious stones from Badakshan, spices, medicines and herbs from the markets of Bukhara. It's been a crossing-place, a migration route, for thousands of years.

Looking from here across to the valley of the Kabul river, you can see the snow-capped ridges of the Hindu Kush, its ranges scored with the ancient passes that lead from central Asia down into India. It was from this region, the Rig-Veda says, that the Aryans spread eastwards into India from the fertile lands watered by the Kabul river, the Khurram, the Gomal and the Swat. From here, as it says in a later text, 'some went east … but some stayed at home in the west', among them the Gandhari tribe, who gave their name to the whole of what is now known as the

ABOVE

'Across many valleys, through rivers and gorges': the landscape of the Kabul river and the Hindu Kush mountains, scene of the earliest Aryan settlements in India.

Northwest Frontier. Archaeology, linguistics and genetics – plus common sense – are all consonant with the idea of a progressive migration of early Indo-European speakers taking place over several centuries. As we have seen, the world portrayed by the Rig-Vedic poets bears no recognizable relation to that of the Indus civilization; it has no memory of vast cities, except as ruins.

While the early poems of the Rig-Veda are set in the Punjab and eastern Afghanistan, the valleys of the Kabul river, the Swat and the Upper Indus, there are strong indications in those verses that this was not the Aryans' original homeland. They were aware that they had migrated from afar: that 'Indra had carried Yadu and Turvasa across the waters, crossing many rivers' going through 'narrow passes'. Remnants of these waves of migration are still traceable by linguists: most famous are the so-called Kaffirs of the Hindu Kush, the pagans of Chitral, descendants of Indo-Aryan peoples who, until the nineteenth century, spread over a much wider area of Afghan Nuristan. Encountered by Alexander the Great in about the fourth century BC, they still speak an archaic Indo-European language, and still worship an ancient 'Aryan' sky god called Di-Zau, who is cognate with the Greek Zeus (Dia) and the Sanskrit Dyaus-pitar. Traces of the migration thus survive to this day. But if their folk memory was that they had come from further west, where had the Aryans originated?

New discoveries in central Asia

Gonur Tepe, Turkmenistan. A howling gale has whipped up a sudden dust storm: grit swirls into our eyes and mouths as our jeep approaches an isolated archaeological site south of the Red Desert and the Aral Sea. We're a few hours along the old road from Askabad in the last days of Turkmanbashi, the idiosyncratic leader who took over this desert state after the fall of the Russian Empire. We have followed the old Silk Route across the plain north of the Elburz mountains to Mary, the ancient city of Merv in the Murghab oasis. Now a vast ruin field destroyed by the Mongols in the thirteenth century, the oasis had been a centre of civilization since prehistory. Finally, with sunset coming on, a low mound rises to the north: near it we see a mud-brick dig hut and a cluster of tents, flaps snapping in the wind. Under an awning Russian and Turkmen archaeologists are examining dramatic finds from a horse sacrifice buried around 1900 BC.

Victor Sarianidi is there to greet us. He can only be described as a living legend. Burly and charismatic, with a mane of white hair, his skin is burnt deep brown by the desert sun, and his voice rumbles like a camel clearing its throat. Sarianidi already has many great discoveries to his credit: it was he who dug up the amazing hoard of Bactrian gold at Tilya Tepe in northern Afghanistan. Great archaeologists have that unquantifiable gift, that nose for the right place to dig, and here he has hit gold again: a hitherto unknown civilization. Sarianidi had mapped more than 2000 Bronze Age sites in the area of the Murghab oasis, sites that seem to have suffered a dramatic collapse due to climate change in the same period as the decline of the Indus cities. Here, he thought, might be the biggest. Sure enough, out in the open desert, he found a huge defended area, plus a separate enclosed space that he interprets as a *temenos* (sacred enclosure).

The finds include not only horses and wheeled vehicles, but curved mud-brick fire altars – like elongated horseshoes – of the same shape and design as those still used in Vedic rites in India. Sunken bowls have also been found, containing traces of ingredients used for a sacred drink based on ephedra, a twiggy mountain plant believed to be the base ingredient of the Rig-Vedic *soma*. When infused in boiling water, ephedra produces quite a powerful sensation of euphoria (as I can testify). But here it's mixed with other ingredients – poppy seeds and cannabis – a fitting tipple for Indra!

The wind blows up in the late afternoon, lifting great swirling clouds of dust from the tractor blades that Sarianidi

BELOW

In camp in the Turkmen desert with the legendary Victor Sarianidi.

A noble or royal burial at Gonur Tepe, c. 2000 BC. What language the people spoke is unknown, but it may have been related to the Indo-Aryan ancestors of Sanskrit.

is using to shift accumulated tons of sand off the upper layers of the site. This is archaeology on a heroic scale: the main enclosure is a quarter of a mile across, while the *temenos*, with round corner bastions, is over 350 feet in diameter.

Sarianidi takes me over to a square pit containing a horse burial; the foal's skeleton is still perfect. 'They practised horse sacrifice as a special ritual – like the Aryans in India and other Indo-European peoples, even as far as the ancient Irish.'

There is no evidence of which people lived on this site: they did not use writing, but the material culture has too many affinities with the texts of the ancient Indo-Iranians and Indo-Aryans not to draw parallels. It is hard to look at the finds – horse burials, spoked chariot wheels, the ephedra-based sacred drink, the fire altars – and not think of the Vedic culture. Sarianidi thinks he may have found the ancestor of the early Iranian branch of the Indo-European migration into Iran and the subcontinent. But he has also found material links with northern Mesopotamia: he believes that the people who settled Gonur Tepe had previously had contact with the culture zone of Mesopotamia, and were part of the movement that left the Indo-European-speaking dynasty of the Mitanni in northern Syria around the fifteenth century BC.

The big picture, then, is that the ancestors of Aryans were part of a huge language group who spread out from the area between the Caspian and the Aral seas 4000 years ago, and whose language lies at the root of modern European languages, including English, Welsh, Gaelic, Latin and Greek, but also Persian and the main modern north Indian languages. They were people with new technology (horse-drawn chariots) and a religion that was, in a broad sense, 'Vedic'. Then, in the second millennium BC, the 'Aryans' were driven by climate change and population pressure to move south in several waves into Iran and India – a momentous event for India and the world.

The wind is up again, catching our tent flaps as the earth-movers rumble back to camp for the night. Beyond the food tent wolves howl in the distance as I write up these notes. So this was one point on the migration of one large and organized group who had come from the west or northwest. Sarianidi sums it up like this: 'They came into the oasis towards 2000 BC and left in 1800 BC or a little later when the Murghab delta dried up.'

So they were caught up in the same big climate change that affected the Indus civilization. From here they followed the water, moving south towards Herat and east towards the Oxus, from where the Hindu Kush rises across the plain of northern Afghanistan on the southern horizon. From the Oxus it is only 200 miles to the Khyber, and the first sight of the plains of India. These migrations will have involved many such groups, and they may have taken place over centuries, a slow leakage across the hills of Afghanistan, fighting along the way to carve kingdoms for themselves in the rich plains of northern India.

'The Great Epic of India'

So the Aryan tribes entered the subcontinent from Afghanistan, perhaps over some centuries in the Late Bronze Age. Despite the massive academic controversy over these matters in India, the evidence of the Rig-Veda shows that the newcomers saw themselves as conquerors, modelled on Indra himself. Entire tribes or groups of tribes entered the subcontinent, conquering whoever stood in their way. Later verses in the Rig-Veda tell something of the battles in northern India as the Aryans expanded their lands eastwards, sometimes fighting against natives with strange, non-Aryan names, sometimes allied to indigenous chiefs, sometimes fighting each other. In places they coexisted with the local powers: one verse says that the forts of one enemy of the Aryans, a king called Sambara, were stormed only 'in the fortieth year'. These all sound like real historical events recorded in the bards' verses. As they moved east, gaining more land, the mountains always 'on the left' (still the Sanskritic term for 'north'), the conquest of the sub-Harappan peoples of the Punjab is a continuing theme in the Rig-Veda: 'You put down 50,000 blacks. You beat thin their forts like a threadbare garment.' Indra himself 'destroyed the ninety-nine forts of Sambara … Indra destroyed a hundred stone forts … and put to sleep 30,000 Dasas'. These figures need not be taken any more seriously than those for the Greek and Trojan heroes in Homer, but the drift is clear. This was not a small-scale trickle; nor was it a more or less peaceful migration.

The poems of the Rig-Veda mention thirty Aryan clans and tribes, but the key books are about the history of two lineages – the Purus and the Bharatas – how they rose to power, fought with each other, and eventually intermarried and joined together. The Rig-Veda implies that the climactic victory of the Purus was the 'Battle of Ten Kings' near the Ravi river. With that, they established a kingdom in the Punjab, which they expanded into the Ganges-Jumna doab. Thus they came to control access to the richest lands in India, using horses, chariots and their superior weaponry (made of iron) to spread their power over the indigenous peoples, the post-Harappan population and the older stratum, many of whom had lived in the

ભીમ   નકુળ   સહદેવ   અર્જુન   યુધિષ્ઠિર

ABOVE AND OPPOSITE

The Mahabharata*: the greatest story ever told. Above: the Pandava brothers. Opposite: the battle of Kurukshetra. Told and retold over many centuries in all Indian languages, the* Mahabharata *became the story of India itself.*

adjacent forests since the Stone Age. The Rig-Veda shows that the Aryans burnt and cleared the forests for agricultural land, building forts with earth and timber ramparts. They used their surplus to enrich the warrior class and to uphold a basic three-tier division of society – priests, warriors and farmers. Below them the workers, servants and slaves came from the majority indigenous population. Here, perhaps, lies the root of the caste system. The divisions were apparently based on *varna* (colour) and *jati* (literally 'births', meaning the level of society or job you are born into). Very likely the colour of skin was used by the paler-skinned immigrants as a means of separation. Later, language and religious rites would become key definers. An inheritance from the Bronze Age, the caste system persists to this day; and even now, the majority of the underclass is descended from the aboriginal peoples.

This time of warfare may be distantly reflected in the most famous work of Indian literature, the *Mahabharata* – 'The Great Epic of India'. Just as Homer's *Iliad*, the tale of Troy, became a defining text of Greek culture, so the *Mahabharata* became the national epic of India, retold countless times and in many forms for over two millennia. For the orthodox Hindu, the war it describes is the dividing line between myth and reality: the beginning of political history.

The *Mahabharata* tells the tale of two clans, the Pandavas and the Kauravas, descended from the same grandfather, Kuru, head of a real clan that took his name and also appears in the Rig-Veda. It is a tale of war. Just as the *Iliad* begins with the wrath of Achilles 'that brought untold sufferings on the Greeks', so the *Mahabharata* starts with a fateful dissension, between the 'wrathful sons of Drita-rashtra, born of Kuru's royal kin … god-born men of god-like race'. The tale tells of a disputed succession of a kind that runs right through Indian history. In the end there is a terrible war and the final victory of the good, but, as at Troy, almost all the heroes on both sides die.

The location of the tale is the same as in the later historical poems of the Rig-Veda – on the river Jumna, centring on the region of Kurukshetra, the 'homestead of the Kurus'. Out of this comes the first defining myth of India, a great sprawling compendium of myths and morals. As a later commentator put it, 'what is here is nowhere else; what is not here is nowhere'. Indian audiences have loved it, admired its characters and referred to its dilemmas and moral judgements as exemplars for action for over two millennia, especially the key idea of dharma – the necessity of doing your duty.

The text as it stands amounts to roughly 100,000 verses – the longest poem in the world – and it probably reached its present shape between the last century BC and the first century AD. But its roots lie in bardic poetry of a much earlier epoch: the Sanskrit of the poem still carries traces of formulas of earlier Indo-European poetry. If we could see the version known to the grammarian Panini in the fifth century BC (only a fifth of its present length), we would no doubt be struck by the similarities to Homer's writings and other Iron Age heroic poetry. A Greek writer in the early second century AD refers to the Indians having 'an Iliad of 100,000 verses', which strongly suggests the text we have today. But the story was still expanding as late as the Gupta period (*c*. AD 320–600) because it mentions the Romans, the Hellenistic city of Antioch, and even the Huns' invasion of India in the fifth century AD.

The 'original' *Mahabharata*, then, was not unlike the *Iliad*, an Iron Age poem with fossilized verse forms from an even earlier time. But in the twentieth century the tale was put on a different footing by archaeological discoveries in the Ganges plain. After the archaeologist Heinrich Schliemann and his successors at Troy, Mycenae and Knossos brought the Greek heroic age to life, Indian archaeologists attempted to uncover a real Indian heroic age, and they began at the place in the story where the Kuru brothers ruled by the Ganges, 'in the royal hall of Hastinapur'.

Separating fact from fiction

We are driving across the cow belt, the Ganges plain, the heartland of Indian civilization, heading from Meerut 50 miles northeast of Delhi towards what is now the village of Hastinapur, the focus of the *Mahabharata*. All around us are green fields as far as the eye can see. The Ganges plain is one of the most fertile places on Earth, and has consequently attracted many people: the population of Uttar Pradesh and Bihar-Jharkand alone is more than that of the USA. Great tracts of this land were cleared for cultivation in the first millennium BC by 'Aryan' settlers from the northwest, led (so the Rig-Veda says) by Agni, the god of fire.

It is 'cow dust hour', the time before sunset when the bullock carts are heading back to the village, and dust churned up by their wheels rises into the warm air and golden light. Soon we enter the village, passing huge hostels for pilgrims, mainly of the Jain religion, who claim the site as the birthplace of two of their prehistoric founders. Presently a hill comes into view behind modern temples: this

OPPOSITE

Cow dust hour near Hastinapur. The Aryans were cattle herders and meat eaters; how exactly vegetarianism and cow protection became so important in Indian culture is not clear: maybe it came from the south, still a stronghold of vegetariansim today.

is the mound of the royal citadel, which in legend was the Troy of India, the residence of the Kauravas, and the place that sparked the fateful war that sealed the end of the heroic age when gods and heroes walked the Earth. But is there historical basis to the story? In India the *Mahabharata* has always been believed to be 'what happened', but colonial-period scholarship was both dismissive of the epic's literary merits and sceptical of any historical basis. Soon after Independence a young Indian archaeologist, B.B. Lal, set out to see if there was more to it. Before leaving for Hastinapur, I visited Lal in Delhi. Although now in his eighties, he is still hale and hearty, with a winning sense of humour and a still formidable command of detail.

Over the years he has been involved in many controversies surrounding early Indian history and archaeology. In his house he showed me black-and-whites slides he had taken in rural India a year or two after Independence – images that now seem almost like ancient history, nearer to the world of the epic than the neon-lit streets of modern Meerut. 'Well, you see the question that was worrying me most of the time was the historicity of the *Mahabharata* because there are two divergent views. According to one, everything in the text is true. According to the other, everything is imaginary. My approach was simply as an archaeologist.'

Fittingly, his was the first great dig by Indian archaeologists in newly independent India. In any state, even a modern democracy, it is crucial to establish a shared past, and the *Mahabharata* had been a crucial part of the Indian peoples' idea of a shared past over many centuries. Historiography, in a modern sense, had been established by the colonial power, the British. But epics such as the *Mahabharata* and *Ramayana* harked back to an older tradition, what one might call the dominant national culture in northern India, through folk plays, poems, songs and stories. To test the historicity of the national epic, Lal set out to examine sites mentioned in the *Mahabharata* on the same principle as Schliemann, Wilhelm Dorpfeld and Arthur Evans had uncovered the Greek Bronze Age. However exaggerated later by the bards, did the epic recall real places and even real events?

Lal went to Hastinapur in the autumn of 1949. The ancient city, named in Jain and Buddhist texts as the capital of the Kurus, had lain on the Ganges, which is now 3 miles away. The northern face of the mound still falls steeply 60 feet into the green farm fields, where a sluggish perennial stream is still known to local farmers as 'the old Ganges'. On the edge of the mound was a shrine to Shiva, 'Lord of the Pandavas', by the look of it not old, but a pointer to the tale that still haunted the local folk memory. Although the river was long gone, one of the old ghats (landing places) that once lay on it was still called after the epic's heroine Draupadi. Taking all this in, Lal scouted around for pottery finds in rain-eroded gulleys at the foot of the mound and soon turned up some distinctive thin, grey ware, often patterned with geometric designs filled with dots. 'It was *thali* plates and bowls, ordinary tableware, just as we use today,' Lal told me, 'and we immediately began to suspect it was prehistoric, a marker of north Indian Iron Age culture. So we came back in 1950 for three seasons. We stayed in tents, though the local Jain community let us use their kitchens. We used bullock carts to move the tools and lifting gear. We decided to put a great trench through the mound where we had found all the grey pottery in rain gulleys.'

The grey pottery proved crucial in dating the site. The citadel had lasted, Lal thought, till about 800 BC, when it was abandoned. Later genealogies, preserved in texts known as Puranas, described the abandonment of Hastinapur and the movement of the rulers to Kausambi, lower down the Jumna, after a great flood. Remembering this story, Lal had an incredibly satisfying 'eureka' moment in the middle of the night, when he went down with an oil lamp to inspect the exposed site and saw that the Iron Age occupation had indeed been ended by a flood. 'There's nothing like that for an archaeologist,' Lal beamed. 'You feel very excited and you think, "Yes, I've got it"!'

None of this, of course, proved that the events of the *Mahabharata* war actually happened, or that its characters were real, but it proved that the bards who composed the earlier layers of the story in the Iron Age were writing about royal centres and clans that were important in the early part of that period: the setting of the story was back in the early first millennium BC.

Emboldened, Lal searched on. He and his colleagues took a look at over thirty other sites mentioned in the *Mahabharata,* all of which produced the same grey pottery. They also looked at the traditional site of the climactic battle at Kurukshetra in a tract of land north of Delhi, which has been the scene of several

ABOVE

Krishna and Balarama from an 18th-century manuscript. Krishna's advice to the warrior Arjuna on duty before the final battle became a key text of the 'right way' in Indian society. Even the secularist Nehru had a well-thumbed copy by his bedside.

great battles in Indian history. This is the *dharmaksetra* (holy field), the centre of the land where the battle is believed to have taken place, and where the god Krishna, disguised as a charioteer, revealed himself to the hero Arjuna before battle commenced, and spoke the famous words of wisdom, the *Bhagavadgita*, a text beloved of all Indians. Again from the pottery, Lal and his team identified an early Iron Age settlement out in the farmland half a mile beyond the medieval city, on a mound occupied by a village and topped with an old and revered Shiva temple.

Tonight is Sivaratri, the 'great night of Shiva', when visiting Kurukshetra is deemed especially auspicious. It's the February full moon, and all day crowds have been streaming from the city down the little country lanes lined with stalls selling pilgrim trinkets and souvenirs, food, and glasses of thick green *bhang* (cannabis), which adds an anarchic edge to the night of the great anarchist god himself. I walk past hostels for sadhus (holy men), retirement homes for old or invalid cows, to the Shiva temple and its bathing tank, festooned with strings of fairy lights. Unlike Hastinapur, this is only a small place, but perhaps realistically sized for a fortified farmstead of an Iron Age royal clan. Maybe this was the site of the real *kshetra* of the Kurus: a royal hall on a royal estate with earthen defences in waving wheatfields by the Jumna.

Lal had not proved that the story was true, but, like Schliemann at Troy and Mycenae, he had shown that the bardic tradition had handed down the names of real places that had existed at a particular time, and that later generations had preserved the names of those places. But what exactly had they remembered? An epic tale or a real event? Or an imaginative mixture of both? The Puranas suggested that a ninth-century date might be appropriate for the war, provided the genealogies had preserved the lineage of real people. Beyond the shadowy data of walls, pottery and 'tradition', Lal was prepared to discern the shadowy lineaments of ancient battles. On the basis of his painted grey ware, he suggested a date for the *Mahbharata* battle of around 860 BC. No more than with Troy, though, can we say that it really took place, but with India's extraordinary tenacity of folk memory, it would be unwise perhaps to dismiss the possibility out of hand.

Identity: a distillation of the past

The sun is setting as we head back to our hotel in Meerut (the town where the Great Indian Mutiny or, as Indians call it, the First War of Independence, began). We eat our meal looking over a packed bazaar, where crowds are out celebrating the festival. When he hears where we have been, our hotelier tells us a Meerut folk tale. Back in the fourteenth century, he says, Tamburlaine's army had invaded India, and the Mongol cavalry swept across the Ganges-Jumna doab, looting, burning and killing, a seemingly unstoppable force. But here in Meerut a heroic resistance was organized by a local scholar and poet, who called on the people to 'remember what Krishna said to Arjuna, and fight even though the odds against them seemed to be hopeless'. Organizing themselves into guerrilla forces that included women and children, they moved through the forests, braving the most brutal reprisals and harassing the invaders 'to defend the people and land of Bharat', until eventually the harried and baffled Mongols withdrew.

Mulling over the hotelier's tale, while Sivaratri fireworks go off in the street like volleys of gunfire, another thought comes to me about the *Mahabharata*. It describes a past that may seem to be timeless, always there, tempting some to see India as a place of thought and inaction. But the reverse is true: the nation was born of struggle. The ancient commentators referred to the epic as *sruti*, which means 'what actually happened'. That intuition is right. It tells of the 'real' world, of war and destruction, violence and betrayal, the vanity of ambition, the futility of anger and hatred. Its heroes have feet of clay, but ultimately good triumphs even in a time of cosmic destruction. The epic then is one of action, and behind all the accretions at its core is a realistic view of the tragedies of history: good men on either side suffer and die; time moves on and the cities of the epic are swept away by the Ganges. New capitals are built. The wounds of history heal in time. Over the next 3000 years Greeks and Kushans, Turks and Afghans, Mughals and British, Alexander, Tamburlaine and Babur, will all come and fall under India's spell. And India's greatest strength, one known only to the oldest civilizations, will be to adapt and change, to use the gifts of history and to accept its wounds, but somehow, magically, to be always India.

2
The Power of Ideas

DAYBREAK IN BENARES. The end of the night is heralded by the sound of birds on my window sill. A pale wash of light touches the crumbling façades of the maharajas' palaces and the prancing tigers on the house of the Dom Raja, the keeper of the funeral pyres. Swathed in blankets against the chill air, knots of pilgrims file down to the water's edge to strip off and plunge in. Gasping at the coldness and holding a handful of water with outstretched arms

towards the first pink hint of the sun, they recite the ancient mantra: 'Giver of life, remover of pain and sorrow, bestower of happiness, creator of the universe, may we receive your supreme, sin-destroying light; may you guide our minds towards good …'

I have come here many times over the years, but familiarity has never dulled the sheer thrill of this scene. For all the ravages of modernity, the crumbling infrastructure and the pollution of Mother Ganges, Benares is still a beautiful city, one of the most evocative on Earth. It is a city of the imagination, which never fails to fulfil its promise of mystery and enchantment. All too often the technological brilliance of the global age of mass communication kills the past and breaks these older allegiances in just a few generations. But not here. In Benares are 2500 years of stories, of life lived in the city's narrow lanes. The Banarsis have their shrines, their music, their customs and dialect, their funeral pyres, their thick, bitter curd cooling in the alleys in handmade earthenware bowls, their jugs of sour green *bhang* for the nights of Shiva the transgressor, the god of excess – invisible topographies ingrained in the minds of those lucky enough to be born inside the old city.

The lodging house teeters on a steeply stepped bathing ghat. From the rooftop the magnificent frontage of the city stretches 3 miles on a great curve of the river, the sun rising downstream across wide sandbanks and jungle, where in heavy monsoons the flood can spread to the horizon. As the sun comes up over the trees, it gilds the water, where skiffs with long oars float along the glittering surface like water-flies on a path of gold. Below me, through the branches of the old pipal tree at our front door, a lady in a yellow sari sprinkles petals of jasmine on a *linga*m (the phallic stone of Shiva) at the foot of the trunk, and pours Ganges water on the vermilioned stones among its tangled roots. In the alley, boys are heading to Vedic school, the master of the wrestling school rakes his sandpit, and the pandits set up their tattered umbrellas and well-fingered almanacs to receive the day's clients. This is a great Hindu city in a time of Hindu revival. But things were once very different.

The story of India brings us now to the fifth century BC, the time when Greek civilization was the powerhouse of the eastern Mediterranean. At that time the Persians ruled the greatest empire on Earth. Darius the Great had conquered the lands from the Aegean to the Indus, and brought the early Indian kingdoms in the Punjab and the Ganges and Jumna valleys into contact with the dazzling imperial kingship of their distant linguistic and cultural cousins. Benares, the place where the Buddha preached his first sermon, was then simply the capital of one small northern Indian kingdom. This was a time when Hinduism as we know it today, with the cults and gods we see in every corner of the city, didn't exist. Although the pandits tell the visitor myths of the city's primordial antiquity (and in India myth has an uncanny way of creating its own reality), the archaeologists tell us that the first urban settlement on the site of Benares began only in the sixth century BC, at what is now known as Rajghat (the king's riverbank), the crossing point of the great historical route that later became the Grand Trunk Road, which today is carried over the river by the Curzon railway bridge. There were brick buildings, perhaps fortified with brick defences, and a clay embankment against the river floods. But the place rapidly expanded in the fifth century to become a centre for long-distance trade and textile production, as it has been ever since. We have no real evidence for its size, but the city of Kausambi, from the same era, has been excavated and had massive revetted, burnt-brick defences, with a 6-mile circuit, all of which suggests a booming population with powerful authorities able to deploy large-scale communal labour. It was this new urban civilization that was the setting for the next stage of the story of India.

The Axis age

The achievements of the great civilizations encompass the whole range of human creativity, from the practical and the artistic to the intellectual and spiritual. And nowhere has this been truer than in India. The pursuit of knowledge has had an almost religious value in Indian civilization, and still does today, even in India's headlong rush into modernity. The formative time happened in the few generations either side of 500 BC. This has become known as the Axis age because so many of the great thinkers of the Old World lived at this same moment: the Buddha and Mahavira in India; Confucius, Lao Tzu and Chuang Tzu in China; the Old Testament prophets; the Greek philosophers; even, it has been suggested, Zoroaster. This idea has recently met with criticism. That Lao Tzu ever existed is a moot point, while Zoroaster clearly is to be dated many centuries earlier among the herders of central Asia. And whether it is valid at all to suggest a relationship between these great developments in the history of ideas has been questioned. Nevertheless, the insight, I think, is useful and broadly true, in the sense that in the Middle Iron Age the old, ritualistic ideas of religion inherited by the ancient civilizations from the Bronze Age were all essentially expressions of the ideology of the rulers. As such, they were subject to profound questioning in urban societies, where the old social order was changing and new mercantile classes were on the rise. Obviously, this was true in several places across Eurasia, certainly in the mixed cultures of the Levant, and in Iron Age Greece where the 'orientalizing revolution' from the Near East transformed Hellenic culture.

Here in the Ganges plain, in the fifth century BC, new cities were developing and trade routes were opening up across the world. Perhaps this was accelerated by the existence of the Persian Empire, whose official language shared a common root with Sanskrit. (In fact, all through the history of India the close relation of the Indian and Persian languages is a factor in the exchange of ideas between the subcontinent, central Asia and the Iranian plateau.) At this time there were many thinkers in different fields – astronomy, geometry, grammar, linguistics and phonetics (indeed, in the third century BC writing would be reintroduced to India for the first time since the unknown writing system of Indus cities). But this was also a time of speculation about the nature of the human condition itself.

Rethinking the world

Since the time of the Rig-Veda, and no doubt long before, Indians had meditated on the nature of the universe and the place of human beings within it. This fundamental obsession was compounded in the fifth century BC by a growing questioning of the moral and social order promulgated by the Brahmin priests in a rigid caste system. What was the meaning of life and what part did humanity play in the chain of being? On whose authority existed the power systems that controlled peoples' lives even beyond birth and death? The Vedic belief in the cycle of life, with its belief in karma and rebirth, had the effect of fixing the poor in poverty, and the rich above them, the pattern being repeated through their children and their children's children. India is still battling with this legacy today. Subject to horrendous discrimination and violence even now, the untouchables and lower castes have only recently found a voice in India's post-Independence democracy, although the debate began many centuries earlier.

In the fifth century BC seekers after truth in the cities of the Ganges plain were as varied and numerous as their contemporaries in the pre-Socratic societies of Greece and the Ionian islands. There were sceptics, rationalists, atheists and determinists. There were those who rejected any idea of an afterlife, and those who proposed that the world is composed of atoms, as did their contemporary, Heraclitus of Ephesus, who believed 'all is change'. There were others who thought all change was illusory and held that the universe is bound together by immutable laws. But there were also those who denied the gods altogether and rejected the Brahminical order.

Among the most important and long-lasting seekers after truth were the Jains, who have had a profound influence on Indian thought and society for more than 2000 years. They have always drawn support from the trading communities, especially in Gujarat in western India, one of the main centres of the Bronze Age

Indus civilization. Their chief leader Mahavira, 'the great soul', was an historical character, a contemporary of the Buddha, who in Jain tradition came at the end of a long line of gurus. Although the religion emerged in the fifth century BC, it probably had much more ancient roots. Some Jain ideas, especially the principle of *ahimsa* (non-harm or non-violence) to all living things, even insects, sound very archaic indeed. (Could they even be prehistoric?) The sect still survives today, and the notion of *ahimsa* is one of the great ideas of Indian culture, percolating right down to Mahatma Gandhi and the freedom movement.

However, the most influential of these early groups, not only in India but the world, were those who followed a teacher whom we know as the Buddha. He was a prince from a land-owning family, whose clan were rulers in the Nepali *terai*, the steamy borderland between India and the foothills of the Himalayas. His ideas spread beyond India to China, Korea, Japan and the whole of eastern Asia, also to Afghanistan and central Asia, the wisdom of India seducing East and West. This phase of India's history, then, is a fascinating story of great empires and giant figures, but it is above all about the power of ideas.

Buddhism: an end to suffering

It is 2 a.m. From Gaya Station we make our way to the Hotel Classic, where we are offered puri and vegetables with hot sweet tea, welcome after the long hours on a delayed train down from Benares. The morning papers are full of the bombings that have taken place in Benares, both at the station and the Hanuman temple. It is a reminder that no society in history has been immune to violence; and for all its great tradition of non-violence, India is no exception. Indeed, India's history has been uniquely violent, and one might think that it is precisely because of this that India has meditated so long and hard about the causes of violence and the need to restrain it. Violence has continued to be a part of the subcontinent's experience since Independence, as evidenced by the wars with Pakistan, the Bangladesh conflict and the war in Kashmir. All are part of the continuing aftermath of the 1947 Partition which took place on the grounds of religion. These events continue to give fuel to the sectarians, hence the demolition of a mosque in Ayodhia in 1992, one of the most charged events in Indian history since Partition, which has spawned further conflict, such as that in 2001 in Gujarat. The world of the Buddha was very different from ours. But like a therapist, the Buddha is diagnosing the condition of the human mind, and that, I daresay, has not changed. We underestimate the people of the past at our peril.

Outside the station approaches, Buddhist pilgrims are heading in rickshaws on the short trip to Bodhgaya, the place where the Buddha found enlightenment.

LEFT

*The miraculous birth
of the Buddha from an
18th-century Burmese
manuscript. The trans-
formation of the Buddha's
tale with fairytale
elements really began
under Kushans in the
1st and 2nd centuries AD
when the story expanded
along the Silk Route to
China and east Asia.*

OPPOSITE

*The giant Buddha at
Bodhgaya today: the
Master himself would
have thoroughly
disapproved of his
deification.*

The journey takes us through green fields alongside the Phalgu river, dried up at this time of year: it is a yellow expanse of windblown sand, edged by jungle and backed by distant wooded hills. The Buddha walked across it from the little homestead where he is supposed to have broken his fasting and austerities to take porridge from a woman whose name the tradition remembers as Sujata. This was to be the last step before his moment of destiny.

The young man had been a prince of an old *kshatriya* (warrior caste) land-owning clan, the Sakyamunis, who came from the foothills on the edge of Nepal. But he was a prince who renounced that life and all its privileges. His reasons for going were said to be four. He saw the reality of the human condition in the spectacle of disease, illness, suffering and death after witnessing an old man, a blind man, a dying man and then a corpse. (These are sights you can still see any day on the streets of India.) The prince left his home and all the pleasures of his rank to seek an answer: an end to suffering He turned his back on the most human intimacies, his loving wife and their helpless child, in order to discover his humanity. A paradox? The Buddha's life is full of paradoxes. Since his time there have sprung up so many myths about him, so many miraculous tales, that it is hard to get back to the man himself and what he actually preached. But that depends on the context. He was arguing with other sects, especially the Brahmins. He was contesting their ritualized vision of the universe and their predetermined conception of human society. His ideas formed a reaction, then, a questioning of the old order. He was a protestor.

So when he lived matters, but, unfortunately, it is not even certain what century that was. Tradition says that he died around a date equivalent to 486 BC in the Western calendar, but recently there has been a growing feeling that the date should be brought down to the fourth century, making him almost a contemporary of Alexander the Great. The controversy centres on the nature of the society in the Ganges plain as depicted in Buddhist texts, all of which were written down much later than his time. These texts assume a backdrop of urban societies, not villages but cities, where the mercantile classes in particular found his message of trust and 'right conduct' congenial. On his travels the Buddha is described as visiting bustling cities, many of which – if they existed at all – must have been new in the fifth century. Another perplexing fact is the apparent silence on Buddhism for more than two centuries after his death, until the accession of the emperor Ashoka in *c.*270 BC. Did Buddhism stand still, remaining an insignificant cult until it was picked up by the emperor and turned into something like an 'official' ideology? This has led many scholars to argue a fourth century BC date, though it may well be that Buddhism stayed a small cult until it was taken up by the emperor (a distant parallel might be Constantine's adoption of Christianity).

As for the cities, some of those excavated, such as Kausambi with its huge perimeter defences, were certainly in existence by the sixth century. So there is still much to be said for the traditional dating. Crucial supporting evidence is the traditional chronology recorded in Pali chronicles in Sri Lanka from the fourth to the sixth centuries AD, which are based on historical material going back to the time of the emperor Chandragupta Maurya (*c.*320–293 BC), two generations before Ashoka. These converge with remarkable precision on the traditional date. So while the eighty years traditionally allotted to the Buddha's life is a suspiciously round figure (did he really spend forty-five years wandering around rural Bihar and northern India?), a fifth-century date for his death, and even a death date of 485/6, is still possible.

On the road to enlightenment

So Prince Siddhartha (as he was) left his family to live the life of an Indian ascetic, mortifying his body. You still meet such people on the road – these days even with their mobile phones – gathering at the annual *melas* (festivals), starving themselves, practising austerities, holding an arm in the air, standing on one leg and keeping a vow of silence. The aim is to break through the fetters of human existence as the young Buddha hoped to do. A wry saying, later attributed to him, rings true to life. It is expressed in what may be his characteristic voice – vivid, self-deprecating and bluntly realistic: 'My legs became as spindly as sticks, my buttocks became as knobbly as a cow's hoof, my ribs looked like a collapsed shed. And it did me absolutely no good at all!'

So he finally came to Bodhgaya. The place stands on low twin hills in a wood by the wide, sandy bed of the Phalgu river. It is one place where archaeology has specifically corroborated the traditional stories. Excavators here found traces of human settlement dating from the Chalcolithic period (third to second millennium BC) until the twelfth century AD, a very long-lasting indigenous culture offering a rare view of precisely what was there when the Buddha came, unmediated by the weight of later tradition. The place is now a scruffy field down a lane just outside the walled enclosure of the Mahabodhi temple. There, unkempt and disregarded, are the footings of ruins going back over three millennia. If the tradition is true, the Buddha attained enlightenment in a place already frequented by renouncers, by Jains and Brahmins and by long-haired fire worshippers, whose culture went back long before the coming of the Aryan Vedic religion. Here he came to the moment of transformation. That night, despairing of the self-punishing techniques of the sadhus, he sat under a pipal tree and resolved not to leave until he had achieved enlightenment.

We are used to our heroes in history being warriors or men of action, which usually means men of violence, for good or ill. That, after all, is what we teach our children at school. These are the makers of history. But here the hero sat under a tree and simply thought. During the course of the night he came up with an idea, a technique for self-knowledge. It was an idea so powerful that it would transform half the world and be spread not by war, violence and coercion, but by curiosity, dialogue and a thirst for knowledge.

The key idea is deceptively simple. The human condition, by its very nature, entails suffering; suffering is caused by the human ego, by desire, clinging, attachment and greed. Humanity can find tranquillity only by removing attachments that are at the root of all human unhappiness, anxiety and aggression. The way to liberation is not through worship of a god (or anything else), but by becoming a fully autonomous and compassionate human being. Those, in a nutshell, are the noble truths, and the Buddha called the way to them the eightfold path – one of right conduct and truthfulness. To expound his system further would need far more space than this book allows, and more conversance with the subtleties of Buddhist thought than I possess. But to this definition one might add a further observation – that the implication of the Buddha's logic is that even

*The bodhi tree at
Bodhgaya is supposed to
be descended from the
tree under which the
Buddha sat and attained
enlightenment. The tale
has an ancient pedigree
in India: images of
a holy man sitting
lotus-fashion under a
pipal exist on Indus
valley seals.*

belief in god is itself a form of human desire and clinging, a product of the ego and another cause of suffering in that it prevents a person from becoming an autonomous and free human being. This was nothing less than a rebellion against history.

The path to Vulture Peak

About 35 miles from Gaya an austere, rocky brown range rises from the green wheatfields of northern Bihar. This is ancient countryside, with poor villages of domed huts, thatched haystacks and mud houses. In the fields, ribby cattle with long horns, lines of egrets along the irrigation dykes, and creaking wooden shadoofs at the wells. All these the Buddha must have witnessed, along with the feudal order of landlords and the impoverished peasantry. The road climbs into the hills and enters the perimeter of Rajgir through Cyclopean walls that snake over bare rugged crags for a staggering 48 miles. These huge, drystone defences with their square towers formed the outer protection of the city in the Buddha's day. By the gate is a gaudily painted Kali shrine above a steep natural pool where women are washing bright cotton sheets and laying them on the rocks to dry.

Rajgir at that time was the capital of the kingdom of Maghada, one of half a dozen increasingly prosperous kingdoms that spread down the Ganges plain, and to judge by the vast circuit of its defences it was a populous place. Today it's a dusty little country town, with a clutch of hotels for the Japanese, Koreans and Burmese (not to mention Westerners) who come through on the Buddhist pilgrim trail. In the centre of town, by the tourist-bus stand and the *chai* stalls, is a bamboo grove. Local tradition says that this was gifted to the Buddha early on by his first important patron, the king of Maghada, and despite all the ups and downs of history, it has remained an atmospheric, overgrown piece of wilderness right in the centre of Rajgir. This was the Buddha's refuge during his forty-five years of walking and teaching, criss-crossing the Ganges plain from one monsoon to the next.

Down the main street you go through a car park on the outskirts, dotted with drink stalls and souvenir shops, to reach the beginning of the path up to Vulture Peak. It's now a well-trodden pilgrim route, a sacred way, with bearers to carry the sick and old on palanquins. At the top is the cave where the Buddha stayed during the rainy seasons over many years, its entrance hung with prayer flags. You have to stoop to go in, but inside there is enough space to walk about. At the back of the cave there is a makeshift shrine with votive gifts and smoking incense sticks. From the terrace outside is a magnificent vista of the ring of hills within which Rajgir nestles. At dusk, when the sun has disappeared behind the hills and long streamers of prayer flags flap across a sky of ultramarine, Vulture Peak is a magical place. Shantam Seth, a Buddhist teacher, tells me: 'The Buddha loved this place. Here you can see him as a man like us. On an evening like this you can feel his breath.'

The story, as we have it, has all the magic of a fairy tale, which is what it became over the centuries as the myth grew. What we can recover in terms of real events comes from the traditions assembled after the Buddha's death. These speak of wanderings, mainly confined to the Ganges plain, and of rainy season hideaways like Rajgir.

So the Buddha walked and talked for forty-five years, speaking to princes and ordinary folk. In terms of eschatology, he seems never to have discarded the idea of reincarnation; in everything he said, he accepts the cycle of rebirths as a given. The goal is to escape it. His ideas were an assault on the beliefs of the Brahmins, and there were even attempts to kill him, but over time he won powerful supporters – merchants, land-owners, even rulers such as the king of Maghada. Towards the end he made his way up to Nepal, near his old homeland in the *terai*. His journey ended at Kushinagar, now a busy little country town on the main truck route to Gorakhpur.

'This is a two-bit place, a nowhere town stuck in the jungle,' said his disciples. 'Can't you hang on and die in a famous place?'

'A small place is fitting,' the Buddha replied.

When British explorers came here in the eighteenth century, trying to find the lost landmarks of the Buddha's life, the place had been long forgotten. The ruins were hidden, covered by tangled bushes. The stupa (the domed relic shrine) erected by the emperor Ashoka long ago, had been plundered by the locals for its bricks and was covered with trees. Clearing the jungle, excavators discovered the remains of conventual buildings, hostels and a small shrine. To their amazement, buried inside the ruined shrine there was an exquisite, larger than life statue of the Buddha reclining in the state of paranirvana – the moment of death. It was a 15-foot masterpiece of the Gupta age (fifth century BC) by a great artist called Dinna, several more of whose works have since been identified. The shrine has been rebuilt and a tranquil garden laid out around it. There are few more atmospheric places than this chapel at sunrise, with the chanting of Burmese monks, the candles and oil lamps casting their soft light, and the quiet fervour of the pilgrims tenderly wrapping the statue in golden silks as if it were the Buddha's real body.

ABOVE

The lotus throne:
an image from the
12th–13th centuries
when Buddhism declined
in the plains of India.
It still survives strongly
in the Himalayas, Nepal
and Tibet.

We return to the main street with its *chai* houses, Internet cafés and phone booths. The poster stalls display their icons of modern India – big laminated images of the Buddha, Vishnu and Lakshmi, alongside 'Pandit' Nehru, the nationalist 'Netaji' Bhose and B.R. Ambedkar, hero of the lower castes. And, of course, the Bollywood stars: Aishwarya, the former Miss World, like a living goddess, perennial image of desire, devotion and auspiciousness.

'Across the world there is huge interest in the Buddha today,' I say to the abbot of the Burmese monastery who looks after the shrine. 'Why do you think that is?'

He smiles. 'You see,' he says, 'the Buddha's message is true.'

Nirvana: the end and new beginnings

The cremation place lies just out of town, down by the river, close to a copse and a Hanuman temple. There's a little cemetery and a cluster of thatched houses where women crush sugar cane on an old wheel press. The stupa, a great eroded red-brown dome of burnt bricks, is set in a verdant lawn behind a screen of ashok trees.

The last scene of the Buddha's life is idealized in all the later narratives and depictions as a cosmic event. In reality, he was old and had been violently ill with

The stupa at Sarnath outside Benares (right), marks the site of the Buddha's first sermon and his last words (below), shown in the death scene at Kushinagar in this Tibetan painting.

dysentery after eating pork (like most ancient Indians, the Buddha was not vegetarian). He knew he was about to die. None of his utterances was recorded at any point near his own time; when there was no writing. They were set down in Pali four centuries later. But there is an utterly convincing realism in the old man's urgent, exasperated response as his disciples – devastated at the prospect of losing him – continue to ask for his guidance: 'What about the *sangam*, the community?' He had, after all, always told them that his teaching was only like a boat or a raft, to get across the river: 'Once you get to the other side, you don't try to pick the boat up and carry on walking with it; you leave it by the water and push on.'

His life ebbing away, he said: 'What do you expect of me? I have taught the truth. I have held nothing back … You are the community now. Be a lamp to yourselves. Be your own refuge. Seek for no other.' His final words were these: 'All things must pass. Strive on. Don't give up.'

In hindsight, the Buddha was not setting out to found a new religion – indeed, one may well question whether that's what Buddhism actually is. Certainly, it is not a religion in the way that the devotees of Christianity and Islam regard their beliefs. Nor was he claiming to be divine. He was adamant with his followers that they should not deify him. Buddhism might have remained a local teaching, one of many in the Ganges plain that arose from the thinkers of the fifth century, many of whom knew each other, crossed paths and debated together. Among these were the Jains, who still survive as an Indian phenomenon and have had a profound influence on Indian civilization.

Today we see the Buddha's message as so compelling, and its worldwide influence as being so great, that its historical trajectory was inevitable, but Buddhism could have faded away like other Axis age cults, such as Ajivikism. We know his teachings were assembled soon after his death by his immediate followers, at a council held at Rajgir. But it was as much as 200 years later that the message began to go out to a wider world. At that time this regional sect was taken up as an official ideology by a powerful local dynasty that had turned itself into the first empire of India. So the next phase of the story is tied up with great historical events. And the catalyst, as so often in history, was war.

Alexander the Great and the coming of the Greeks

Back in 500 BC – perhaps during the Buddha's lifetime – the Persian king Darius the Great invaded the Indus region and exacted tribute from its peoples. On his inscriptions the people of Gandhara (around Peshawar in Pakistan) are listed among his subject peoples, and on the walls of the great palace at Persepolis the ambassadors of 'Hindush' (the Indus valley) are shown paying tribute with (among other things) what look like bales of fine Indian textiles. The Persian attempt to go west ended with their decisive defeat by the Greeks in 480 BC. The Greeks, however, never forgot the Persian desecration of their temples, and in 334 BC Alexander the Great invaded Asia in a war of conquest and belated retribution. Indian elephants and soldiers were among the terrified ranks in the dust storm at Arbela in October 331 BC, when Alexander overcame the great king's army and destroyed the Persian monarchy. Four years later the Macedonians burst into the plains of India. In 327 BC the army crossed the Khyber Pass, bridged the Indus, and occupied the Indian city of Taxila in the Punjab. That May, as the monsoon rains fell, Alexander forced a crossing of the Jhehum river and won a savage battle against the local raja in the Punjab, whose name the Greeks report as Porus, perhaps one of the ancinet Aryan clan of the Purus. Fragments in later Greek sources show the reactions of Alexander's army to India – to its climate and monsoons, its flora and fauna. Greek botanists and philosophers offered the first observations on the country, even the connections between the languages (Greek is affiliated with the eastern Indo-European linguistic group, which includes Old Iranian and Sanskrit). It was the beginning of a long and fruitful interaction.

Believing India to be a narrow peninsula whose eastern borders bounded the shore of the 'Great Ocean', Alexander moved east through the Punjab during the monsoon season of 327. He crossed the Chenab and Ravi rivers in early September, and stopped at the Beas river in the pleasant countryside outside Amritsar. This was a strategic tract of land, where battles have been fought since the days of the Rig-Veda right up to the Sikh wars against the British. What intelligence the Greeks had about the road ahead is unclear, and they seem to have known that there were powerful kingdoms down the Ganges, but after a debate among the leadership, the weary army turned back. They fought bitter battles and sieges along the rivers south of today's Lahore, where the ancient cities around Harappa were sacked, but the Greeks suffered heavy losses, from fighting and sickness, and Alexander himself nearly died from his wounds. Eventually he made his exit from the Indus delta via the inhospitable wastes of the Makran desert. However the Greeks dressed it up, the Indian campaign ended in anticlimax. Despite his ambition to rule India and to see the ends of the Earth, Alexander never stepped on Indian soil again.

The first Indian empire

So Alexander came and saw, but India was not conquered. For all his glamour in Western history, Alexander is mentioned in no early Indian source. Nonetheless, the Greek–Indian contact would prove fantastically enriching. In culture and politics, particularly in the northwest, the synthesis would have a lasting impact. The world had opened up. His expedition, together with the political upheavals it set in motion between Iraq and the Indus, were to be the catalyst for the first great Indian empire. It was led by Chandragupta Maurya, one of the greatest leaders and organizers in Indian history. An adventurer from the land of Magadha, around Rajgir, the young Chandragupta – so the Greeks later reported – had met Alexander, and been inspired by his power, charisma and the glamour of his violence. The tale of his rise from nowhere, complete with divinely inspired omens, survives in Greek sources.

Having been driven into exile by the Nanda king in Maghada, Chandragupta led a revolt to expel the Greek garrisons from the Punjab, and after a series of battles, he overthrew the king himself and seized power in Maghada. This bitter warfare left grim memories in the Buddhist tradition of 'eighty corpse dances', of gibbets and impalings. Chandragupta then extended his power over northern India from the Indus to the Ganges. The Greek king Seleucus Nicator, Alexander's successor in the eastern Hellenistic empire, now moved against him with a great army, and fought in the Indus valley, but was unable to defeat him. By 302 BC Chandragupta found himself ruler of the first great Indian state – a state that can be fairly described as the first predecessor of today's India.

Wary, suspicious, masterful and surrounded by a personal guard of female warriors – Indian Amazons – Chandragupta understood the nature of power with a cool-eyed clarity, and ruthlessly deployed spies and assassins in a surveillance state. The chief surviving testimony to his rule is the famous *Arthashastra*. This is India's first great text on statecraft, which tradition says was composed by his wily chief minister Kautilya, who masterminded Chandragupta's triumph over the Nanda king. Although the text as we have it has many accretions (it proved useful to a number of later emperors), that tradition may well be true. Written long before Machiavelli, the book's psychological insight into human nature and its weak points has impressed all who encounter it, and is even now used as a model by modern Indian business schools and military analysts.

The central idea of the work is the *artha* (prosperity) of a kingdom – how to get it and how to keep it. Kautilya advocates the application of agents, surveillance and diplomacy beyond the frontiers to ensure the maintenance of power ('My enemy's enemy is my friend' is one of the *Arthashastra*'s many memorable sayings). The state is not seen as a moral order, but

BELOW

The tale of Chandragupta in the famous Amar Chitra Katha series of comic books.

AFTER RAKSHAS BECAME CHANDRAGUPTA'S CHIEF MINISTER, CHANAKYA DECIDED TO LEAVE.

PLEASE STAY WITH US, GURUDEV.

NO CHANDRAGUPTA, I AM A TEACHER AND MY PLACE IS IN THE ASHRAM.

REMEMBER MY DREAM!

30

purely as a system of power relations defined by the limits of what is practically feasible. At the centre is the king, whose natural enemies are his immediate neighbours; his enemies' further neighbours are his natural friends. The ruler's ability to hold power, says Kautilya, depends on the seven pillars of power. These were: the king's personal quality and that of his ministers, the wealth of his provinces and of his chief city, his treasury, his army and, last but not least, the success of his diplomacy in the cultivation of allies. In all this Chandragupta proved as adept as any ruler in history.

Around the year 300 BC Chandragupta cemented his power by diplomatic exchanges with Seleucus Nicator. This provided him with 300 war elephants ('and certain powerful aphrodisiacs'!) in exchange for an agreement defining India's 'natural frontier' – a goal sought after by all imperialists in India, right down to the British. India would now be bounded by the Hindu Kush, the Afghan mountains and the Baluchi desert. As part of the deal, he married a Greek princess, so his grandson Ashoka, perhaps the greatest ruler in Indian history, may have had Greek blood, and perhaps even spoke a little of the language.

It was in the aftermath of these events that the first Westerners, so far as we know, reached the heart of India. In about 302 BC a Greek embassy, led by ambassador Megasthenes, visited the Ganges plain. Megasthenes wrote a book about his time in India, which is now lost, but it survives in fragments quoted by other writers. It is the first foreign description of India, and the first datable account of its social order, customs, caste system and kingship. Its anecdotes provide a fascinating window on the world of early India.

After their long journey from Babylon, the Greeks made their way through the Khyber Pass and down the old highway across the Punjab from Taxila (the ancestor of the Grand Trunk Road). En route they passed Alexander's altars on the Beas river, where a Greek source, Plutarch, says Chandragupta was later accustomed to do puja, a prayer ritual, in memory of the Macedonian king. Then they made their way by boat down the Jumna and the Ganges past the cities of Kausambi and Benares, no doubt remarking, as all later travellers would, on the fertility and beauty of the countryside. Surviving fragments of Megasthenes' book give us a vivid sense of the Greeks' open-mouthed entry into an alien world that Alexander had only ever encountered at its fringes, and then with violence. Sailing down the Ganges, they saw at first hand 'the greatest river in India, worshipped by all Indians, which is all of a hundred stadia [11 miles] wide, sometimes so that one cannot see the far shore'.

At last they came in sight of Chandragupta's capital, Pataliputra, today's Patna, in Bihar. This bustling city of 1.5 million inhabitants is seldom mentioned these days on the tourist trail, but it is one of most important and interesting places in Indian history. Founded in the sixth century BC, it would be the chief city of northern India until the Gupta age in the fourth century AD, and through all the later phases of its life down to the Mughals, the East India Company and the freedom movement. It is a living witness to the drama of Indian history.

Patna: India's first imperial city

We sail at dawn with a Patna boatman from Collectors Ghat, the upstream landing place where the British built their offices, villas and opium warehouses from the eighteenth century onwards. Floating slowly downstream, as the Greeks did so long ago, we pass early morning bathers and head straight into the rising sun – for the Ganges flows almost due east as it passes the city. Viewed from the river, Patna is still low-rise, with woods, gardens and clumps of palms. The shore is dotted with gaily painted shrines, both Hindu and Muslim. During the Middle Ages Patna became a noted centre of Islam, and can boast over a dozen important *darghas* (tombs) of Sufi saints, their white onion domes dotting the riverbank. Soon the boat is drifting past immense ruined palaces, medieval Mughal fortresses, drum towers keeling over into the water, their huge walls displaced by the relentless flow of the river, their crumbling bastions silted with thick mud the colour of chocolate. As the sun rises above the city, it is as if we are sailing in slow motion past an Indian Rome.

Gradually, the silting of the river pulls the channel away from the line of the old walls, and the boat drifts alongside a great shoulder of whitened sand about 20 feet above the water. On the shore between the city and the river are a dozen

LEFT

Dawn at Patna. Sailing down the Ganges reveals a spectacular panorama of ruined fortresses, palaces and shrines.

BELOW

*Street in Patna in
c. 1825, by which time
the city had contracted
within its medieval
defences to a third of its
ancient size; it was still
estimated by the British
surveyor Francis
Buchanan as having
300,000 people.*

towering brick-kiln chimneys rearing up one after the other, some with long smudges of smoke hanging in the dawn air. The whole scene begins to take on the feel of a dystopian fantasy in science fiction. At the landing place are three big wooden sand barges with giant skeletal stern rudders and huge lateen sails, their torn and patched grey canvas hanging limp in the still air. Beside them women are cooking at a fire, while others in bright saris are bathing and laughing. We pull in under long, bending bamboo poles with snapping flags, and scamper up the bank past the shrines of Shiva and the monkey god Hanuman under a spreading tree. From the riverbank it's a 100-yard walk through a brickyard with towering chimneys up to what was once the medieval waterfront, which crowns a steep rise lined with red-brick mansions and old shrines. The former landing place is now high and dry, crowned by a lovely Sufi shrine that once commanded beautiful vistas over the river. And so we enter the old Mughal and British town, the eastern end of the city that played such a role in Indian history for nearly ten centuries, and which, after Delhi, was India's greatest imperial city.

Buddhist tradition tells of the Master's prophecy that Patna would be the greatest of all centres of trade and population. In the first century BC the author of the text known as the Yuga Purana saw Mauryan Patna as the fruition of urban life in early India. He wrote: 'On the southern and most excellent bank of the Ganges the royal sage will cause a lovely city to be founded, filled with people and flower gardens. And that pleasant city will endure for 5000 years.'

Chandragupta Maurya's capital, so the Greeks recorded, stood at the junction of the Ganges and the Erranoboas (the latter derived from the ancient Sanskrit name for the river Son, Hiranyabahu, meaning 'golden armed'). The city stretched for nearly 10 miles along the Ganges, and was about $1\frac{1}{2}$ miles deep, making a circuit of 22 miles. According to Megasthenes, the city had sixty-four gates and 570 towers. These seem almost incredible figures, but remnants of stockades and tower bases found a century ago in the British period tend to confirm his story. Given the strength of the seasonal inundations, the defences were mainly wooden, consisting of huge palisades with piles sunk along the riverside to give better protection against the flooding of the Ganges. The main gates had wide, timber-floored walkways through the ramparts, with bridges across an outer ditch system fed by water from the Son, which was 600 feet wide on the landward side and fed a network of smaller canals. Inside the city were massive buildings of burnt brick, with stone and wooden columns, and decorated plaster. 'I have seen the great cities of the east,' wrote Megasthenes, 'I have seen the Persian palaces of Susa and Ecbatana, but this is the greatest city in the world.'

From a distance the townscape of gardens, trees, ornamental woodland, parks and menageries might have given the impression of a vast pleasure garden, rather like Kublai Khan's magic world of Xanadu, or the peony and cherry gardens of imperial Xian celebrated by the poets of the Tang dynasty in China. In other words, the Asiatic city might be seen as a royal ritual enclosure, and a far cry from today's bustling, proletarian Indian city. But on closer inspection – and Indian ministers and equerries plied them with mind-boggling facts (some no doubt exaggerated for effect) – the Greeks rapidly came to understand that Pataliputra was, in fact, a vast military base. Outside the walls to the south was an enormous cantonment of the kind later laid out by the British, a semi-permanent camp for the royal army, which, so the Greek visitors were informed, amounted to 40,000 men (out of a full military establishment claimed to number 400,000, with 3000 war elephants). As for the ruler's own residence, the palace area lay in a great oblong to the south, inside separate moated defences. There Chandragupta Maurya himself kept court, ever vigilant for insurrection, 'never sleeping by day', as Megasthenes reports, surrounded by his female bodyguard 'loyal only to him', yet still 'by night obliged to change his couch from time to time to thwart plots against his life'.

Portrait of early Indian society

Even in the fragments preserved in the pages of later historians, the Greeks' first view of India is one of those texts from history – like the letters of Cortes from Mexico – that tells us how it feels to encounter another world. 'There are one hundred and eighteen separate nations in India,' noted Megasthenes with amazement (and presumably his informants could speak only of the lands under Mauryan rule). No wonder the Greeks overwhelmed by the scale of it all, and by the sheer exoticism, which at times led them to descend to literally fabulous fairy tales. There were sections on climate, custom and even on the physiognomy of the Indians. There were lengthy digressions on elephant hunting and tigers, on cotton and banyan trees. The Greeks noted disapprovingly that the Indians did not make eating the social ritual that it was in the Mediterranean, where the communal meal was also a religious rite, as it still is today. 'The Indian people,' Megasthenes remarked, 'take food at any time of the day, and even singly if they wish.'

Like every modern visitor, Megasthenes noticed the Indians' 'love of adornment', especially gold jewellery and precious gems, and their 'brightly coloured cotton garments, a brighter colour than any other'. He adds, 'For since they esteem beauty so highly, they do everything they can to beautify their appearance.' But a cultural trait that particularly impressed the Greeks was the Indian respect for 'the superiority of wisdom above all', and their emphasis on simplicity, frugality, 'orderliness' and 'self-restraint' in daily life. Even more striking is his observation that 'No Indians ever set out beyond their own country to wage aggressive war because of their respect for justice'.

Coming from a literate society, the Greeks were surprised by 'the lack of written letters' in a memorizing society, where 'everything is regulated from memory'. Given that, one of the most surprising elements in Megasthenes' account is the level of organization Chandragupta achieved over such a wide empire. With government departments for the supervision of public works, roads, prices, markets and harbours, and with joint administration of military affairs, transport and naval supply, the degree to which memory and custom regulated Indian society is revealed in one of the most fascinating sections of Megasthenes' lost text, which gives the first outside account of the caste system:

> The population of India is divided into seven castes. The first is
> formed by the collective body of the philosophers [Brahmins].
> These in numbers are inferior to the rest, but in dignity are pre-
> eminent. They are exempt from public duties, but are engaged by
> private persons to perform the necessary rituals of life and death.

For they are believed to be most dear to the gods, and most conversant with matters pertaining to the world of the spirits. In requital of such services, they receive valuable gifts and privileges.

Elsewhere (as recorded by the geographer Strabo), Megasthenes talks about the Brahmins of the mountains worshipping Dionysus (Shiva?) and in the plains, especially around Mathura, worshipping Heracles (Krishna?). He also adds a fascinating and little-noticed reference to a huge annual gathering, 'the great assembly, as it is called'. This took place each year in January in northern India when 'all the philosophers [Brahmins and holy men] come together at the gates of the king', where they perform rituals and iron out issues of civil and religious law. Such a gathering, accompanied by a great royal distribution of alms, is described by the Chinese Buddhist pilgrim Hsuan Tsang in AD 640 as 'having gone on since ancient times' at Prayag, today's Allahabad, where great annual *melas* are still held, and where every twelve years the *Kumbh Mela* takes place, the largest gathering anywhere on Earth.

Megasthenes also describes the other ranks of Indian society. He writes of the peasant cultivators, who formed the mass of the population, and 'who pay a land tax and a fourth of their yield', the cattle herders and shepherds, the hunters, trappers and bird-catchers, and the artisans, craftsmen, wood- and metal-workers. The fifth caste in his scheme is the military (*kshatriyas*), a numerous class, who lived at leisure in time of peace. They were 'well organized and equipped for war, with a huge establishment of elephants and war horses'. Megasthenes also tells us that there was a royal fleet, with shipbuilders and a 'first sea lord' who let out ships for commercial purposes in time of peace. Going outside the customary fourfold division of castes we find in early Indian texts, he assigns a separate category to the civil service (*ephors*), 'whose duty is to enquire into and report everything that goes on in India to the royal government or magistrates'. Similarly, he makes a seventh caste, the smallest in numbers, of councillors, administrators, governors, judges, army commanders and chief magistrates. Megasthenes concludes by noting caste rules – 'no one is allowed to marry outside his caste, or exercise any calling but his own: a soldier cannot become a peasant; an artisan cannot become a [Brahmin] philosopher.'

Megasthenes' fascinating account is the first of Indian society and the caste system to be written by an outsider. It is interesting that he expands the basic four castes of the ancient texts – Brahmins, warriors, traders and farmers – to a sevenfold division, which is in fact found in southern Indian Brahminical accounts of the caste system, though no doubt then, as now, there were thousands of subcastes. Essentially, though, he corroborates the information in the *Arthashastra*, which is

ascribed in its earliest form to the time of Chandragupta. He also mentions what are clearly Stone Age indigenous tribes in a number of areas, with whom the Mauryans had contact, among them 'wild people' living in the Himalayas around the source of the Ganges. Many such peoples survive today. The one section of society he may not have come into contact with as a foreigner (though its members are mentioned in the *Arthashastra*) was the *chandalas* (untouchables). These lived outside towns and were viewed as polluted, so they were forbidden, for example, from using the wells of other castes. How this form of oppression arose is still disputed, but it has been sustained over millennia and is still very strong, despite India's democratic constitution and the further legislation on untouchability since the 1980s which has sought to abolish it. In general, caste rules were not as rigid as Megasthenes makes them sound, and medieval Muslim and later British observers were equally misled by the possibilities of diversification within the castes and movement between them. But the core principles of caste are still functioning, as can be seen from any marriage column today in India's Sunday newspapers.

The legend of Chandragupta

Of the physical remains of the city of Chandragupta there are few traces. The broad topography is still there, with the Ganges , 5 miles wide in the rainy seasons, defining the northern edge of the city. The Son river has shifted and now meets the Ganges 20 miles upstream. For such an important site, there has been very little excavation. Indeed, it was only a century or so ago that British archaeologist Laurence Waddell, with growing excitement, was able to prove that the physical remains of ancient Pataliputra lay underneath the modern city. Even the wooden walls described by Megasthenes were exposed. They were made of sal tree trunks, their tops 20 feet below the present ground level, and the remains of the great moat described by Megasthenes, an old channel of the river Son, also still existed. It was 200 yards wide and still known in one place as Maharaj Khanda, 'the emperor's moat'.

But of Chandragupta himself there is one specific and remarkable survival. This is at the Kamaldah Jain temples, which lie on a picturesque wooded peninsula inside the city. They are set in a beautiful lake, the 'lotus pond', where fishermen still cast their nets from boats only a few hundred yards from the railway track. The lake shore, with its fruit orchards, is now being encroached on by Patna's burgeoning urban sprawl, but here it is still possible to imagine the city of pools and pleasure gardens described by the Greeks. The main shrine stands on a deep mound of ancient debris, its crumbling brick plinth surrounded by trees. You climb a flight of steps on to a sun-baked plastered platform with a little sanctum on top. According to the custodian, it commemorates not one of the twenty-four Jain

OPPOSITE

Top: At the Kumbh Mela *2001. This greatest of all festivals reached its present form in the British period, but its forerunner was perhaps the 'great synod' described by the ancient Greeks, and by the Chinese in the same place in the 7th century AD. Below: Sadhus queue up to bathe at the* sangam, *the junction of the sacred rivers, at the most auspicious moment astrologically for 144 years.*

tirthankars (great saints), but the muni (guru) of Chandragupta Maurya himself, Sthula-badra who is said to have died here. In this almost forgotten corner of his imperial city, perhaps a real connection and a living tradition has survived from the age of Alexander the Great.

The Jain tradition brings us to the most fascinating of many legends about Chandragupta. After a life of great deeds and conquests, so the story goes, he resigned his kingship to become a Jain monk. The custodian of the Kamaldah shrine tells me what happened as we sit on a golden evening overlooking the lake at Patna against a distant background roar of rush-hour traffic and the claxons of crowded commuter trains. The tale that the Jains still tell goes like this. At the height of Chandragupta's rule, a Jain teacher warned him of the limits of his power. Soon afterwards a terrible famine decimated the population, and, despite all his caparisoned elephants, his vast palaces, his numberless bodyguard and his magnificent tiger hunts, the king was powerless to prevent it. He sat in his gilded throne-room while the smell of death and the sound of lamentation rose up from the streets. Eventually he summoned the teacher and submitted to him as his guru. Chandragupta's son Bhimbisara would become king, and he himself would take the cloth and begging bowl. With that, he said goodbye to his palace staff and his family, and walked out of the gates on a pilgrimage that led him far south into the rugged mountains of the Deccan. There he ended his life by ritually fasting to death in a cave at the most sacred Jain site of Sravanabelgola. This is still a great place of pilgrimage today. In 2006 millions of Jains from all over the world gathered for the twelve-yearly *mela*, pouring great vats of coconut milk, sandal paste, saffron and vermilion over the giant statue of Bahuballi (an ancient Jain guru who also renounced his kingdom). He is depicted standing naked and impassive, rapt in contemplation as the creepers grow around his body, his eyes fixed on what lies beyond. In one dramatic image, the statue encapsulates the ancient Indian faith in the power of knowledge to break the bonds of human existence.

All around this magical landscape are rocky hills and weathered outcrops where Jain ascetics still live, making offerings to images of the gurus and living on rice and pulses. On one crag the cave where the great Chandragupta passed his final days is still pointed out , its entrance smoothed by the fingers of centuries of pilgrims. On the floor is a worn carving of stone feet and a scatter of pale rice grains and hibiscus petals stirred by the warm breeze. Fierce light floods in from the cave mouth. Here the former king died, his body wasted to skin and bone, his mind floating above the emerald green hills.

'Chandragupta Maurya came here to find *moksha* [salvation],' one pilgrim told me. 'He did penance here, and when one does penance one does not eat. And so he died. But he found *moksha*.'

PREVIOUS PAGES

The Sravanabelgola mela *in 2006 when millions of Jains from all over the world gathered to pour great vats of milk, paste, saffron and vermilion over the giant statue of Bahuballi.*

Ashoka and the rule of reason

The first great political genius of Indian history, Chandragupta, died in about 297 BC. His son Bhimbisara extended the empire further, justifying his name, the 'killer of foes'. There are even later Tamil legends of a Mauryan attack on the southern kingdoms of the Cholas and Pandyas. Bhimbisara also continued diplomatic relations with the Greeks. One delightful tale tells of his request to Antiochus of Syria to purchase consignments of figs, Greek wine and a Greek teacher of rhetoric. Antiochus sent him the fruit and wine with a note saying that 'unfortunately Greek law does not permit the sale of professors'!

Then, in 268 BC, following a power struggle after Bhimbisara's death, Chandragupta's grandson Ashoka came to power. Ashoka is one of the great figures in history, and his story is told across southern Asia and the Far East in legends, folk plays and wisdom literature in the manner of the Western tales of King Arthur or Charlemagne. As a young man, the legends say, he was unattractive and ungainly in appearance, with bad skin, and was disliked by his father. But he was a capable administrator and was made viceroy of Ujain. While living there, he met and fell in love with the beautiful daughter of a merchant from the town of Vidisa, a woman called Devi. They had two children, though there is no suggestion that they married. Both the children, a boy called Mahinda and a girl called Samghamitta, are later associated with Ashoka's Buddhist mission to Ceylon. Indeed, it is Buddhist sources from Ceylon that say Devi herself was a Buddhist. They also claim that she was a member of the Sakya clan, a branch of the Buddha's family, who had emigrated to Vidisa. Whether this connection with the Buddha is a fiction or not cannot now be decided, but Buddhist tradition insists she was Ashoka's inspiration in eventually adopting Buddhism.

When Ashoka eventually became king (he was perhaps now in his thirties), Devi stayed in Vidisa rather than moving

BELOW

Ashoka, subject of novels, histories, cartoons, and even a recent Bollywood movie since his career was rediscovered in the 20th century.

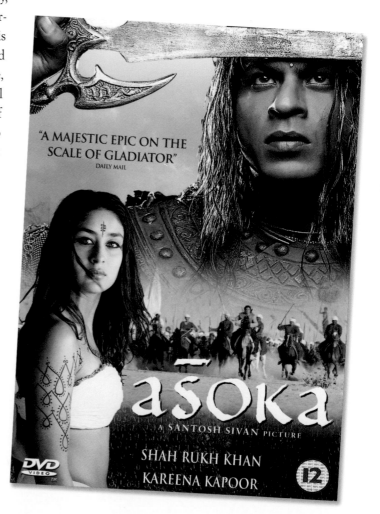

"A MAJESTIC EPIC ON THE SCALE OF GLADIATOR"
DAILY MAIL

aśoka

A SANTOSH SIVAN PICTURE

SHAH RUKH KHAN

KAREENA KAPOOR

to Patna. Some said this was because the court did not favour Buddhism, though it is more likely (if any of these tales have a kernel of truth) that she may have stayed in Ujain because she wasn't a legal wife and was inferior in social status. But when he became king, Ashoka married other women, including one of high rank, Asandhimitta, who became his chief queen.

At his father's death, Ashoka, it appears, was not the designated heir, and in some versions of the tale there was a four-year power struggle for the throne. One later legend says that his father's guru, an Ajivika holy man, told Bhimbisara that Ashoka was the most able of his sons, and prophesied he would be a great king. A Chinese story says the Buddha himself appeared to Bhimbisara in a dream and foretold Ashoka's rule, during which he would unite all of India. Some key ministers at court supported him as the best candidate, but his brothers opposed him, and later legends say he put down their revolts and killed ninety-nine of them, sparing only the youngest. A less dramatic, and perhaps more plausible, version says he had six of his half-brothers put to death. Fairy tale or not, in the light of the murderous succession struggles between royal brothers in later times, the basic story is certainly plausible enough.

Let's stay with the legends for a little longer. In the early part of his reign the Buddhist stories say that Ashoka spent many years in a life of pleasure, and gained the nickname Kamashoka, a pun on his name that loosely translates as 'Follower of Desire', or perhaps even 'Lover Boy Ashoka'. Then came a period of extreme violence and wickedness, as a result of which they called him Candashoka, 'the Cruel'. Only after that, in this exemplary moral fable, does he convert to Buddhism and lead a life of piety, giving rise to his being called Dhammashoka, 'the Just', the follower of the divine law. Such stories were no doubt fabricated by later Buddhist apologists, though they were in existence in the first two centuries AD, and the stories of his cruelty were surprisingly long-lived and widespread if there is no truth whatsoever in them. 'Intensely wicked' as a young man, he even had some of the women of his harem killed when they told him how ugly he was!

In the most famous story Ashoka's chief minister tells him that to be a great king he has to be cruel, and that he needs a staff of torturers as it is unseemly for kings to do the dirty work themselves. So he made a 'hell on Earth' in the form of a prison in Patna, with torturers and fiendishly ingenious implements of torture. The scene of these events, according to a still-current legend, was the Agam well in Patna. Ashoka himself went there, watched, and invented his own methods of interrogation. Then, according to one version of the story, his conversion to Buddhism took place when a Buddhist monk being tortured in the 'hell' was unmoved by his treatment and the king became fascinated by the man's almost miraculous powers. The Jains, of course, have their own version, making the torture victim one of their own.

How to untangle history from all this? Historians regard the portrayal of Ashoka as an extremely wicked man who suddenly turned to the good as pure fantasy. Like all really great rulers in history, from Alexander and Genghis Khan to Napoleon, Ashoka gathered an incredibly fertile afterlife of legend. All we can say is that at his father's death there may have been a power struggle and that Ashoka, like some of the Mughal rulers, may have killed one or more brothers who opposed him. There is, though, no sign in the early years of his reign of the ruler who would emerge. That comes with the dramatic events eight years later.

Like all early empires, the Mauryan state was aggressive. It demanded tribute from its neighbours, and its kings were expected to be warlike. Ashoka's grandfather and father were both conquerors, and early in his reign he followed in their footsteps. In his eighth year on the throne he moved against the independent kingdom of Kalinga on the eastern seaboard in present-day Orissa (a kingdom that Greek sources say, only a generation before Ashoka, could muster 60,000 infantry, 1000 cavalry and 200 elephants). The date was probably 262–261 BC. The story we have is in Ashoka's own words on stone edicts he raised later, but until 2006 there was no evidence of the actual battle on the ground. Then a dramatic archaeological discovery offered a possible solution to one of the most fascinating questions in Ashoka's tale. Where was the site of the battle that changed the course of Indian history?

Orissa and the Kalinga war

Night is falling on the National Highway 300 miles south of Kolkata, on the old coast road that winds its way from the Ganges valley in Bengal down to the southern tip of India. It is one of the great routes in Indian history, and one of the best Indian journeys – one to savour over several days, if you have the time, exploring the byways that lead to sleepy little backwaters once frequented by Greek, Roman and Arab traders. The journey takes you along a fertile alluvial coastal plain backed by the jungle-clad blue hills of the Eastern Ghats. Orissa is one of the most enchanting landscapes in India. On its surf-beaten shores are magical inlets, such as Chilka Lake, 50 miles long, dotted with islands and crowded with migrating birds in winter. It is criss-crossed by flat-bottomed boats with lateen sails of bamboo matting. Further to the south is ancient Kalingapatnam, the 'port of the Kalingas', situated on the southern border with Andhra Pradesh and the Dravidian-speaking lands. It consists of just a little beach and a British lighthouse today, but in the ancient world Orissans traded from here with Tamils, Sinhalese and Romans, and with kingdoms straight across the ocean in Java and Sumatra. As late as the nineteenth century there was a steamer service from here to Rangoon. So Kalinga was an ancient kingdom with ancient contacts, and throughout its history Orissa has remained a distinct geographical unit with its own distinct cultural and political history.

With darkness coming on, we cross the Mahanadi river and come into the flat green coastal plain, still covered by monsoon floods. It is night before we reach the little country town of Jajpur. Our small hotel is hung with a waterfall of fairy lights for the festival of the goddess Durga, and wild firecrackers thump late into the night as the townsfolk celebrate in the streets. That night I reread Ashoka's own account of his Kalinga war.

'After he had been anointed for eight years, King Devanampiya Piyadasi ['the beloved of the gods', as Ashoka was known] attacked the Kalingas. Then 150,000 living persons were carried away captive, 100,000 were killed in the war, and almost as many died afterwards …'

After the testosterone-fuelled rush of war came the body count. Kalinga had been crushed. Then came the great moment, the turning point …

'After the Kalingas had been subjugated there arose in the king a striving or a conflict, a yearning for law [or meaning?], now a remorse for the conquest. For a free people to be conquered means killing, massacres and the enslavement of human beings. Now the king finds this a source of anguish, a profoundly serious matter.' (Rock Edict XIII)

Thinking today of the current murderous events in Darfur or the sectarian disasters in Iraq, it is clear that Ashoka's words remain as relevant as ever. He had hit on one of the most dangerous ideas in history: that aggressive war is wrong. As he goes on to point out, we are all bound together by the common bond of humanity.

> The many people who live here – Brahmins, Buddhists and other sects, the householders – all share the same basic human values, among which are respect for parents, being well disposed, respecting their elders, showing kindness and firm attachment to friends, acquaintances, companions, kinsmen – and to slaves and servants – but they will all suffer injury and killing, cut off from the ones they love. This is a tragedy for everybody, and to the king it is a desperate matter.

And so, the king tells us, he decided to renounce violence and resolved to conquer 'by persuasion alone'. 'He desires for all creatures non-violence, self-control, detachment, happiness.' One should never take politicians' words at face value of course, but Ashoka's edicts are so personal, so idiosyncratic and self-recriminating, that it is hard to think this is not his voice. The tale has echoed down the ages, through the violent histories of India and the world, down to Gandhi and the freedom movement. In modern times it would lead to Ashoka's lions being chosen as the emblem of modern India, and his wheel of dharma (law), which topped his monuments, to be set on the Indian flag against a white band (signifying peace) between the orange and green fields of Hinduism and Islam.

But where was Ashoka's place of destiny? The kingdom of Kalinga extended nearly 300 miles south of the Ganges mouths. The war must have been fought over a wide area, but the chief battles must have been for royal centres, and there were two of these: one near the present temple city of Bhubaneswar, the other to the north near Jajpur, controlling the river crossings from the north of India. And this is where Orissan archaeologists have made a dramatic discovery.

Site of the Kalinga battle?

In the early light we cross the Brahmani river and turn south on a winding country lane towards the sea. Soon we find ourselves in a soft, hazy green plain fringed by three dramatic domed hills. In the fields there are long-horned cattle pulling wooden ploughs, and ox-carts with wooden wheels. Later Buddhist pilgrims described ten great stupas built here by Ashoka, and in Queen Victoria's day British district officers made finds of Buddhist sculpture, especially near Udaigiri, 'the hill of dawn'. Now Dr Debraj Pradhan has uncovered the base of a great square stupa on a high hillside over the plain and, nearby, Buddhist rock-cut figures with dozens of small, commemorative stupas. Even more exciting, cut into the rock is the name of Ashoka.

'We think we have found Ashoka's stupas mentioned by the later Chinese travellers,' says the archaeologist, bursting with excitement. 'But then came the crucial discovery. It was right under our noses. Following the trail of earlier finds and local oral traditions, we surveyed the fields around a little village recorded in the old gazetteers as Rajanagar, which means "the enclosure of the kings". And there it was.'

It would have been so easy to miss, but in the low, early sunlight we can make out the line of the defences snaking through the paddy fields; a rampart with two gates protected by large, projecting entrance bastions, and nine other tower bases. All in all it is a rough, irregular square about 1300 yards along each side. Under the trees are brick defences over 40 feet wide and still in places 20 feet high.

'Inside it in the ploughed fields the deposit in places is 26 feet deep. Think of it!' says Dr Pradhan breathless with excitement:

> Then the final clue. So far we have only made one trial excavation on the rampart, but we got immediate results. The place had been founded in the sixth century BC and had lasted for about a thousand years. People were still living here in the fourth to fifth centuries AD. In fact, of course, they still are. It's shrunk, but there is still a little village here by the lotus pond. Inscriptions on the polished black ware give the name Tosali, which we know was the name of the Kalinga capital. And, even better, we found a terracotta image of a king, one with earrings, turban and an inscription identifying 'Raja Ashoka'.

He saved the key find to the last. Back in the dig hut, as the August heat of Orissa turned the storeroom into a stifling oven, he unwrapped plastic bags full of corroded metalwork. Inside was a mass of arrowheads and spearheads from the Mauryan period. As he turned them over, he nodded reflectively: 'All this came from one small area of a few square feet on the ramparts. It must have been a blitzkrieg, a blizzard of arrows.'

Ashoka's conversion and the law of life

Piecing the story together from the dates on Ashoka's edicts, we can recover something of what happened next. The following year, now ten years into his reign, Ashoka went on a countrywide pilgrimage to the sacred places of Buddhism, ending up in Bodhgaya at the foot of the bodhi tree. This became his own personal

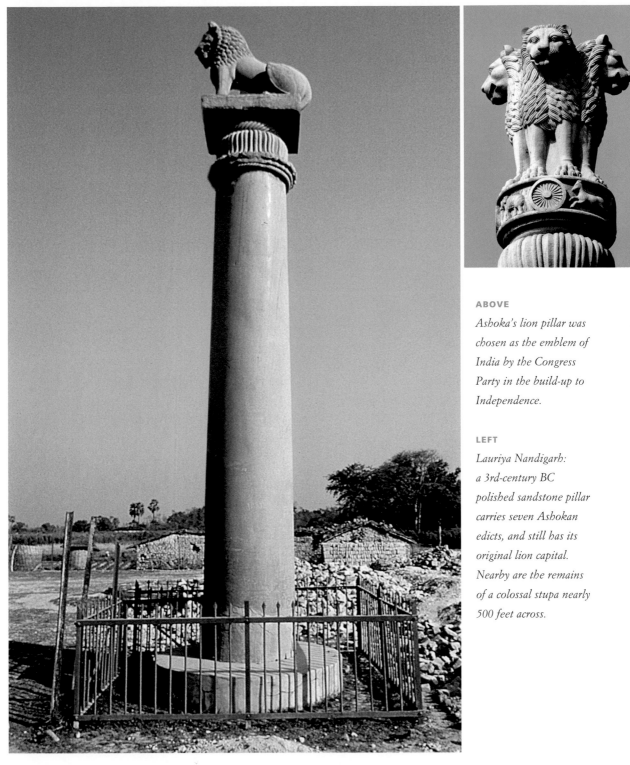

Ashoka's lion pillar was chosen as the emblem of India by the Congress Party in the build-up to Independence.

Lauriya Nandigarh: a 3rd-century BC polished sandstone pillar carries seven Ashokan edicts, and still has its original lion capital. Nearby are the remains of a colossal stupa nearly 500 feet across.

pilgrimage place in the legend too, with the added twist that the tree would be the cause of a fateful dissension with his queen, Tissarakha (see page 92). One legend says he asked for a guru to resolve his questions, and a Buddhist monk Upagupta came forward, the son of a perfume-seller in Mathura. Contemporary texts say nothing of this, simply that at Bodhgaya Ashoka gave charitable gifts to the poor and conferred with his leaders about 'how to implant good in a kingdom'. In his mind was forming a kind of political order, which had never been seen before.

This marked the beginning of the new order. What Ashoka would try to do was take the Buddhist ideas of compassion and self-possession, and the Jain ideas about non-violence, and use them as the basis not just of personal morality but of politics too. The record of his thoughts and actions survives in a series of often garrulous edicts carved first on rocks in prominent places across the empire, and later on great polished stone pillars – some already standing, some newly erected. About sixty have been found so far, twenty of them, astonishingly, discovered in the last five decades. They begin in year thirteen of his reign (*c.*258 BC), announcing his 'conquest through dharma [righteousness], not violence', and there are twenty-five separate edicts over the next sixteen years. The early ones are ecumenical; the later ones more Buddhist in tone. Ashoka seems to have got more heavily into Buddhism as he grew older, though he never converted and was only ever a lay member. In that he was a typical of the Mauryan dynasty, whose members, whatever their personal leanings, had no interest in pushing what we would call a state religion. The edicts are found from the Bay of Bengal to Kandahar in Afghanistan, and from the Northwest Frontier of Pakistan to below the Krishna river in southern India. They give us a sense of the extent of the territories over which Ashoka claimed to rule. Building on his grandfather's kingdom, his is the first state in history that ruled the majority of what is India today.

In the edicts, the nuts and bolts of his new ideas on politics are enunciated in detail. The first key idea is the sanctity of all life, which is especially a Jain idea. The king does not renounce violence in self-defence, but the death penalty was removed, as also appears to have been the case under some later dynasties, such as the Guptas. Meat-eating was widespread in early India, so the king tried to limit it rather than ban it altogether. Remarkably, Ashoka's laws also attempted to stop environmental destruction. 'Forests must not be needlessly destroyed,' he said. Other injunctions call for the preservation of many species, from the Ganges porpoise to the rhino, and even the white ant.

Another key idea was toleration for, and sympathy with, the beliefs and practices of other religions. Speaking of the diversity of India, Megasthenes says there was a huge number of 'nations', and many sects that often violently disagreed among themselves. A special edict (XII) is concerned with just this. People must abstain from speaking ill of a neighbour's faith, Ashoka said, 'for all religions aim at the same thing in the end: that is, gaining self-control and purity of mind'. Thus they agree about the essentials, however much they may differ in externals, so 'All extravagance and violence of language should be carefully avoided'. It hardly needs pointing out that every ruler of India has grappled with this issue since ancient times. It was a key issue for the greatest Mughal, Akbar (1542–1605), and for the framers of India's modern constitution. Of course, such ideas are still painfully relevant today to the wider world as a whole, where absolute truths are claimed by one faith or another, and where death threats are issued every day for perceived religious insults, real or imagined.

Practical ideas for good governance are also contained in Ashoka's edicts, among them civic amenities and provisions for travellers. The Mauryans were great highway builders. One assumes that the Grand Trunk Road must go back to them, and on the road up to Lumbini from Patna there are still Ashokan columns in four places. Megasthenes had already been impressed by this aspect of Mauryan rule. He wrote: '… every ten stadia there are placed pillars showing the by-roads and distances', and 50 years later Ashoka tells us: 'On the roads I have planted banyan trees to shade men and beasts.' Wells were dug by the main highways, groves of mangoes planted and rest houses erected, and there were watering places with distance markers on pillars. It was an old Indian tradition, still widely followed, to feed, shelter and look after merchants and pious travellers, who then, as now, moved around India in a constant circulation.

Of course, there is a world of difference between what a government says it wants to do and what it actually does, between its ideals and how it enforces them. The edicts suggest that Ashoka's was, in our terms, a very moralizing nanny state in which you could think or believe what you wanted, but you had to do what you were told. It is unlikely that Ashoka relaxed the surveillance state of his grandfather with all its mechanisms of state control, such as the Special Ministry of Censors, to enforce not only the rules on the sanctity of animal life, but 'respect for elders', the food laws the sacrifice laws and even 'female morals'.

It is probable that some aspects of this customary law have come down to the Indian society of modern times. In Kashmir even into the last century there was a special court of five Hindu pandits, hereditary officers from the deep past, maybe descended from Ashoka's, who tried breaches of the Hindu scriptures. And hereditary Brahmin officers specifically supervising breaches of caste rules existed in many places in the Deccan during Queen Victoria's day. One tiny detail of the Mauryan state will be familiar to anyone who has attended a rally in today's India. When the ruler was on the move through the streets, Megasthenes reports, attendants stretched out ropes to keep the crowd back and 'to cross the rope was punishable by death'. While the death penalty no longer applies, even today the crowd obeys the rope.

Spreading dharma to the world

Ashoka's ambitions for his dharma were not confined to India. The edicts tell us that he sent his Buddhist embassies to Gandhara and Kashmir, to the Himalayan regions, and overseas to Sri Lanka, Thailand and Burma. But of special interest are the missions to the West. Ashoka sent his ambassador Dhamaraksita (who is described as being Greek himself) to the Yonas (Greeks) in what is now Afghanistan and Pakistan; and further embassies went to the Mediterranean world, to the Greek kings of Egypt, Syria, Anatolia, Cyrene, Epirus and Macedonia. So three generations after Alexander had brought fire and sword to the Indus valley, India looked for the first time to the West, sending envoys to preach the dharma and spread Ashoka's message of friendship and brotherhood. We know that Greek ambassadors visited the Mauryan capital too; for example, Dionysius from Ptolemaic Egypt stayed in India for some time and, according to Pliny, wrote a book 'enlarging on the power and vast resources of the Indian nations'. It is tantalizing that, as yet, no record of these exchanges has been discovered in Western sources, though an interesting story told by the geographer Strabo gives an idea of how difficult it was to make the journey from the Ganges plain to the Mediterranean, a round distance Ashoka describes as being some 600 yojanas, nearly 5000 miles. The party reached Antioch in Syria with gifts carried by eight servants clad only in loincloths: 'three had survived, the others died on the long journey.' On the missions to the Eastern world things are less clear. We know Ashoka's son led one to Sri Lanka; later stories say others went over the Himalayas to Tibet and the Tarim basin, and even to China, but these are less certain.

Death of a dream

In his later years there are signs that Ashoka lost control. In the last ten years of his reign there were no new edicts. There are hints that before his death Ashoka partitioned the empire between his sons. In the twenty-ninth year of his reign his chief queen, Asandhimitta, died. Four years later, in 237 BC, he raised one of his lesser queens, Tissarakha to the rank of chief queen. She was young and beautiful, and Ashoka succumbed to her charms. In later Buddhist legend she occupies the role of the wicked queen, evil enough to match any counterpart in Western fairy tales. She is portrayed as vindictive, proud and foolish, while Asandhimitta had been a good queen, friendly towards the Buddhists. Two years later, the story goes, jealous of Ashoka's deepening devotion to the bodhi tree at Bodhgaya, that she in some way fatally injured the sacred tree by piercing it with a thorn steeped in a magic potion or poison. The tree withered away (according to a Chinese version it was cut down). Ashoka was devastated, prayed that the tree might still live, and offered fervent puja, as the Buddhist monk who is the present custodian of the tree at Bodhgaya told me: 'Ashoka poured libations of holy water and the milk from a thousand mares, and sure enough, though the tree was dead, there was a miraculous revival of the root.' The present-day tree, plus others, including one in Sri Lanka, are supposed to be from cuttings, but there seems little doubt that the original tree died, though modern botanists say it is impossible to kill a tree by scratching it with poison. Perhaps this is just a fairy tale told by the Buddhists to blacken the queen?

The last legend of the wicked queen is darker still, and hints at wider dissension within the royal house. It is told in the wonderful *Asokavadana*, a collection of stories about the king from the second century AD. The legend goes as follows: Ashoka has a son, Kunala, who is very handsome, a gifted musician and singer, with extraordinarily beautiful, captivating eyes. But an oracle says he will lose his sight. In the story his stepmother, the wicked Tissarakha, is infatuated with him, rather like the Greek legend of Phaedra and Hippolytus. The prince repels her advances, and she plans to harm him in revenge. When Ashoka falls ill, she cures him by her magic and in return asks for a boon. She takes control of his royal seal and sends a letter in his name to Taxila (where Kunala is suppressing a revolt). The letter orders the governor to blind Kunala and then kill him. The governor cannot bring himself to kill the young man, but carries out the blinding. Shedding his identity as a prince, Kunala now becomes an outcast, walking across India, playing the vina and singing, a nameless wanderer. Then one day, in the streets of Patna, the frail old king Ashoka hears his song from a palace window and recognizes his son's voice. On being told the whole story, Ashoka has the wicked queen put to death.

And what is the truth? Ashoka may have been beset with revolts in the empire, and may have had troubles with queens and princes in his last years, but first-hand sources are simply lacking. From some of the edicts we get the impression of a driven man sometimes working day and night, available 'at any hour and any place'. 'I am never fully satisfied with the end product of all my work, my exertions and the conclusion of my business … But work I must for the public good.' (This brings to mind Philip II, scribbling his late-night missives in the Escorial, or Napoleon in Jacques-Louis David's famous 4 a.m. painting.) Twenty-five edicts passed in thirteen years, the wear and tear of ceaseless royal itineraries, bombarding his councillors with ideas: Ashoka sounds to me like a man who worked too hard. 'Let the highest and the lowest both do their bit,' he urged. Perhaps he believed too much in the possibility of changing human nature. A fatal

RIGHT AND ABOVE

Sanchi, the greatest surviving stupa of thousands originally built by Ashoka, rebuilt in the 1st century BC. What connection the place had with the Buddha's life is unknown, though Ashoka was viceroy in the nearby town of Vidisa, from whence his first wife came.

mistake in a politician? One of his later edicts has this admission: 'now I realize how hard it is to persuade people to do good.'

Ashoka died in 233 or 232 BC, his thirty-seventh regnal year, aged about seventy-two.

There is one last story. Ashoka wanted to give all his wealth at his death to the Buddhists, but his ministers and sons conspire to stop him. When the time comes for the customary royal gift of alms to the monks of his favourite monastery in Patna, all the dying Ashoka can give them is his sole possession, half a mango. 'Tell me now,' he says to his councillors, 'who now is lord of the Earth?' It is a story that, like the best fairy tales, turns a full and perfect circle. But did he really die sad and disappointed, stripped of all his power? According to the Buddhist legends, since suffering on Earth is the lot of every human being even the great Ashoka had to face his share of it. For him, however, it was all the greater, since it came so hard at the end of a glorious reign.

The Mauryan Empire did not long survive Ashoka. Although its end is shrouded in mystery, it is clear that it was overcome finally by the resurgent Greek kingdoms of northwest India and Bactria. Buddhism itself has long ceased to be a great force in Indian society. In the cold light of day Ashoka's dream, you could say, vanished, a heroic failure, leaving edicts on weathered rocks and cliffs from Kandahar to the Bay of Bengal to be deciphered millennia later by young men from a distant land. But Ashoka created one of those great moments in history when we can see the power of ideas working in the real world. The Mauryans laid down a template for the future of India. A ruler on the Ganges plain calling himself king of India, a ruler who used ideas to define the morality of politics. We moderns can often admire ideas of the past without necessarily thinking they are relevant to us today. But Ashoka's dharma – however imperfectly executed – was one of the great ideas of history, like the American Declaration of Independence or the Communist Manifesto. His edicts go to the key moral question of human life on Earth. How do you persuade human beings to do good? In their commitment to the power of ideas, they are like a bolt of lightning across the pages of history.

India's Buddhist legacy to the world

Buddhism itself disappeared in the heart of India, submerged by the Huns, Turks, Afghans and Mongols, by Islamic iconoclasts and also by its Hindu Brahminical enemies. It lingered on in the south until the fifteenth century, and in eastern Bengal until modern times. Today it survives in strength only in the Himalayan regions and Ladakh, though these days many young Indians are attracted to its teachings, and many *dalits* (untouchables) are converting to Buddhism in an attempt to escape the chains of caste. In the western parts of Ashoka's world – the great Buddhist lands of Gandhara – it vanished completely under the tide of Islam. But the Buddha's message, distilled into the blood of India and throughout the subcontinent, permeates the country today, 'strewn and diffused everywhere in the thought world of India' as Akbar's biographer Abul Fazl so acutely wrote.

The ideas of the Buddha have had a tremendous impact on the rest of the world. In the West, Buddhist influence on the ancient world was probably greater than has been recognized. The Greek Sceptic philosophers, for example, traced their ideas to Indian philosophers, who were clearly Buddhists. The core of the Sceptics' doctrine was a quest to attain *ataraxia* (unperturbedness), that is tranquillity and peace of mind, with the goal of removing mental conflict and pain. 'A wise man,' said the philosopher Pyrrho, 'keeps himself in a state of inner calm.' Sceptics believed that through reason and discussion one can cure human ills, namely self-centredness, rashness and dogmatism. These ideas had a profound influence on European thought during the Renaissance, and subsequently on the whole of modern Western philosophy.

But it is in China and east Asia that Buddhism has had its greatest influence. It was the most successful ever export of Indian culture. It became a unifying cultural idea across Asia over the last two millennia, and now unites hundreds of millions of people. And it happened without coercion, which cannot be said of Christianity or Islam. Now, in the twenty-first century, as Asia rises again and the dust settles on the colonial era, cultures that were great long before the brief heyday of the West are rediscovering the common set of ideals, customs and beliefs they share in Buddhism.

We live in challenging times, and the problem of suffering in the world, posed by the Buddha 2500 years ago, has not gone away. Indeed, it is compounded today by the pervasive pressures on the individual to desire and possess, and by the revelation of human responsibility for environmental destruction, the extinction of species and global warming. In all these areas Buddhist thinking is as relevant now as when the tradition began. As the Buddha said in his last words: 'Be a light to yourselves. Seek no other. Never give up'.

3
The Growth of Civilization

NIGHT IS FALLING off the shore of Cranganore, close enough to the Kerala coast to waft the fresh smell of palm forests after rain. Our boat is a 120-foot ocean-going *uru*, the same size as the Roman ships that plied between the Red Sea and India 2000 years go. Ours is a boat out of Cuddalore, with a Tamil-speaking crew, trading between the Andamans, Sikkal in Gujarat and the Gulf, carrying a cargo of cement, pepper and spices. After four months at sea the crew are looking forward to the thrills of the old port of

Dubai: the steersman stirs cardamom and ginger into our coffee, spits out his *pan* and grins: 'There a man may be free!'

Trade is one of the key factors in civilization. By allowing civilizations to make contact, to share and test ideas, trade also allows them to grow. Our image of India, influenced by colonial writing and historiography, has so often been of a civilization stopped in time, stuck in the past, but in fact Indian civilization has always grown and changed through dialogue with other civilizations. The tidal waves of Indian history have produced great native dynasties, but also great foreign rulers, and receptivity to outside ideas has always been part of the Indian experience. Many of the greatest developments in the story of India have been shaped by dialogue with other civilizations, which began back in the Harappan age, when Indian ships traded with the Gulf. Contacts with the Persian world had grown intensive from 500 BC, but it was only in the last centuries BC that regular sea routes opened up between the Mediterranean and peninsular India. The opening of the Spice Route to the Mediterranean spurred contacts between Rome and the kingdoms of southern India, while the development of the Silk Route established contacts between China, Europe and India. This was the time of Hadrian and the Antonine emperors in the West, a time the historian Edward Gibbon thought the happiest in the history of the world. And in the beginning the chief motivation, believe it or not, was the produce of a weed: pepper.

Our boat is heading up to Gujarat via the old port of Mumbai. Indians have sailed this coast up to the Gulf since at least the third millennium BC. And in the harbours of the Indian Ocean, the picturesque old dhow ports from Oman to Gujarat and the Kerala coast, you can still touch on the commerce that became one of the earliest long-distance international trades in world history, uniting the Indian Ocean and the Arabian Sea, and opening up the sea lanes to Southeast Asia and China.

They still use the old technology too. The construction yards at Beypore near Calicut almost died in the 1980s, when their manpower and skills passed to the Gulf, where the money lay. But the old shipbuilding arts have been rekindled in recent years – for good economic reasons. The old boats quite simply are still good value. The builder's boast is that an owner will make his or her money back in four years, when the lifespan of a good boat is over forty. Construction here in Kerala was often in the hands of the Mopylas, descendants of Muslim traders and crafts-men, long naturalized, who married Indian women and had their own guilds in the Middle Ages. The *mestiry* (master builder) here, though, is a Hindu: named

Gokuldas, he is only in his thirties, and his father and ancestors were also boat carpenters 'since 500 years'.

ABOVE

The old construction techniques in the boatyard at Beypore.

On the forested estuary of the Beypore river his construction yard is at the end of town, behind warehouses and chandlers' shops. Inside the gates piles of cut timber and two tree trunks lie outside two enormous wooden sheds, where two boat frames, each the size of a large house, rise under a rattan roof. Beyond the fence in the somnolent heat brightly painted ferries with tall prows criss-cross the river, emerging from creeks in the palm forests fringing the other side, just as they must have done in Roman times.

'We use no plans, even for boats this size,' says Gokuldas. 'There is a lot of secret calculation and mathematics involved in the process of building an *uru*. All the secrets are passed on from father to son. That's how we do it with no technical drawing – how we make such big ships to full perfection. The curve of the ship and the overall shape and structure come from working out in the mind.'

Incredibly, here on this sleepy backwater, Gokuldas has just built one *uru* boat over 170 feet long, with a 40-foot beam. High as a three-storey house and weighing in at over 1000 tons, it has a cargo capacity of 1500 tons, and now trades between the Gulf and Gujarat. Careened and recaulked in the old dhow yards of Dubai or Sikkal, it will have a good lifespan and pay for itself many times over. 'Working the old way, we get no complaints,' Gokuldas went on. 'The boats are stable and strong, and no change is needed.'

This gives you a sense of the scale of ancient ocean-going shipping: the big Greek and Roman cargo boats that in the Roman period plied from Myos Hormos on the Red Sea, 120 of them every year; or the five-masted trading junks that roamed the South China Sea down to Vietnam and Java well after 1949. (You could still see them in the early 1980s, as hulks and houseboats on the Shanghai river.) Similarly, the big Arab dhows that dominated the China trade in the Middle Ages are still constructed in the yards of Karachi and Dubai, though now with engines as well as sails. Scratch below the surface of the modern world, and the old ways are still there, especially in India. This is the antithesis of globalization: the persistence of local knowledge.

At the jetty down by the river in the little port of Beypore are five big *uru* boats, the largest a vessel from Tuticorin, from whose cavernous hold a crane is unloading sacks of soda ash amid clouds of choking white dust. The ship has one big, stubby mast with a giant main spar and lateen sail; she's sailing on to the Andamans. His face burnt black by the sun, the captain offers me tea heavily spiced to hide the taste of the bad water.

'We've sailed to the Yemen, Aden, Iraq, Iran and Somalia,' he tells me. 'From there you can come "straight over" in the summer months with the southwest wind.'

That's just as the Roman navigators used to do. Like them too, his cargo includes sacks of pepper. This is what first enticed the Greeks and Romans here.

(The word 'pepper', incidentally, like 'rice', comes from the Tamil.) At its peak, tons of the stuff were heaped in the pepper barns by the Tiber. The cost was huge. According to Pliny the Younger, 'By the lowest reckoning, the India trade takes from our empire 100 million sesterces a year – *at the lowest reckoning.* That's what our luxuries and our women cost us.' That's about 10 tons in gold – probably equivalent to the annual yield of the Roman imperial gold mines in Spain. And Pliny was perhaps only talking about the sea trade via the Red Sea, not the overland route. Interestingly enough, India is still the biggest importer of gold in the world – £9 billion worth per annum; the addiction went both ways, and still does.

The Roman craze for pepper was all about food, of course. Nothing better underlines the idea that the story of civilization is also the history of food and cooking; and Indian cooking – now a mainstay in Britain – was perhaps the first international cuisine in the world. In the Roman Empire the celebrity chef Apicius wrote a famous cookbook in which 350 of the 500 recipes – from spiced flamingo and curried ostrich to dormice stuffed with peppercorns – used pepper and southern Indian spices. Read Apicius and you get the impression that to go to a high-class dinner party in imperial Rome was to risk having your taste buds irreparably blasted. Pliny raged at the stupidity of it all: 'It's incredible that pepper has become such an obsession. With some foods the appearance is what is appealing; with some, taste or sweetness. But pepper has nothing to recommend it other than its pungency. For that we go all the way to India! Who first thought that up?'

An ancient guide to the Indian Ocean

In the pages of their geographies and gazetteers we can follow the Roman obsession down the Red Sea and all the way across to the west coast of India. The *Periplus of the Erythraean Sea*, a Greek merchant's guide to the India trade from the 70s or 80s of the first century AD, is one of them. In fact, to my mind it is one of the most fascinating of all historical texts. An old Alexandrian salt who had travelled all over the Red Sea and the Indian Ocean, Hippalos, adds his own details of winds and tides, of good and bad harbours, of where to buy and what to sell. Over the years I've tracked many of them, camping at night stops on the desert route from the Nile valley; picking over dumps of Roman pottery in sweltering Red Sea ports, such as Berenike or Adoulis; waiting in coffee shops in old Massawa, Eritrea, for the winds to change; sleeping on white sands strewn with pale crimson coral at the heavenly anchorage of Qana in the Yemen. The *Periplus* lists them all. From its pages drift the exotic substances of the ancient world: malabathron and spikenard, pepper, cloves, coral, antimony, red and yellow orpiment, along with other riches that the Mediterranean world coveted: elephant ivory, fine cotton, Chinese silk and Argaritid muslins, pearls from the Gulf of Mannar.

The *Periplus* names twenty ports on the west coast of India, but the most important in the south – Pliny calls it *primum emporium Indiae* (the first market of India) – was Muziris. This was the place where Greek navigators, beginning with Hippalos himself, made their landfall after the long direct voyage from the Red Sea. A recently discovered papyrus contract between a second-century ship-owner and an Alexandrian merchant tells us about the organization of the Muziris trade, showing how they mixed their cargoes, with several merchants bearing the costs and insurance for one voyage, 'the loan repayments as per the deal agreed at Muziris'. From the Indian side the town is recorded in Tamil poetry as Muchiri-pattanam – a *pattanam* being a 'trading port' in southern speech. A softly perfumed and much sought-after place it was too, one imagines, fanned by what the Greek sailors called the tropical *zephyrus*. A haven for lotus-eaters, maybe: a place so home from home that the Greek and Roman colonists even erected a temple to their own gods, with a special niche for the deified emperor Augustus. (So British Calcutta was by no means the first Indian city to erect statues of an emperor from the West!)

The town is marked on a beautiful, coloured Roman map called the Peutinger Table, but the location of Muziris has never been identified. We know it must have been close to Cranganore, north of Cochin, and that it lay 20 stades (2 miles) inland from the mouth of a big river, most likely the Periyar. The trouble is that rivers here alter their courses, and the Kerala coastline is notoriously prone to change, creating new shores out of sandbars and floating islands, which over time become long strands of dry land covered with forest, separating the sea from the intricate filigree of lagoons in the Kerala backwaters. But in 2005 archaeologists from Kerala found Muziris exactly where it should be. The site is now 4 miles inland, behind a double line of tranquil backwaters, and it lies by an old bed of the Periyar river, which has shifted a couple of miles up the coast since Roman times. The main mound is 650 yards across, in a shady grove of palms, bananas and jackfruit, festooned with twining pepper vines. Coins of Nero and Tiberius have been found near by, and a preliminary excavation has revealed that the mound is stuffed with Roman amphorae, broken terracotta pots, Mediterranean glass ornaments and precious stones. On top stands a very ancient brick shrine of the goddess '2000 years old' according to a local man. Her name is Pattana Devi, and her village is Pattanam, no doubt the site of the famous port known to the Greeks and Romans as Muziris.

Cosmopolitan influences

The town of Muziris had a quay and warehouses, with Arab and Jewish quarters. It was a foreign enclave, perhaps resembling those Roman trading ports in the Red Sea and Indian Ocean that are specified in the ancient gazetteers and geographies as 'designated ports' – that is, places set up under treaty with the local rulers.

The native town must have sprawled among the palm groves near by, rather as the British in their day laid out their 'Black' and 'White' towns.

So Kerala has long been a cosmopolitan place. No wonder, then, that this coast is so rich in traditions. The Arab trade with Kerala began long before Islam, and the earliest mosque in India is said to be the pretty old wooden prayer hall at nearby Cranganore, where the imam tells a story that the mosque was built by Muslim merchants, companions of the Prophet, who traded here even in the Prophet's lifetime. The Jewish community has been here at least from Roman times, originally sailing down the Gulf from Charax, near Basra, bringing with them their Iraqi rituals, and even the ancient board game excavated in third millennium BC Ur, which until recently was still played by old Indian Jewish ladies in Cochin. The Jewish trade with southern India in spices, pharmaceuticals and dyes can be traced through the Middle Ages in the fascinating traders' letters that have survived from the *geniza*, the storeroom of the Jewish synagogue in Old Cairo. During the nineteenth century Baghdadi Jewish families, such as the Sassoons, built spice warehouses in 'Jewtown' in old Cochin. Even today there are still a few Indian Jews in the vicinity of Muziris, with a lovely pillared synagogue in the forests close by at Chendamangalam.

Near Eastern Christians also settled here on the Malabar coast very early on. Exactly how early is not clear. The Apostle Thomas is supposed to have landed at the Periyar river around 50 AD with the aim of introducing Christianity to India, and a gleaming white Syrian Christian basilica stands on the spot today. The earliest Greek traditions place him – more plausibly perhaps – up in the Indo-Greek court at Taxila in the Punjab. But Muziris was a major trading place for the merchants of the eastern Mediterranean in the first two or three centuries AD, and the landing of a Roman-Jewish traveller on the Periyar river around the time of the *Periplus* is certainly plausible. It is an idyllic spot where, no doubt, many Jews, Christians and Arabs from Palestine made their landfall in the heady days of the Roman spice trade, and as evensong drifts over the swaying cocoa palms by the church of Mar Thoma (St Thomas), who would wish to doubt it?

Today red-and-green-painted passenger ferries chug across the estuary from one landing point to another; the evening catch is landed; and ladies in billowing lemon or scarlet saris skip on to the landing stage and hurry home with their shopping. It is easy to imagine foreigners settling here of all places in India, servicing the annual influx of Western boat crews. Here they could enjoy their home comforts – wine from Arezzo or Kos, Italian olive oil and fish paste (imported in the amphorae found all over the site of Muziris) – happily melding their own gods with the native ones. Is that how an Indian ivory statuette of the goddess Lakshmi found its way to Pompeii, where it was buried in the eruption of AD 79? Tamil poetry of the later Roman period talks of the Greeks as mercenaries, merchants and even sculptors in southern India. It was the beginning of a long love affair.

The spice trade between India and the Mediterranean lasted until the fourth century, when it was taken over by the Persians, and then by Arabs and Arabic-speaking Jews in the seventh century after the advent of Islam. But it left many remains, both in material traces and in ways of seeing the world. Roman coins have long been found in the antique dealers trays in Cochin, Trichy and Karur. Even today it is the custom in southern Indian marriages to give the bride a necklace of small gold coins, as it was in ancient times when the coins bore the heads of Trajan and Hadrian. Another Indian borrowing is even more curious: it is an Indian source that claims a Mediterranean origin for the oil lamp – the 'Yavana [Greek] light'. If true, how delightful that one of the greatest pleasures in southern Indian temples today should come from the homely terracotta lamp found over so many Roman sites, from Hadrian's Wall in chilly northern England to balmy Muziris: the wise maiden's lamp of first-century Palestine still burns as the flame at puja time in India's tropical south.

Madurai: the first great civilization of the south

The early train from Quilon climbs away from the sea coast of Kerala and winds eastwards through the forested hills of the Western Ghats. At Tenkasi Junction we head north by road into the plain of Madurai, passing through Srivilliputtur, where the magnificent gate tower of the Vishnu temple soars 250 feet over the little town. Bursting with sculpture, its giant medieval halls are carved with scenes from the *Mahabharata*, the national epic. For travellers arriving from Kerala the temple is their first glimpse of classic Tamil architecture, as characteristic of India's south as the Gothic cathedral is of Europe.

Marco Polo spent two months here in 1273, and he found it 'the most noble and splendid province in the world'. Approaching Madurai in the early morning before the onset of the heat, you can see why. The sky is clear and the air fresh, and apart from a gentle haze over the city, you can see all the way to the giant brown rock of Tirupparakunram, the home of the god Murugan, whose hill shrine there has been celebrated in Tamil poetry and song since the Roman period. We skirt the city and reach our lodgings, an old British house on the wooded edge of Pasupatimalai (wild beast hill). From there a magnificent view opens out over the whole of the Vaigai plain, like a natural theatre widening out into the blue haze in the direction of the Bay of Bengal 50 miles or so eastwards. From the Kerala coast we have crossed the bottom of the Indian peninsula. This plain was the heartland of Pandyan civilization, the southernmost of the three great historical cultures of Tamil Nadu, and the mightiest power in southern India at the time of the Roman spice voyages. Down below us, at the heart of this ancient and renowned city, are the towers of the great temple of Minakshi.

Madurai is one of most fascinating places in India. The second city of Tamil Nadu after Madras, it is a thriving commercial city of a million people, with textile mills and transport workshops. Auto-rickshaws buzz up the narrow lanes around the temple like angry hornets in a cacophony of horns. Today the city is as famous as it was in ancient times for its busy commerce and its craftsmen quarters with goldsmiths and tailors. New buildings are going up everywhere, but the modern city is still shaped by its ancient layout and by the ritual calendar of a traditional civilization. The streets form a series of concentric circles around the temple, a layout that has always determined the city's topography and that probably goes back to at least Roman times. The inner streets are named after the Tamil months, and were part of the pattern of the city from its earliest days. This is city planning as laid out in the religious Shastras. The idea of a sacred city is an ancient one, but most, such as the Forbidden City of Beijing, exist only as museums. Here in Madurai it is still a vibrant, living entity.

At the heart of the city is the great temple with its huge gate towers and labyrinthine corridors. In my experience, it's a building hard to beat anywhere in the world for sheer atmosphere. It's a Shiva temple, but is actually dedicated to Shiva's wife, who is still regarded as the real patron of the city. Here she is called Minakshi, 'the fish-eyed goddess', a very archaic name, which probably goes back deep into the cultural and linguistic prehistory of the south. The goddess of the city is mentioned in Tamil poetry as far back as the Roman period, but her name and attributes may point to a more distant connection with the culture of the Bronze Age and before.

The culture here grew over many centuries, and to sketch its background we need to go back for a moment to the aftermath of the Indus cities, the age of the Rig-Veda in the north. Here in the south the first recognizable culture begins in the Pandyan lands on the coast, 50 miles south of Madurai at the mouth of the Tambrapani river. Excavations here at Adichanallur over a century ago found a large, megalithic settlement dating back before 1000 BC, with clear links to later Tamil culture. Particularly striking was evidence for the worship of a male god, whose emblems were a leaf-bladed lance and a peacock – very like the Tamils' favourite god today, Murugan, the 'red one', the lord of the hills. There were even signs of devotees piercing their jaws with mouth-locks, a custom still practised. The excavation was reopened in 2005 with immediate and fascinating results. Archaeologists uncovered a mud-brick fortification wall faced with stone, a potters' quarter, a smithy, a place for bead manufacture, and numerous high-status burials in a huge burial ground extending over some 150 acres. Among the most remarkable of the new finds were pieces of a burial urn beautifully appliquéd with raised motifs depicting a horned deer with raised tail, a crocodile, a crane sitting on a paddy stalk, a sheaf of standing paddy, and the tall, slender figure of a woman with palms spread out – perhaps the earliest examples of art in the south yet known.

The finds at Adichanallur strongly suggest that some living Tamil traditions, such as devotion to Murugan, are very archaic indeed: so too, no doubt, is the bull-running festival, which draws 2 million people every year to Madurai and is mentioned in early Tamil poetry. The sensational find in 2006 of a votive stone axe head bearing four signs in the Indus script, unearthed on the Cavery river near the ancient town of Mayavaram, has added to these tantalizing hints. Deposited in the Iron Age, but probably an older heirloom, how it got there is a moot point. Did it come after the Indus age? Was it brought by migrants or by trade? Was the stone itself quarried in the north or the south? The find might even point to the ancient links with the northwest claimed in the oral traditions of some surviving clans and castes in the deep south, one of which (close to Adichanallur) in a poem of the Roman period is credited with an ancestry going back forty-eight generations!

This Iron Age culture developed in the last centuries BC into an urban civilization with writing that was adopted after contact with the Mauryan Empire in the third century BC. The three historical kingdoms of the south – Cholas, Pandyas and Pallavas – emerge into the light of history at that time in the edicts of the emperor Ashoka. But already Megasthenes in 300 BC had information about the Pandyan kingdom, whose goddess, he was told, was 'a daughter of Heracles', and whose army could muster 500 war elephants, 4000 cavalry and (improbably) 120,000 infantry. Nevertheless, it is clear from Ashoka's edicts that these were sizeable and powerful kingdoms. Lying beyond the Krishna river and the austere fissured plateau of the Deccan, it was never possible for the Mauryans to incorporate them into their empire. All of this helps us to understand the amazing cultural continuities of the south.

Western contacts with early Tamil kingdoms

The Pandyan kingdom was known to the Greeks from the first century BC, and Madurai later appears on Ptolemy's world map. In return, Greeks appear in Tamil poems – as royal mercenaries living in some sort of colony, and walking around the streets gawping like tourists: 'dumb *mlecchas*' (foreigners). There are even fascinating references to Graeco-Roman sculptors working here, a picture coloured by hoards of Roman coins picked up in the city and across Tamil Nadu – further proof of commercial links with the Roman world, which we saw in Muziris. In 21 BC, during the reign of Augustus, a Pandyan embassy went from Madurai all the way by sea to Rome.

The cultural pre-eminence of Madurai dates from this period. Tradition holds that the city was the centre of the *sangam*, or academy, of Tamil poets. In Tamil

ABOVE

'In earlier times', wrote the Greek historian Polybius (2nd century BC), 'the world's history consisted of a series of unrelated episodes, in widely separated localities, but from this point history becomes an organic whole: the affairs of Europe and Africa are connected with those of Asia and Greece, and all events bear a relationship and contribute to a single end.'

literature there are, in fact, legends of several still earlier, antediluvian *sangams*, but the one in the Roman period is real enough. Already in the second century BC this poetic tradition was the subject of linguistic analysis: the *Tolkapiyam*, the earliest Tamil treatise on grammar and poetics, presupposes older and now lost poetry. Only fragments of the corpus survive, among them the *Purananuru*, an anthology of 400 poems of love and war from the first century AD, which draws on the work of 150 poets. These are written-down performances of a class of poets, male and female, that was building on an oral tradition. The works include praise poems to kings on events, deeds and battles – robust, bloodthirsty and life-loving – completely different in tone from the great medieval tradition of Tamil devotional poetry that came to dominate popular culture in the south. Although already influenced by the Brahminical culture of the north, the picture they portray of the early Tamil kingdoms gives us a hint of the culture of pre-Aryan India. It is plainly no accident that the Tamil anthologies of the Roman period contain not only great poetry about war, but also about love; relationships between men and women are depicted with great psychological realism and sexual explicitness.

> What could my mother be to yours?
> What kin is my father to yours anyway?
> And how did you and I meet ever?
> But in love our hearts are as red earth and pouring rain:
>   mingled beyond parting.

Another fascinating aspect of this early Tamil literary tradition is that the city itself is a subject of poetry, a place of glamour, riches, luxuries and overseas contacts; of freedoms, social and sexual. Urban life opened up horizons, physical, cultural and mental, and there are great descriptions of crowded bazaars, temples and debating halls. The foreign presence is hinted at through mentions of Greek mercenaries and references to the consumption of foreign wines by Tamil kings and chieftains. A famous *sangam* poem, 'The Garland of Madurai', paints a brilliant image of the city in the days of the Pandyan king Nedunjeliyan. Then, it was said, the city could be smelt from miles away by the perfume of flowers, ghee and incense: 'a city gay with flags, waving over homes and shops selling food and drink; the streets are broad rivers of people, folk of every race, buying and selling in the bazaars, or singing to the music of wandering bands and musicians'.

In one passage the poem describes the stalls around the temple, selling sweet cakes, garlands of flowers, scented powder and betel *pan*. In another it lists some of the craftsmen working in their shops – 'men making bangles of conch shell, goldsmiths, cloth dealers, tailors making up clothes; coppersmiths, flower-sellers, vendors of sandalwood, painters and weavers'. All this could be today's city, as Madurai has known an amazing continuity from that time to this: the Pandyan dynasty had its ups and downs, but a distant scion of the dynasty that ruled when Greeks and Romans were here was still ruling when the British Raj took over in 1805.

Throwing light on a lost classical civilization

Tamil literature is as rich as any in western Europe – only Greek and Latin are older. However, the Tamil literature of the late Roman and early medieval periods was largely lost until the nineteenth century, and some that was written by Jains and Buddhists was lost for good. As print took over, Western forms of education came to the fore and their European Christian canons of literary value deemed the old palm-leaf manuscripts to be no longer of worth, so they were destroyed. In the mid-nineteenth century the task of recovering those lost writings began when the scholar Swaminath Aiyar, a young student at the time, met a district magistrate who revealed that manuscripts of the ancient classics still survived. As Aiyar describes in his great autobiography (1941), over the next few decades he laboriously criss-crossed the south by train and bullock cart, gathering up ancient palm-leaf manu-scripts before they were thrown out or burnt as rubbish. To his utter amazement, as he delved around temple towns such as Kumbakonum, he even stumbled upon living chains of tradition, such as the annual readings of ancient poems by the Tamil Jains, a tradition of expounding that I was astounded to discover even now (just) survives in some small Jain communities in rural Tamil Nadu.

Today, of the canonical five epics most admired by the scholars of the Middle Ages, two remain lost, and one has yet to be translated from Tamil. But although much of the early poetry has been lost, even today manuscripts are still being found in private hands, as I discovered while we were filming, when a Tamil scholar I had contacted in Madurai phoned me with a new discovery. We arranged to meet at the Minakshi temple one gorgeous spring morning, light slanting across the gate towers and glinting on the golden roof of the goddess's shrine. We sat down under a neem tree in a small, sunlit courtyard near the temple office, while Dr Sivakkolundu carefully unwrapped a manuscript that had come from an old family in a village outside the city. The manuscript was an eighteenth-century copy of the epic called *Silapaddikaram*, which was composed in the fourth or fifth century, and is set partly in Madurai.

The leaves were tied together on a loop in long, thin strips. The text had been incised with a sharp metal point, then rubbed with lamp black to bring out the letter forms. *Silapaddikaram* is rather like one of the late Shakespearean romances:

a tale of love and passion, mistaken identities, shipwrecks and sea changes, and fateful coincidences. It's a tale whose characters and locations reflect the age of the *Periplus*: wealth made on overseas voyages, grand mansions, captivating courtesans, precious gems, fine clothes … There are the young lovers, the captain's daughter Kannaki, she of 'a body like a golden creeper', and the merchant's son Kovalan, who was 'Murugan incarnate'. At the centre of the tale, malign as Desdemona's handkerchief, is the lost anklet that brings disaster on its possessors. And the background is the age when international commerce was opening up, when 'handsome great ships of the Yavanas came splashing on the foam' to the greatest port on the Tamil coast, Puhar, or Kaveripatnam. This morning, as the sun rises over the brightly painted *gopuras* (gateways), and temple bells ring deep in the interior, Dr Sivakkolundu begins to read India's oldest living classical language:

> Great and renowned kings envied the immense wealth
> > of the seafaring merchants of the opulent city of Puhar.
> Ships and caravans from foreign lands poured
> > in abundance rare objects and diverse merchandise.
> Its treasure would be untouched through the entire world,
> > bound by the roaring seas.
> The lotus-eyed Kannaki and her loving husband were fortunate:
> > they were high-born and, like their fathers, heirs to untold riches …

The tale moves between Madurai and the now-vanished city of Kaveripatnam, whose temples and 'tall mansions' stood at the mouth of the Cavery river before they were washed away by the sea or covered in dunes. Now underwater archaeologists are scouring the shallow seabed to find fragments of broken buildings. In the hinterland, down wonderful forested lanes, are ancient red-brick foundations of lost palaces, and old temples where the priests still tell legends of the fabled city that sank into the sea: the 'emporion Khaberis', as Pliny and Ptolemy call it. The Tamil epics celebrate it as 'the city of Puhar, which equalled heaven in its fame and the Serpent World in its pleasures', a town crammed with foreign merchandise 'which came by ship and caravan … Himalayan gold, pearls from the South Seas, red coral of the Bay of Bengal, the produce of Ganges and Cavery, grain from Ceylon and the rarest luxuries of Burma'.

ஆ சிவங்கொ௲ந௲கௌ௬அ௲ப௲வ௭ர்

New worlds: the trade with China

Combine the Tamil poems with the Greek and Roman gazetteers, contracts and geographies, and together they tell us a big story about India opening up to the world. But the *Periplus* also offers fascinating clues to the very beginning of Indian commerce with China. According to the *Periplus*, it was the Tamils who ran the trade up the east coast of India, with big, sea-going catamarans made of split logs. Sailing north from the Tamil lands along the coast to Orissa, says the author,

> … the shore begins to curve eastwards, ocean on right, land on left; then eventually the Ganges appears in sight … the greatest river of India, which has a seasonal rising like the Nile. On it is an important trading post with the same name as the river, Ganges town, through which are exported malabathron and spikenard and pears, and the finest quality muslins called 'Gangetic'. Beyond this country there lies a very great inland place called China, from which raw silk and silk yarn and Chinese cloth are brought overland …

The port of the Ganges mentioned by the Greek navigator, where goods were transported by land towards China, we now know from recent excavations was Tamluk, which stood, and still stands, on a tributary of the Hooghly river 30 miles south of Calcutta in West Bengal. Now silted and overgrown with palm forests, this is one of those fascinating forgotten corners of India. It was once ancient Tamralipti, where a thriving port existed from Ashoka's day. Mentioned by the geographer Ptolemy in the second century AD, it became a famous Buddhist city and a major centre of scholarship, with twenty-two monasteries when the famous India traveller Hsuan Tsang stayed here in the seventh century AD. Indian and Chinese accounts show that this was the most important jumping-off point for China because it stood at the junction of three great trade routes. First was the sea route we have just travelled, down the east coast to southern India and Sri Lanka and across the Arabian Sea to the west. Then there were the two ancient routes to China: the sea route across the Bay of Bengal to Java, Sumatra and Indochina, and the land route through northern India across the Himalayas to Khotan on the Silk Route. Still an important Buddhist town in the seventh century, the port is marked on Chinese gazetteers and portolans as late as the fifteenth century, but lost its

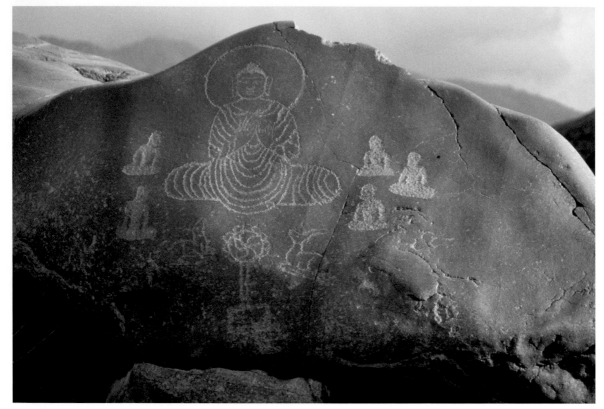

ABOVE

*A Buddhist carving
of the Buddha giving
a sermon on a branch
of the Silk Road. From
the 1st century AD the
Chinese Buddhist
missionary journeys to
India would be a great
influence in the history
of China and east Asia.*

importance when it silted up, to be superseded by the East India Company's
Diamond Harbour, and ultimately by Calcutta itself.

We have reached a fulcrum point of history, then. 'The city of the Ganges
mouth' was a junction of world trade routes on the verge of a new world order; it
is the last place in the *Periplus*, which stops here after listing the ports all the way
from the Red Sea to East Africa as far as Zanzibar, Arabia, the Gulf and the coasts
of India. From there onwards the routes were then still unknown: 'This China is not
easy to reach,' concludes the author of the *Periplus*, sitting with the old salts in his
taverna on the shores of the Mediterranean around AD 70 ('like frogs around a
frogpond', as Plato said). 'People seldom come from it, and not many go there.'
Beyond that were only travellers' stories of migrants, nomadic traders who carried
goods over the passes to China. Our sailor from Alexandria, the 'capital of
memory', ends with this enigmatic final note: 'The lands beyond these places [i.e.
China], on account of excessive winters, hard frosts and inaccessible country, are
unexplored – perhaps also on account of some divine power of the gods …'

So that is where geographical knowledge stood in the 70s of the first century
AD. But knowledge was about to expand with astonishing rapidity as the Silk Route

opened up and the first direct contacts were made between East and West. For at the very same moment that the old navigator put down his pen in Alexandria, events were unfolding far to the east that would open up another spectacular phase in the story of India – an incredible tale of lost treasures, forgotten empires and personal drama – the tale of an empire that may have been as influential as the Mughals or the British, but that is almost unknown today. And the tale begins far from India, near the border of China, beyond the Han dynasty's first Great Wall, where a people the Chinese called Yueh-chi were defeated in battle and driven westwards around the scorching wastes of the Taklamakan desert, to a new destiny and a place in world history.

The long march of the Kushans

These days we are used to understanding human geography, making our mental maps in terms of the boundaries of nation states. Most of history, though, has not been like that. Often the migrations and movements of peoples have resembled matter dissolving and re-forming, coalescing, spreading huge distances across the face of the Earth. Standing at the centre of the Old World, India has experienced such flux from prehistory to the present. Although often portrayed as a static civilization, resisting change, India has, in fact, been amazingly fluid and dynamic: the borders of her civilization have spread far beyond the boundaries marked on today's maps. Dravidians, Aryans, Greeks, Turks, Afghans, Mongols, Mughals, British ... all played their part, bringing new languages, cultures, foods and ideas to the deep matrix of Indian identity. The tides of her history have been a constant interaction between the indigenous and the foreign. And so it was with the Kushans, whose tale opens almost incredible vistas, even by Indian standards.

The story begins out in the wastes of the Taklamakan desert in Xinjiang, central Asia, under the eroded fingers of the Flaming Mountains in the burning oasis of Turfan and the gravel wastes of Lop Nor. Here a strange discovery was recently made: the mummies of red-haired people of Caucasoid physiognomy, whose writings preserved in Buddhist caves reveal that they were speakers of an Indo-European language, the easternmost of the huge language group related to Sanskrit, Greek and the Western languages. Among the various names these people gave themselves, one is still (astonishingly) remembered by today's farmers near the banks of the Jumna river south of Delhi at Brindavan, the town of Krishna. Here, at Tochari Tila (the mound of the Tocharians), a family shrine was built by their rulers at the height of their power, when they ruled from central Asia to the Ganges. We know them as the Kushans, for reasons shortly to be explained.

Their first appearance in history comes in the annals of the Chinese historians, who call them Yueh-chi, a people threatening the edge of China in the wilderness beyond the mud-brick predecessor of the Great Wall, whose remains still snake out into the sandstorms of the Taklamakan from the Gate of Heaven at Jaiyuguan. This first wall of China had been built by the Han dynasty around 200 BC to keep out such peoples, nomads and migrants. The Chinese tell a terrible legend of a treacherous parley, in which they murdered the paramount chief of the Yueh-chi and made his skull into a drinking cup. Assailed by Chinese armies, the Yueh-chi packed their tents and moved westwards into the Tarim basin, the lands above Tibet. There for a while they ruled in Khotan, before their migration further westwards into central Asia and Bactria between the 160s and 120s BC.

Within a century they had established themselves as a power in the region of the Oxus river north of the Hindu Kush. The Chinese then speak of them as 900,000 people in four great tribal groupings, one of which gives us the name by which we know them today: the Kushans. Chinese chronicles mention a king whom we know as Kujula Kadphises, the first significant ruler of the dynasty. He unified the 'great Yueh-chi tribes' and invaded the Kabul valley, Gandhara and Kashmir, before dying at the age of eighty, perhaps around AD 80. Over the next ten or twenty years his son Vima Takto added northern India to the Kushan realm, and 'from this time,' say the Chinese, 'the Yueh-chi became extremely rich'. By now we pick them up in Western sources: Greek historians, who report that Bactria, the old province of the Persian and Greek empires in northern Afghanistan, had fallen to mysterious outsiders. So by the late first century AD, just the time that the *Periplus* gives us its wonderful portrait of the world between the Mediterranean and the Indian Ocean, Kushan power had extended from Bactria across the Hindu Kush into Gandhara and northwest India. In a relatively short time the Kushans had become a world power and come to control two of the most important land routes in Asia.

Once in Afghanistan and the Indus valley, when they came into contact with Indian and Indo-Greek civilizations, Kushan culture began to undergo an extra-ordinary transformation. The Indo-Greek kingdoms in those parts had long been multilingual, even minting coins using Greek and Sanskrit. Now the Kushans adopted the Greek script and language for their own inscriptions and coins. Then, in the early second century, they introduced their own 'Aryan' language, but still using a modified Greek script. Their language, which we know today as Bactrian, has only recently been deciphered with the help of new inscriptions, and an astonishing cache of letters, deeds and other documents written on leather, cotton and wood, from a Kushan site north of the Hindu Kush. These finds also reveal that their language continued to be used for centuries in northern Afghanistan, into the

Islamic period, and it is fascinating that there are many words from it still in common speech there today, including some deriving from Greek.

From the Hindu Kush and the Kabul valley the Kushans, within a generation or two, came down from the Khyber to Peshawar, crossed the Punjab and overran northern India as far as Mathura on the Jumna. Exactly when and how this happened is still unknown. According to the Chinese account of the rise of the Kushans, a son of Kujula Kadphises was the conqueror, who then 'appointed a general to rule India on his behalf'. This was surely Vima Takto, who minted coins with a Greek inscription that called him 'Kings of kings – great saviour'. It may have been Vima who inaugurated a new era in AD 78, which survives as the Shaka era and is found today on the front page of Indian newspapers alongside the AD dating of the Christian era. With that the Kushans could justifiably call themselves 'kings of India'.

That remarkable tale has been pieced together only recently with the decipherment of the Bactrian language; and into that picture we can now place some of the most tantalizing and brilliant archaeological finds of the modern era, the most amazing being made at Bagram, north of Kabul, on the eve of the Second World War.

The treasure of a forgotten empire

Bagram, near Charikar. The giant airstrip that formerly belonged to the Soviets in their war against the Afghan resistance is now the US military base in their war on the Taliban, where giant Hercules transport planes thunder in day and night, and F-116s rise into the sky with an ear-splitting crack. The strip lies in the plain of Kabul, and looking north there is a wonderful view towards the snow-capped mountains of the Hindu Kush. In the foreground, across green fields dotted with brown mud-brick houses – typical Afghan fortified farmsteads – a promontory sticks up over a steep drop to the Panjshir river, a place called Abdullah's Castle. The citadel is about 300 yards across, and the fortifications of the outer city are nearly half a mile further to the south. This is the site of a Greek city founded by Alexander the Great – Alexandria under the Caucasus, later known as Kapisa, the summer capital of the Kushans. Here, in 1937, French archaeologists found the greatest single hoard of artistic treasures ever discovered in Afghanistan: a wonderfully eclectic mixture of Silk Route artefacts from as far away as China and the Mediterranean, and dating from the second century. There were ivory-backed chairs of Indian origin, lacquered boxes from Han China, and Greek glass from Alexandria and Syria, including a unique glass painting of one of the Wonders of the World, the Pharos of Alexandria. There were also Hellenistic statues and silverware, stucco mouldings, and images from the Greek myths, including Cupid and the rape of Ganymede by Zeus. This extraordinary mixture is a testimony to the cosmopolitan nature of the Kushan rulers of the city, evoking the brilliant age when Afghanistan was the stepping-stone between central Asia, India and the Mediterranean.

As the site was the summer capital of the Kushan kings, the building excavated in 1937 may have been a palace storeroom. The fabulous delicacy and discernment of the pieces almost suggests the taste of an art connoisseur, or perhaps a collection of diplomatic gifts, and it gives us a vivid sense of the high culture behind the Kushans' embassies to Han China and Hadrian's Rome. This was a time of diplomatic and commercial exchanges between all the great powers of the classical age, with the Kushan Empire standing in a central position at the junction of the land and sea routes between East and West. The first East–West meeting took place at this time in central Asia on the Silk Route, when caravans of Greeks and Romans met the Chinese at the White Tower of Tashkurgan, on the border between Xinjiang and Tajikistan, the mid-point between Europe and China. This was a time when there was peace in most of the lands from the Yellow River to Hadrian's Wall, which is why the historian Edward Gibbon in a famous passage described it as 'the happiest time in the history of the world'.

The greatest ruler of Kushan India is remembered even today in the Buddhist legends of China, Mongolia and Tibet. In Japan he even appears as the evil genius of one of the most famous *manga* comic books. In Sri Lanka and southern Asia he is remembered as one of the four pillars of Buddhism, even though his shrines and coins show he also worshipped the Iranian fire gods, and Hercules and Athena. In India he is remembered as a tyrant, and may even be commemorated in a famous cycle of religious dramas. But the real ruler is a man so mysterious that until very recently we were not even sure in what century he lived: Kanishka the Great.

Surkh Khotal, 'the Red Pass'

Crucial inscriptional evidence for Kanishka has come to light in Afghanistan since the 1950s, surviving despite the cycle of war and destruction that has followed the Russian invasion of 1979. And the ten years since I last visited have been particularly fruitful.

A few miles out of Pul-i- Khumri, north of the Hindu Kush, is a wide valley, covered in springtime with alpine flowers. The road north to the Oxus runs along the bottom, and the traveller might easily pass through, unaware that the hill terraces off to the left were artificially created in ancient times and were the setting for a splendid royal sanctuary. This included a temple standing in a paved courtyard surrounded by a colonnaded portico, which was approached from the valley bottom by a great stairway of five flights, each one leading to a spacious terrace. This was the site of one of Afghanistan's greatest archaeological finds: the family temple of the rulers of the Kushan Empire. In the sanctum stood a great statue of the ruler in a patterned Kushan kaftan and riding boots, with an inscription noting that the shrine was dedicated by Kanishka himself. The image of the king was smashed by Taliban iconoclasts in Kabul Museum in April 2001, when the minister of information, prompted by Mullah Omar, the de facto head of state, ordered a five-day rampage to pulverize all human images. Kanishka himself, standing in pride of place on a plinth at the entrance to the museum, was reduced to a pile of dust and rubble, but an almost identical full-length portrait found in another Kushan royal shrine – at Mathura, deep inside India – shows us the man in the same baggy trousers and overcoat, with ceremonial staff and broadsword, and the same great riding boots. And what boots! With their big, built-up toes, one can imagine them trekking across the gravel wastes of the Lop Nor, and the rocky screes of the Pamirs and the Hindu Kush.

Like other foreign dynasties in India, the Kushans were ecumenical in matters of worship and had no interest in establishing a state religion. The inscription from Surkh Khotal shows that Kanishka's ancestors worshipped Iranian gods, and they later added Greek deities when they came into Gandhara. Kanishka names Helios, Hephaistos and Selene among his patron deities, along with Babylonian gods, such as Nana, and even the delightfully syncretic Greek–Egyptian–Babylonian Serapis. Indian names appear later on the coins of his son Huvishka, such as Mahadeo (Shiva) and his son Skanda. One of Kanishka's most striking coins shows the Buddha with halo and toga, bearing the name 'Boddo'. Here at Surkh Khotal, just a mile or so away across the valley and lined up with the grand staircase, there is a ruined Buddhist temple of the same period, with monumental figures. This, then, was the place where the first fusion of Bactrian, Persian and Greek art took place, and led to the wonderfully expressive Gandhara art of northern India, one of the most vital artistic traditions in the world, which would play a foundational role in the history of Indian art.

From the top of Surkh Khotal there are wonderful views of the plain of Pul-i-Khumri and the distant whaleback massif of the Hindu Kush above the Khawak Pass. In the last ten years, unfortunately, the site has been devastated and plundered: the great terraces down the hillside, with their ceremonial stairway, have been gouged and slighted; the site of the temple with its Greek-style columns is hard to make out now, the column bases having been thrown aside. But it is the place to reflect on the enigmatic Kanishka: his interest in Eastern and Western gods, his support of Buddhism, his munificent patronage of the arts, his economic astuteness in putting his empire on the Roman gold standard ... He has left legends across the Eastern world to China, but the man behind the deeds is a shadow.

BELOW

Gold coin of Kanishka with typical central Asian coat and riding boots, and perhaps a hint of a rugged personality?

To imagine him at Surkh Khotal in the Afghan hills is to catch a sense of a vigorous, dynamic, self-assured and egotistical man at the centre of a truly expansive age.

Discovery in the Kaffir's Castle

Kanishka's date, and even his century, have long been controversial. So too are the order and the names of those in his dynasty who ruled before and after him until their eclipse in the third century AD. But the veil has been lifted on the mystery in the last few years by an inscription found in 1993 during the Taliban war. The text, which has revolutionized the history of this period in central Asia and India, was found in the territory of Sayyed Jaffar, the local governor and head of an old Shi'ite family of Pul-i- Khumri. By a strange chance, I stayed with Jaffar after crossing the Hindu Kush to northern Afghanistan in the winter of 1995. At that time he showed me a photograph of the stone from which one could immediately see it was in the Bactrian language in Greek letters. But of its significance, no one at that stage could have been aware as the Bactrian language was still imperfectly understood. The stone had come, Jaffar said, from a place called the Kaffir's Castle, not far from Kanishka's shrine at Surkh Khotal. Deciphered in the last few years, it has turned out to be one of the most significant recent finds in early Indian history, for it is about Kanishka, not just as king of the Kushans, but as what one can only describe as the emperor of India:

> Architect of the great salvation, Kanishka the Kushan, the righteous,
> the just, the autocrat, the god, worthy of worship, who has obtained
> the kingship from Nana and from all the gods. He inaugurated the
> Year One … and issued an edict in Greek, and then put it into Aryan
> … In the Year One it has been proclaimed unto India, unto the whole
> realm of the ksatriyas … his rule as far as the city of ——, the city of
> Saketa, the city of Kausambi, the city of Patna, as far as the city of Sri
> Campa … [to] whatever rulers and other important persons who
> submitted to his will, and he had submitted all India to his will …

The inscription has an astonishingly eclectic mix of gods: Nana and Umma, from Mesopotamia, the Zoroastrian god of wisdom Ahuramazda, and the Iranian deities Sroshard, Narasa and Mir, whose images were all placed in the royal shrine. This positively international polytheism echoes the coins of Kanishka and his son, which also depicted an eclectic choice of gods – Iranian, Greek, Indian and Buddhist. Crucially for the historian, the inscription at the Kaffir's Castle also includes a list of Kanishka's ancestors:

… for King Kujula Kadphises his great-grandfather, and for King Vima Taktu his grandfather, and for King Vima Kadphises his father, and for himself, King Kanishka, king of kings, the scion of the race of the gods … [As for] these gods who are written here, may they [keep] the king of kings, Kanishka the Kushan, forever healthy, fortunate [and] victorious, and [may] the son of the gods [Devaputra] rule all India from the Year One to the Year 1000 …

So now, for the first time, we have the order of the Kushan kings, and we can place Kanishka in history. He was a contemporary of Hadrian, who built the great wall across northern Britain, and of Antoninus Pius, with whom he exchanged embassies. He ruled around AD 120–150, his first year possibly AD 127. The inscription also gives dramatic new evidence about the extent of his empire: he was 'ruler of the peoples of India' all the way down the Ganges plain, from Saketa (the present-day city of Ayodhia), past Ashoka's old capital at Patna, to Sri Campa, the giant unexcavated mound of Bhagalpur in the plain of southern Bihar, which has produced a huge amount of early Buddhist material.

So now it is possible to map the Kushan Empire from the Silk Route city of Khotan in Xinjiang, down through Afghanistan, with the summer capital at Kapisa-Bagram, across the Khyber to the spring residence at Peshawar, into the plains of India, with the main winter residence at Mathura, then down the Ganges to the edge of Bengal – an extent of nearly 3000 miles. Of course, it is hardly possible that this was a unitary empire: we must imagine provinces ruled by kinsmen, sub-kings and satraps (governors), who kept control through gifts and fiefdoms, exacting hostages and taking tribute. But theirs was an orientation in Indian history that looks forward to the Mughals, and will cast its shadow right down to Partition.

Peshawar, 'the city of flowers'

'Ah, Peshawar, Purushpura – the city of flowers,' says Zahoor Durrani, his eyes sparkling. We first met twelve years back, when he had helped us through Peshawar when we were following Alexander's route down from the Khyber and up to Kaffiristan. Immaculate in his tweed jacket and silk cravat, Zahoor is an enthusiast, an enabler, with an encyclopedic local knowledge, and a deep love for his native city, which I must say I share. Peshawar is, without question, one of the best places in the subcontinent.

'Babur, the founder of the Mughal dynasty, was very fond of the city for its green and magnificent gardens, and beautiful fertile valley bedecked with flowers and laden with fruit: it's a little different today, of course!'

Zahoor comes from an old Peshawari clan. The family house still stands in a warren of streets in the old quarter of the Bukhara and Samarkand merchants, at the top of the old town, near the Mughal caravanserai. With their elaborate timber frames, carved balconies and extravagant ornamental flourishes, these palatial town houses make old Peshawar one of the most picturesque places in the subcontinent, and Zahoor is involved in a UNESCO project to save them before it's too late. We pause at a gorgeous timber mosque from the eighteenth century in a sun-drenched courtyard. Although the city goes back at least to the age of Darius the Great, Zahoor believes it was the opening of the Silk Route that really changed the city's fortunes: 'See the wood carving? The marquetry? It was all brought from Bukhara on camel trains. Every piece! You see, this place has been a kaleidoscope of cultures and a melting pot of peoples for centuries, a haven of refuge for the wandering humanity coming down from the Afghan hills since the beginning of history.'

We had come down from the Khyber on a fabulous sunny day, when the road from Afghanistan was open despite growing rumours of worsening conflict in southern Helmand province and Kandahar. This ancient road is the great lifeline for Kabul, and vast queues of articulated lorries were waiting to cross over.

Coming eastwards from the viewpoint at the end of the pass, the plain of Peshawar stretches out, with its great old fort Bala Hissar 12 miles off. From here, even in the 1970s, you could see great camel caravans winding their way down into the plains to reach the serais and bazaars of Peshawar (see page 128).

We stop for tea in the Qissa Khawani bazaar, the 'bazaar of storytellers'. Its name comes from olden times, Zahoor says, when this was the place where travellers and caravanners met, news and views were exchanged, and professional raconteurs enthralled audiences of merchants and passers-by. 'In Queen Victoria's day,' says Zahoor, 'the British commissioner in Peshawar, Sir Edward Herbert, described this as "the Piccadilly of central Asia".' And although the storytellers are long gone, the street still throbs with activity. Colourful fruit stalls and sweet shops compete for your attention, and wayside restaurants sell a bewildering variety of kebabs, grilled meats and freshly baked flatbread. The aroma of tea and cardamom, mingled with sandalwood, incense and tobacco, fills the air, and walking through the narrow side alleys, you find yourself engulfed by clouds from cooking fires and steaming samovars.

We are heading for Pipal Mandi, where an ancient pipal tree spreads its shade over stalls selling clothing and woollens, nuts and dried fruit. It's a famous place in Peshawari lore because this is where Kanishka is supposed to have enshrined the Buddha's begging bowl. The story goes that Kanishka's elephant bowed down to the bowl: unable to move it, the emperor built a monastery and a stupa around it. The bowl became a great pilgrim attraction in the fifth century AD, when the poor worshipped at it, throwing flowers and having their food blessed in the Hindu manner. Kanishka was also said to have planted a sapling here of the bodhi tree under which the Buddha had achieved enlightenment at Bodhgaya. The tree too became a stopping place on the Buddhist pilgrim trail, and one early Chinese pilgrim says that its 'branches spread out on all sides and its foliage shuts out the sight of the sky'. Beneath it there were four giant, seated Buddhist statues. They have gone, but today's bodhi tree still thrives, with shops built into and around its trunk, its long branches sticking through their roofs, while rickshaws jostle and splutter up the lane and the blanket sellers call out their wares.

Even now it has a real central Asian feel: the bazaaris offer silver coins of Alexander, huge copper rupees of the East India Company decorated with Hindu gods, and silver coins of Victoria as empress of India. Also on sale are old British Enfield rifles and hand-painted china teapots made in the imperial factory at St Petersburg before the White Russians' fragile polity collapsed. Here, in short, you can see the bewildering detritus of history from wars ancient and modern. The big news is of Kushan coins in numbers, especially from a legendary hoard out in the hills near Gardez, beyond the Tora Bora. Over tea we are shown copper and silver coins of Kanishka – relics of the days when Afghanistan was not a black hole eating up lives, armaments and munitions, but a place of peace, a bridge and transmission point of the world's cultures.

The greatest building in the inhabited world

I'm heading out of the Lahore gate at Peshawar by taxi with Zahoor on another apparently hopeless historical quest. As we've seen, Kanishka supported all religions – uncannily like other great Indian rulers, such as Ashoka, Chandragupta, Harsha and Akbar the Great, and perhaps, above all, for good, pragmatic commercial reasons in a trading empire. But he was also remembered as a pillar of Buddhism, and here in Peshawar he built what with little exaggeration one might call the eighth wonder of the world: a Buddhist stupa 300 feet across at its base and, according to Chinese pilgrims, who described its giant metal and wood umbrellas and finials, soaring 600 feet high. If these Chinese eye-witnesses are to be believed, it was the highest building yet built on Earth, and it was still standing when the monk Fa Xien came here 250 years later. 'Of all the stupas and temples the travellers saw in their journeys, there was not one comparable to this in its solemn beauty and majestic grandeur. There is a current saying that this is the finest stupa in the Jambudvipa ['rose apple continent', that is the inhabited world].'

Many miraculous stories were later told of the construction of Kanishka's stupa. One of them, repeated in legends across China and Tibet, says that the Buddha himself prophesied the stupa and the name of the king who would build it and protect Buddhism; and that when the moment came for the prophecy to come true, a magical child led Kanishka to the spot.

More details come in the AD 640s from another Chinese pilgrim to India, the famous Hsuan Tsang. But these deepen the mystery. Hsuan Tsang's extraordinarily intricate description of the structure, half a millennium after it was first built, may reflect a rebuilding after several fires, destructions and lightning damage, not the original conception. But he says the base was 150 feet high, the stupa dome itself was 400 feet high, and above it were a cupola lantern and a metal pillar with twenty-five copper umbrellas or discs. The whole structure he estimated at 500–600 feet in height. Relics of the Buddha were placed beneath the stupa by the king. A monastery was constructed on one side of the great courtyard, with a host of smaller relic stupas and shrines. By the side of the stupa in Hsuan Tsang's day there was also a great pipal tree about 100 feet high, which it was said had been grown from a sapling of the original bodhi tree at Bodhgaya.

If these stories are true, the stupa was the greatest building before the skyscraper age, soaring higher than the spire of Salisbury Cathedral or even the

LEFT

The Sufi shrine on the site of Kanishka's stupa outside the city of Peshawar. It is the latest of the Buddhist, Hindu and Muslim layers on the site.

tallest of all Gothic cathedrals, Old St Paul's in London. But could that really have been possible? It hardly seems likely, though the biggest stupa in the world today, at Nahkon Pathom in Thailand, a nineteenth-century restoration of an ancient building, stands at a staggering 412 feet. Following the clues in the Chinese pilgrims' accounts, archaeologists first went looking for its remains a century ago. The French Silk Route explorer Alfred Foucher identified the site; then a British archaeologist discovered the stupa's footings in 1908–9 and ascertained that its base was indeed nearly 300 feet across, roughly the size reported by the Chinese. But could it really have been 500–600 feet high, as the Chinese visitors claimed? It seems incredible that the technology existed to create, raise and support the vast superstructure with its copper umbrellas, though interestingly enough, the story is told that Kanishka's builders couldn't raise the great 90-foot iron post on which the umbrellas were mounted until pillars were erected at the four corners of the stupa to support scaffolding with a windlass system. Only then was the huge column lifted in the presence of the king and royal family, accompanied by prayers and libations and swirling clouds of incense. Looking at the proportion of base to height compared with other great stupas, and including flags and umbrellas, the whole structure could well have exceeded 400 feet. Certainly this would rank among the wonders of the ancient world – and even if the Chinese reports are exaggerated, construction of such a building could not have been imagined except in an age of incredible ambition and technical and artistic capability.

The site is forgotten now, a hundred years on from the British dig. It was out in the middle of open fields and graveyards then, but in the last twenty or thirty years, the suburbs of Peshawar have engulfed it. Asking directions to it under the old name, Shah-ji-ki Deri ('mound of the great king'), draws a blank in the streets outside the Lahore gate – even with the local traffic police, who send us the wrong way. With Foucher's sketch-map, I feel we are on the right track when we reach a vast graveyard, but we still have no luck asking the locals for directions. I am on the point of giving up when a local man with an Afghan hat and shawl comes over. He knows about the history of the place and tells us he's been fascinated by the legend of the stupa since school. He points to a ridge a couple of hundred yards off crowned by a warren of brick houses: 'That's the place you are looking for – the site of the stupa of Rajah Kanishka. That's where the Britishers dug when my grandfather was a child. Many ancient bricks here were used for building; bits of sculpture are always turning up, and coins.'

In front of us stretch thousands of tombs, gaily coloured tinsel offerings blowing in the breeze, and a big pipal tree with a shrine at its foot, where the Muslim mourners do their rituals for the dead. I recall the sacred pipal by the foot of the stupa seen by Hsuan Tsang in the seventh century: could this by any chance be a descendant? Zahoor is beginning to be excited. Perhaps our search is not going to be as hopeless as I feared. Our guide leads us on through the lanes of tombs, and then we discover that, as so often in the subcontinent, the site is still a place of worship. We walk through the graveyard towards the houses, and there at the base of the hill, through a tall brick and plaster gateway, stands a picturesque, white-domed Sufi shrine in an overgrown walled garden. The custodian who has kohl-rimmed eyes and henna-dyed hair, comes to greet us and offers tea. He's been here fifty years, and the tomb, he says, belongs to the Kwadja order, and is related to the famous pan-Indian shrines of the Chistis at Ajmer, Fatepur and Delhi. Sufi pilgrims still come here from India. He sits down with us and begins to tell the tale:

> In the days before Independence all those houses on the hill were lived
> in by Hindus. This was an old Hindu part of town. By then there was
> no Hindu temple any more, as there was in the old days, though they
> still had shrines to their gods in their houses, and pilgrims still came
> here from far away, even from Delhi. They used to have a Hindu *mela*
> – I can't remember when, but I think some time in the summer.

I recall Foucher speaking of a Hindu festival here a century ago, around the time of the festival celebrating the conception of the Buddha. Could this have been a hangover from the commemorations established under Kanishka, which continued until the end of Buddhism here after the Muslim conquest?

We sit in the custodian's garden, again marvelling at the continuities in the memory of the people, despite the tidal waves in the history of the subcontinent, the rise and fall of its empires. This is another of those wonderful moments on a historical search where one stumbles on a living link, however tenuous, with the lived past. The custodian refills our cups and regales us with another story …

On the flat roofs of the village children fly kites, on long lines so high that we almost lose sight of them in the kingfisher sky. And as I look up, in my mind's eye the giant stupa appears before me, its huge square base rising in five tiers, with friezes of the life of the Buddha, then the giant dome, which one story said was hung with fine netting sewn with pearls that made little sparkling points of light whether lit by sun or moon. Witnesses claimed that the dome was 300 feet high, shining with painted plaster and gilt, and on top was the decorated pinnacle, which is represented in later illustrations and votive models: thirteen tiers in wood, capped by copper umbrellas mounted on an iron-clad pillar, with huge flags snapping from the apex like dragons' tails in the wind. One of these banners, presented by a Han Chinese queen, was made of sewn silk and was more than 300 feet long. The whole edifice would have been a monstrous, garish thing to our taste – gleaming colours, burnished copper, painted wood and gilt, variegated streamers of silk – but what a sight! And don't forget the sounds that went with it: the tinkling of a myriad puja bells and wind chimes, the mysterious susurration of flags, the clatter of rattles … It was like a vast sounding chamber: a Buddhist wind orchestra.

Zahoor shakes hands with the custodian as we leave and gives his card to our guide. At the edge of the graveyard we turn back for a last look. What an incredible spectacle it must have been across the plain of Peshawar, a beacon visible from the Khyber or from the route down the Indus gorges at the end of the perilous journey from central Asia – a vision from a lost world.

The emperor's casket

'Here you are,' says the keeper of Peshawar Museum as he turns the key to the old glass case. 'I challenge you not to be excited! Now you will feel you can almost touch Kanishka.'

We are back in the museum, a cavernous colonial building with classical pillars and varnished wooden floors, to look at some of the world's most amazing collection of Gandharan art from the Kushan age, when this foreign dynasty changed the way the Buddha was represented and his story told. All around the galleries stand larger than life, polished black stone images of the Buddha and Bodhisattvas from the Kushan age, looking for all the world like 1970s rock stars, with their long, wavy hair and moustaches, their bare, muscled chests dripping

*Gandharan Art: a
Buddhist statue typical
of the Kushan period,
mixing Greek, Indian
and Buddhist elements.*

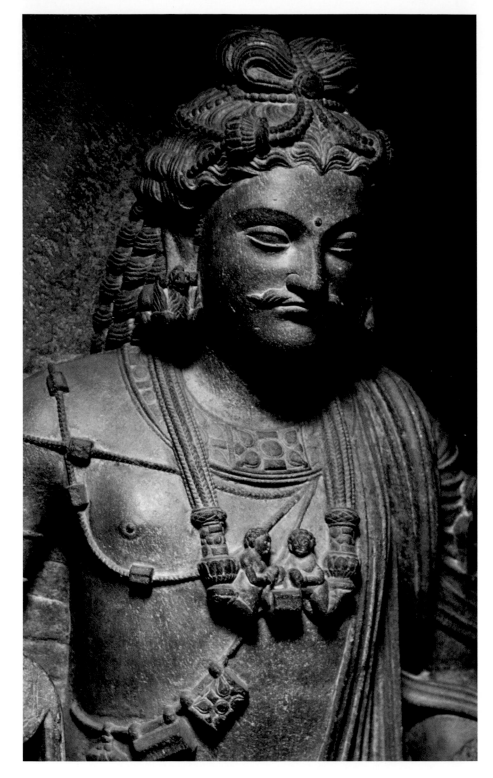

with chunky jewellery. The Kushans, it has to be said, took the look of Buddhism – and, indeed, its ideology – into a very different place.

In the base of the great stupa at Peshawar, according to the Chinese pilgrims, Kanishka deposited a sacred relic of the Buddha himself: a casket with a small quantity of ashes. The casket, dated to the first year of Kanishka's reign, was discovered in a tiny chamber under Kanishka's stupa during the archaeological excavations of 1908–9. The tiny reliquary inside contained three bone fragments of the Buddha: these were given to the Buddhists in Burma, and remain today in Mandalay. The empty casket, though, is still here: the keeper takes it out and very carefully hands it to me. I experience a little shiver, as if the thing still has a faint charge of spiritual radioactivity. The keeper continues:

> There is some discussion today about whether it is actually of his time, or if it was put under the stupa by his successor. The text is signed by the maker, who is possibly (though there is argument over this too) an artist with a Greek name, Agesilas, who oversaw the work at Kanishka's foundation. The inscription has been read like this: 'The servant Agesilas, the superintendent of works at the vihara [shrine] of Kanishka in the monastery of Mahasena'. But other readings are possible.

ABOVE

This casket found under Kanishka's great stupa contained a small reliquary with ashes of the Buddha.

The decorations on the casket form an eloquent – and intimate – testimony to the eclectic bent of the Kushans. The lid shows the Buddha on a lotus pedestal, worshipped by Brahma, the creator god of the Hindus, and Indra, the old sky god of the Rig-Veda. I turn it over in my hands. The matt bronze finish is unblemished and looks almost new. On the edge of the lid is a frieze of flying geese, Buddhist symbols of the achievement of enlightenment. On the casket itself in relief is a Kushan monarch, probably Kanishka, with the Iranian sun and moon gods at his side. The king wears the same big nomadic boots and greatcoat he wore on the smashed statue in Kabul Museum and on his vivid portrait coins – could this perhaps have been a mass-produced, 'authorized' image? On the sides are two images of a seated Buddha, worshipped by royal figures. A garland, supported by cherubs, goes around the scene in typical Hellenistic style. The casket is a tiny artefact, tucked away on one of the lower shelves in the museum, but as a symbol of the Kushan age, it's perfect.

The happiest time

At the top of the town is Ghor Khuttree, the huge walled Mughal caravanserai built by Akbar, towering above the houses like a fortress. Until recently it was the police station, but now it's a public garden with a tea shop, and over to one side of the courtyard is a deep, rectangular pit, scene of the most ambitious recent archaeological excavation on the subcontinent.

'We think this may be the oldest continuously inhabited town on the subcontinent,' says Professor Ihsan Ali. Gingerly, we pick our way down rough steps cut into the earth down the side of the hole. The dig already descends through more than 50 feet of strata, with each of the main periods labelled: so far they have reached the Kushan age: 'Look, you can see: you British are already 2 feet down!' he says smiling.

> The last two or three centuries have left 6 feet of habitation deposits.
> The deeper layers are still to be uncovered, but it certainly looks like
> the oldest city in the subcontinent so far verified scientifically by archaeology.
> And the point is that, as you can see, its life has been continuous.
> This is why it is such a wonderful opportunity for the archaeologist to
> see the whole pattern of human society here – the continuities of the
> material life over a vast span of time through all the changes of rulers
> and dynasties.

We stand in the bottom of the pit by the Kushan levels, the later history of the subcontinent above us, each phase neatly labelled: Guptas, Ghaznavids, the

RIGHT

With Ihsan Ali in the huge excavation pit at Ghor Khuttree in Peshawar.

Sultanate, Afghans, Mughals, British. The Kushan Empire reached its greatest extent and power from around AD 120 to 150, the time of the Antonines in Rome and the Han emperors in China, both of whom avidly exchanged their most exotic products for the spices, gems and cosmetics of India and Sri Lanka, and the precious stones and furs of central Asia. The Kushans, situated exactly midway on the Silk Route, certainly made the most of their advantageous position. As one of the Chinese chronicles puts it, 'after they conquered northern India, the Yueh-chi became very rich indeed'.

I asked Ihsan Ali why he thought it was such an extraordinarily international epoch. 'It's simple,' he said. 'Civilization is ravaged by war and prospers with peace. The answer is peace.'

Commerce and the spread of Buddhism

Evening is coming on, and there's a sudden chill in the air as the temperature drops. It's December on the Northwest Frontier. I'm standing on top of the great gate of the Ghor Khuttree caravanserai, looking over the packed wooden houses of old Peshawar, with their flat rooftops and timber *balakhana* screens (source of our word 'balcony'), where secluded women took their private exercise. Beyond the city there's a fabulous view of the Afghan mountains, with the Khyber Pass clearly etched against an eggshell sky. In the clear, wintry light it seems close enough to touch. From here you understand something about the history of the subcontinent; you see why Peshawar has been so important, and why several historic capitals in India were out here controlling the foot of the pass. For the Kushans especially it was the key link in the route between central Asia and the Indian plain.

The biggest cultural product of the peace was the spread of Buddhism across the East – to China, Korea and Southeast Asia, finally reaching Japan 150 years later. This was one of the great movements in history. Standing on the road to central Asia, Peshawar was at the heart of these political, religious and commercial activities. There were already Buddhist monasteries in the city, but things moved on to a different level when Kanishka decided to support Buddhism. While the evidence from coins and inscriptions at Rabatak and Surkh Khotal shows that the Kushans maintained Iranian religious beliefs and practices, other inscriptions provide abundant evidence of the patronage of Buddhism under Kanishka and his successors. The ideals of Buddhism were very congenial to the merchant classes, and Buddhism initially spread through Kushan merchants from Gandhara and Kashmir travelling through the mountains of northern Pakistan to the Tarim basin and into China. We can recognize the ethical message of Buddhism, but it is easy to forget what the ancients saw as its commercial ethos.

So it was the Kushans who began the first formal relations between China and India. It is said that Kasyapa Matanga was the first to go from Peshawar and take Buddhism to China in the first century AD. The Kushan monk Lokaksema in the second century became the first translator of Buddhist scriptures into Chinese, and established a translation bureau at the Chinese capital of Loyang by the Yellow river. These were followers of Mahayana Buddhism, as are the majority of Buddhists in the world today, and it was Kanishka who patronized and propagated this sect of Buddhism. (Earlier, Ashoka had supported the more austere Hinayana Buddhism.)

One characteristic of this new school of Buddhist thought was to stress the miraculous life and personality of the Buddha, and this seems to have been officially sanctioned by Kanishka in his patronage of Buddhist art and literature. This humanization of the Buddha led directly to a desire for a representative figure of the Buddha who had, until this time, been depicted by such symbols as a wheel, an empty throne, a riderless horse or a footprint. Hence, it was here in Gandhara that the image of the Buddha we know today, wearing a Greek toga, was created. The revival of Buddhism by Kanishka, and the attendant emergence of Gandharan art, are among the enduring legacies of Kushan culture, and are the reason why, in eastern Asia, Kanishka is still seen as the third pillar of Buddhism.

The magical city of Mathura

Three hours down the Grand Trunk Road on the new highway from Delhi stands Mathura. From the road you can see Aurangzeb's mosque over to the east on the horizon, a memorial to later, less open-minded days (see page 215). It's a great pilgrim centre for Indians, though the tourist coaches pass it by rushing on to Agra and the Taj. But it's a magical city. Coming down the Grand Trunk from Peshawar, said an early traveller, 'it is only when one reaches Mathura, with its monkeys in the streets and sacred turtles in the river, that one feels the real character of Hindustan'.

Today it is still one of the seven sacred cities of India, with its picturesque river frontage lined with temples, pilgrim shops and hostels. It is the centre of the cult of Krishna, as it already was in the ancient world. Inside the town many of the numerous shrines perch on the massive remains of ruined Buddhist and Jain structures from the Kushan age. Meanwhile, the city's ancient earthen defences still encircle it in a great crescent 1 mile across and 2 miles from north to south – a sign of its huge size and importance 2000 years ago.

The Kushans captured Mathura in the late first century AD under Vima Takto. The city had long had connections with the northwest: indeed, Mathura had been ruled by Greek dynasts for over a century in the age after Ashoka, so the arrival of another 'Aryan' dynasty perhaps was not such a great shock. The Kushans

LEFT

*Krishna plays at Holi
in a temple in
Brindavan.*

BELOW

*The drama in Mathura
is recorded in inscriptions
from the 1st century AD.*

OVERLEAF

The Holi festival.

refurbished the outer defences and erected a rectangular inner fortress 650 yards long, with semicircular bastions and round towers at the corners. The contemporary *Harivamsa* describes the newly rebuilt city: 'crescent-shaped behind its high defences and moats, well established and laid out, prosperous, cosmopolitan and teeming with strangers.' Under Kanishka and his successors it became 'large, prosperous and beneficial, abounding in people, and a place where alms are easily obtainable,' says the *Lalitavistara* (a contrast with the 'poor dusty village' of the Buddha's time, where charity was reputedly hard to come by). To another writer, Mathura was 'simply perfection on Earth, rich in money and grain, full of noble, wealthy folk, a city of the highest excellence'. Along with Kapisa-Bagram and

Peshawar, it would become a main place of residence for the Kushan kings, and their winter capital. From here, according to the Afghan inscription found at the Kaffir's Castle, Kanishka mounted an expedition down the Ganges and annexed Saketa (present-day Ayodhia), Kausambi, Patna and Champa (now Bhagalpur). By then his empire dominated the heartland of Indian civilization.

Revolutions in ways of seeing

It often happens with foreign dynasties – the British and the Mughals are other cases in point – that outsiders who want to improve their understanding of the lands they rule seek to record, codify and explain the indigenous culture. Several great figures in Indian culture are associated by later tradition with Kanishka's court. In the indigenous Indian tradition of medicine, Ayurveda, the physician Caraka (or Charaka), one of its two traditional 'founders' (whose works are still passed down in lineages by oral teaching), is said to have been the guru of Kanishka, and is the subject of many legendary tales as far away as China. It is also likely that during this period revisions of the early epics the *Ramayana* and the *Mahabharata* were produced, just as they were under the Guptas, the Cholas and the Mughals, all of whom had a great interest in 'imperial ' and 'national' epics. Indeed, new evidence suggests that it may have been under the Kushans that Sanskrit, hitherto a sacred language that was the preserve of the Brahmins, began to be disseminated as a 'classical' literary language, eventually assuming the role across southern Asia that Latin would have in the medieval West.

Another important intellectual figure at this time was Asvagosh, a Buddhist teacher, who was a poet and a dramatist, but also the author of a great collection of Buddhist *jatakas* (magical birth tales), which were transmitted across eastern Asia, and have been described as the forerunners of *The Arabian Nights* and Boccaccio's *Decameron*. Asvagosh's work as a playwright is especially interesting in view of the still continuing tradition of miracle plays in Mathura. The earliest evidence for acting troupes in India comes from the Kushan age in Mathura, with inscriptional references to a courtesan from a 'family of actresses' and a travelling company of 'players from Mathura' working across northern India.

But perhaps the most fascinating product of the Kushan age is the art developed in Mathura: a uniquely cosmopolitan art that would influence the whole history of Indian and eastern and southern Asian art. Under the Kushans a revolution in Indian art took place, driven by Kushan and native Indian traditions, and by the Greek–Buddhist art of Gandhara. Its characteristics are a vigorous sense of life, a roving curiosity and an eclectic mind borrowing from many sources. It was an art that served its purpose of mass communication better than most in history to that time, so was multiplied everywhere that Indian culture took root. It was humanistic and people-centred (including fine portraits); it handled long narrative; it revelled in technical experimentation. And there were some surprising inventions. For example, the tradition in Indian religious art of many-armed, many-headed gods seems to have started in Mathura, defining forever the representation of the Brahminical deities. Sometimes particular artistic innovations are so useful that they transform ways of seeing: and this meeting of Greek, Indian and central Asian styles on Indian soil in the second century AD proved so successful that regional cultures across the subcontinent swiftly adapted it to their own uses, galvanized by the extrovert energies of the day.

The museum at Mathura houses an unrivalled collection of Kushan sculptures. Among them is a famous statue of Kanishka, closely matching the famous statue from Surkh Khotal in Afghanistan. Carved in the characteristic local red sandstone, it came from a mysterious Kushan family shrine at Mat, on the other side of the river Jumna. The site was excavated badly a century ago, and the findings were never published, but the place is still known as Tochari Tila (the mound of the Tocharians), a reference to the old racial identity of the Kushans before they ever came to India. From the same time are wonderful images of young nobles in turbans, and voluptuous bacchic scenes, a hint of the courtly culture of this multiracial empire in the mid-second century AD, when the Old World was largely at peace from Hadrian's Wall to the Yellow river.

The beginning of a world economy

It is at this time that we begin to detect the coming shape of a world economy. The Kushans inherited a run-down currency in the northwest, but soon started to supplement the debased silver and copper coins with newly introduced gold coins on the weight standard of the Romans, which had a very wide circulation. Beautifully designed and minted, the coinage is one of the most fascinating and unexpected aspects of their rule, both practical and symbolic. Like later foreign dynasties – the Mughals and the British, for example – the Kushans aimed at a high-value currency that would enable large-scale commercial enterprise. Wholesale business could now be conducted in a vast area from Bactria to the Ganges basin, and perhaps in the internal economy of India part of the flow of bullion into southern parts from the Roman spice trade found its way north to be recoined by the Kushans.

Historical economists over the last twenty years or so have been attempting to calculate the history of the world economy based on a complex series of calculations and hypotheses, which by the time we get to AD 1500, begin to be more reliable. For the Kushan age it is largely a matter of guesswork based on such things as the widespread circulation of money, a population boom, and increased settlement, but the upshot is the first of a series of graphs of the rise of the world economy. Estimates for the population of India suggest that the subcontinent might have had 75 million in an entire world population of perhaps 250 million; so India perhaps had more than a quarter of the world's people (the 2007 figure for the subcontinent is around a fifth of the world total). The estimated wealth of Kushan India in terms of gross domestic product (the total value of goods produced and services provided in one year) is nearly 30 per cent of the wealth of the world – more than Rome or Han China because of its dominant position in the Eurasian landmass at the centre of trade systems. In fact, India would retain this superiority until around 1500, when the European conquest of the New World gave the western European powers access to the natural resources of an entire continent and altered the balance of history away from the ancient civilizations of Asia.

Kanishka's death

It goes without saying that neither the rule of Kanishka nor that of the Kushan dynasty approached the thousand years hoped for in the inscription found recently in Afghanistan. Kanishka died in the mid-second century AD, though his dynasty retained power for another seventy-five years in India, and longer in Afghanistan. There is no good evidence about what happened to him. Later legend tells fabulous tales of his death. He had conquered three-quarters of the world, it was said, but could not rest till he had gone on and taken the last quarter. Assembling a great army, he marched to the northern mountains, led by a vanguard of Hu barbarians on white elephants. But in the snowy heights swept by blizzards, even his magic speaking horse protested. Eventually, he turned back, to be assassinated by his own people. A strangely specific detail about his death appears in a Chinese tale that may just have an element of truth. When he was sick in bed, so the story goes, conspirators murdered him by suffocating him with a bed quilt or mattress.

This last tale is set in Mathura, where archaeology suggests that the family shrine outside the town was at some point deliberately and vindictively smashed, Kanishka's statue overthrown and decapitated. All the more strange, then, that if Kanishka was assassinated in Mathura, there is no whisper of these events in the Indian tradition. (Later Indian tradition, though, in the final version of the *Mahabharata*, preserves a hostile opinion of the Kushan-Tocharians, who, it says, did not obey the ancient Indian code of chivalry and were guilty of 'terrible and cruel deeds'.) But there is one great corpus of legends that may cast light on this. In Mathura, where drama has flourished since ancient times, a series of plays is enacted every year telling the tale of Krishna, the avatar of Vishnu, who appears in

the *Mahabharata* as an indigenous chief of Mathura. This cycle of over thirty plays developed in its present form in the sixteenth century, with all the parts played by children: and in them the central theme is of the tyrant of Mathura, Krishna's wicked uncle, who is eventually overthrown by his nephew. His name, Kans or Kansa, is still attached to many ancient Kushan mounds around the city. Could this, I wonder, be a folk memory of the great Kushan?

If so, here's a last twist. On the northern edge of Mathura, overlooking the river, is an ancient mound deep in debris, littered with fragments of Kushan Buddhist sculpture. A footpath leads up to a cluster of yellow-painted houses and a Hindu shrine of Gokarneshwar, an incarnation of Shiva. You enter through a gateway that leads into a little courtyard and a marble-floored chamber. The inner sanctum is lit by a strip light, and a fan in the ceiling gives a bit of relief in the 47-degree heat of Mathura before the monsoon. The image of the god is a giant statue of a king with great saucer-like eyes, sitting on a kind of throne, holding a wine bowl and grapes, and wearing a pointed Kushan cap. Backed with green floral tiles and holding a big brass trident, he stands in for Shiva now, with strings of wilting marigolds around his neck, his bulky shoulders covered with purple powder. But this was once a Kushan king. In the city of his demise, the 'son of the gods' Kanishka is perhaps worshipped still today.

Although virtually unknown in the West, Kanishka's legend is remembered across China, Mongolia, Tibet and Japan. Recently the king was even portrayed in one of the biggest Japanese *mangas* (adult comics), which sold 30 million copies, and has spread in cartoon versions and films to Europe and the USA. Here he is Ganishka, the grand emperor of the Kushans, head of a demonic empire, who can throw lightning bolts and who uses his familiars, his demon soldiers and his dark magic to conquer the entire world! Coming out of eastern Buddhist legends, it is a strange fate for the king who opened up the world and brought the art and ideas of East and West to Afghanistan and India; the king who sent embassies to Hadrian in Rome, and Buddhist missionaries to China.

The legacy of the Kushans

It had been an extraordinary journey. We had followed the Kushans all the way from the Merv oasis across the Hindu Kush to Kabul, Peshawar and Mathura, and the journey confirmed to me that the story of the Kushans is one of the most fascinating in history. Their empire collapsed in the third century AD under pressure from Sassanians and then Huns, but it left a permanent legacy. In northern Indian history the Kushans are the link between the ancient world and the great era of the Guptas (see Chapter 4), defining some of the key features of later Indian civilization.

4
Medieval India: Age of Gold and Iron

SUNSET FROM THE GOGRA BRIDGE in Ayodhia, a small country town in the Ganges plain: the sky looks molten – vivid red-gold underneath a huge bank of deep blue monsoon clouds. The air has freshened up with reviving rain after a muggy day, and now the evening is simply glorious. The river is rising with the coming of the rains, waves whipped up by the wind and rushing over the shallows, spreading wide to the horizon like an inland sea. To the right is open countryside, the

riverbank fringed with waving reed beds, and beyond that is what the locals call *jangal* – a wild landscape of lagoons and groves of trees through which are glimpses of a thatched village. To the left, across the bridge, are the painted domes and towers of the city: twenty or thirty mosques, tombs and temples lit up by the setting sun. On the bathing ghats pilgrims still throng, taking a last bath, squeezing out their clothes, saying sunset prayers, orange flags snapping around them in the breeze. The light dips, becoming peach-coloured; then, as the sun disappears, it fades into a soft blue. It's a beautiful sight, conjuring feelings of pure elation. One can almost believe in fairy tales, or at least see why this place was chosen by medieval poets to be the earthly location for the golden age of the Ramrajya, the rule of Rama. Golden ages, though, are problematical things, for they never exist in reality; they are imagined pasts – literary creations made for a purpose, and capable of very different readings, both creative and destructive. They perhaps tell us less about the past than about the present – and about our imagined futures.

Between about AD 400 and 1400 – in European terms, from the time of the fall of Rome to the Renaissance – Indian civilization enjoyed a series of brilliant flowerings in its regional cultures, but also went through great changes, in some places suffering violent rupture. The coming of Turkic and Afghan conquerors bearing the faith of Islam would set the north on a new path that would eventually lead India, the largest Muslim land on Earth, to be partitioned on religious grounds in the mid-twentieth century. The fact of this change is clear among the writers of those early times. At the end of the tenth century northern India ('Hindustan' to Muslim geographers) was seen as a land whose people were all 'idolaters', that is, followers of the native Indian religions – what we today would call Hindu, Buddhist and Jain – along with the many folk religions and cults. But in the Middle Ages northern India would become one of the greatest Muslim civilizations in the world, both in numbers and in creativity. (If we include Pakistan and Bangladesh, the subcontinent still has much the biggest Muslim population today.)

These changes were tremendous historical events that are still profoundly influencing the history of India. The next stage of our journey, then, takes us into those times when some of the key lineaments of modern Indian civilization were laid out: the rise of great kingdoms across India, in Bengal and Orissa, the Chandalas in Khajuraho, the Cholans in the south, all of which, though speaking different languages, saw themselves as belonging to an Indian 'great tradition', sharing the same complex of religions that since the nineteenth century has been called Hinduism. In the northwest, Muslim kingdoms were created, forerunners of the modern state of Pakistan. This was a time that saw the gradual decline and disappearance of Buddhism, except in the Himalayan regions and Bengal. Out of these great tides of history, with their waves of creation and destruction, an even more diverse India would grow. The story begins at the time of the fall of the Roman Empire, in the fifth century AD, and it led me first of all to one of India's most famous cities: a name to conjure with in Indian history, and what one recent Indian writer has called 'India's Ground Zero'.

Inside Ayodhia, the city of Rama

Early morning and the heat is already rising. The Hotel Ram lies on the edge of the sacred zone of Ayodhia. It's scruffy but friendly: in the dining room there's a tasty vegetarian breakfast of puri and vegetables with purple pickled onions – no meat, eggs or alcohol are permitted in God's city. Upstairs skinny builders in loincloths and headbands are already banging away, mixing pink cement in the bedrooms opposite mine. In the foyer a large TV sits alongside a big poster of Rama as the just king – a handsome, square-jawed young warrior, with bare chest, limpid, movie star eyes, helmet and bow. Next to him is Sita, his wife, the ideal woman, his brother Lakshman, and Hanuman, the half-human, half-monkey beloved across India, who in the legend saves Rama in his climactic battle with the demon king. In the modern revival of Hindu nationalism that began in the 1920s and has peaked in the last twenty years, Rama has come to be seen, in northern India at least, as the supreme godhead himself, and Ayodhia is held to have been his birthplace.

Turn right out of the front door, and you are immediately in the heart of things. In a street, already heavy with sun, you walk past the corner *chai* shop, where a resident cow hovers to share customers' leftovers, and in a few yards you come to the police lines. Beyond them the sacred centre of the city stretches down to the river in a mile of fabulously crumbling lanes and alleys, a labyrinth of 300 temples, hostels, mosques and Sufi shrines. Two minutes away from what passes for calm, I find myself swept up in a scene of fantastic vitality, which goes on day and night, and it is fascinating just to wander, hang about or sip *chai* as an unending stream of pilgrims floods past, millions of them every year, all drawn by the tale of Rama.

As you walk, you notice everywhere on the stucco façades of mansions and shrines great plaster fish, their scales painted bright blue – the badge of the Muslim nawabs of Ayodhia, or Awad (as it was known). In 1722 the rulers here, who were Shi'ites, became effectively independent of the great Mughal in Delhi. Curiously enough, it was under them that most Hindu temples here were built in the century-long heyday of Awadhi culture, whose twilight is portrayed in Satyajit Ray's great film *The Chess Players* (1977). The town's greatest Hindu temple, dedicated to Hanuman, was paid for by a Muslim nawab. Since then, Ayodhia has had its ups and downs: sectarian fighting flared in 1855, first between followers of Shiva and Vishnu, then between Muslims and Hindus, but for much of the last 300 years

ABOVE

The TV Ramayana *produced in the late 1980s had a tremendous effect on the popular culture and communal politics in India. In the countryside whole villages gathered to watch it on a single, battery-powered TV set.*

Ayodhia was as good an exemplar of religions living together as could be hoped for in the often troubled sectarian world of northern India. But since 1992 the city's name has become associated with horrors that have threatened the whole Indian body politic. In that year, inflamed by a flagrantly sectarian campaign by their politicians, Hindu fundamentalists descended on Ayodhia in their thousands and demolished a Mughal mosque that they claimed had been built on the exact site of the birthplace of Rama himself. In the bitter aftermath, riot and murder occurred across northern India, and many of the Muslim population of Ayodhia were killed or forced to flee for their lives. That night the prime minister, Narasimha Rao, spoke to the nation on television:

> Fellow countrymen, I am speaking to you this evening under the grave
> threat that has been posed to the institution, principles and ideals on
> which the constitution of our republic has been built. ... What has
> happened today in Ayodhia is a matter of great shame and concern for
> all Indians. ... This is a betrayal of the nation, and a confrontation with
> all that is sacred to all Indians as the legacy we have all inherited ...
> I appeal to all of you to maintain calm, peace and harmony at this
> grave moment of crisis. We have faced many such situations in the past
> and have overcome them. We shall do this again ...

In the narrow lane outside Hanuman's shrine the pilgrim stalls are heaped with pictures and cassettes, and the bookshops are piled high with copies of the *Ramayana* (the famous Gita Press edition has sold an incredible 65 million copies). Long fundamental to the popular culture of northern India, the Rama legend has become a giant presence in the rise of the Hindu nationalist movement in the last hundred years, and especially since the 1980s. Originally a hero of early epic, so scholars tell us, Rama is believed by devotees to be an avatar or incarnation of Vishnu, who comes down to Earth 'at times whenever injustice thrives'. (Another famous incarnation is Krishna, but on pilgrim stalls up and down the Ganges plain one will also see images of the Buddha, and even Jesus and the Shi'ite imam Hussein portrayed among the avators).

In the north Rama's name has been used as a synonym for God since the Middle Ages. But he is also the ideal man and ideal king, an exemplar for human action. And the incredible popularity of the tale was underlined by a blockbuster TV series in the late 1980s, which in the popular eye has increasingly become the received version. In Ayodhia its seventy-eight episodes blare from every bookshop and pilgrim stand. For many, though, the astonishing success of the series was offset by a deep unease at the use to which it has been put – as the focus of a communal rendering of Indian national history, supplanting in the popular imagination the myriad other tellings, often contradictory, unorthodox or subversive, but still part of the great *Ramayana* tradition. But in the electronic age the tale is still changing, still shaping views of the Indian past. And the town of Ayodhia is the theatre where myth has been translated into modern metaphor.

The legend of Rama

'The soil of Ayodhia has been sacred for nearly 1 million years,' the head of the temple tells me. Burly, white-bearded, his forehead marked in damp sandal paste with the yellow sign of the Vaishnavaites, like an inverted tuning fork, he has been a driving figure in the campaign to erect a temple to Rama on the site of the demolished mosque. He is sitting cross-legged in a cramped, oven-hot study heaped with pamphlets and books. Around the walls are religious images depicting the legend: gods and goddesses with jewelled crowns and kohl-rimmed eyes; Sita in a crimson sari. In the sweltering, pre-monsoon summer heat sweat beads trickle down my forehead and my shirt is soaked as the mahant continues:

ABOVE

An 18th-century image of the marriage of Rama and Sita: ideal husband and ideal wife, but like all the greatest stories, shot through with a dark strain of tragedy which religious interpretations have never quite been able to iron out.

We consider Ayodhia was built by the first human being, Manu, but as a human artefact, it is merely a resemblance of the eternal city of the gods. Hence its name, which means 'unconquerable'. You see, Indian time is without beginning and end, and goes beyond counting. To call one thing present and another thing past is against the idea that all is permeated by the One. What we call one moment is in fact indestructible time … We can only see the divine setting of Ayodhia with an Indian eye. The knowledge of Europe is of no avail to reach the depth of ancient India.

The mere historian feels a little powerless in the face of such certainty. But the point is that the tale told by the traditional Brahmins and pilgrim guides here takes place in another aeon. Our era, the Kali Yuga, began a mere 5000 years ago, after the great war described in the *Mahabharata*. The time of the *Ramayana*, the Treta Yuga, is much further back, nearly 1 million years ago. A different view of the tale's beginnings, though, might suggest its origins in myth and folk tale. Three figures in Indian religion and myth have the name Rama, which (like Krishna) means 'the black or dark-skinned one'. One of these is 'the bearer of the plough'. Now Sita means 'the furrow' and is the name of a goddess of agriculture in some ancient Sutras; in one text, the *Harivamsa*, she is the goddess of farmers. Perhaps these clues point to an aboriginal or pre-Aryan origin to the tale? Whatever, the tale as we have it almost certainly arose in the last centuries BC, out of oral stories and bardic tales. Its setting is quite narrow: a small area of the kingdom of Kosala, between the Ganges and the Jumna; and, for what it is worth, the sites associated with the tale have all yielded pottery of post 600 BC, later than the *Mahabharata* sites (see page 50).

There are hundreds of tellings of the story in twenty main languages across southern Asia, some offering fascinating and radical variants, but the core story, the most widely accepted, goes like this …

Rama is a prince of Kosala, residing in the city of Ayodhia in the Ganges plain. Unjustly exiled from his father's kingdom, he lives in the forest with his faithful wife Sita and his brother Lakshman. This golden time is broken when Sita is abducted by Ravana, demon king of Lanka ('island' in Sanskrit). Ravana, the charismatic, tragic anti-hero is supremely intelligent; he can appear in any guise (the most famous has ten heads and twenty arms) and cannot be killed by gods, demons or spirits. Ravana begins to lay waste the Earth and destroy the deeds of the good Brahmins, the upholders of dharma (the universal moral law), so Rama is born a human to defeat him.

Lanka is now identified with Sri Lanka, but this is not recorded as an early name of that island, and it is possible that the city of the demon king was originally

LEFT

The siege of Lanka by Rama and the monkey armies shown in a 17th-century Mughal painting. The Ramayana *was a great source of interest to the Mughal emperors who commissioned translations into Persian.*

*Sita tested by fire:
the story of Rama has
sometimes radically
different endings in its
many regional traditions.*

envisioned by poets as much nearer to hand. More likely, though, it is a fairy-tale city, part of a geography that is not to be found on this Earth. The eleventh-century Muslim historian al-Biruni says that 'according to the Indians, Lanka is thirty yojanas above the Earth, and no sailor who has ever sailed in the direction ascribed to it has ever seen anything that tallies with the legend'. As with Homer's *Odyssey* or the *Argonautica*, over many centuries mythic geography shifts to accommodate the expansion of real geography, just as the *Ramayana's* setting in time eventually had to be put back to a mythic age a million years ago. According to the Brahmins, the *Mahabharata* was 'what happened' in the heroic age, just before 'real' history; the *Ramayana* is 'what is always', which means it is disengaged from historical chronologies. It is in another aeon, a paradigm. This is not 'history' like the *Iliad* or the *Mahabharata*, and in such myths it is best, if at all possible, that mental maps stay magical.

While living in idyllic exile in the forest, Rama offends the demonic world by rejecting and insulting the sister of the demon king. Captivated by Sita's beauty, Ravana diverts Rama with a golden deer and, disguising himself as an old holy man, abducts her. To cut a long story short, the tale ends in a great expedition to Lanka, where in a tremendous battle Ravana is overthrown with the crucial help of the faithful monkey Hanuman. Sita is restored to Rama, and in some versions rules happily ever after in Ayodhia, though only after she is tested to see if her virtue was sullied by Ravana. But the dark strain of tragedy and jealousy in the epic emerges in an ambiguous and troubling epilogue, which may in part be a later addition (and which was initially not filmed in the Indian TV version). This final denouement has all the power of the greatest myths, where the tale finally imposes its own logic of destiny on the protagonists. Just as there was a long tradition in the Greek myth that Helen never went to Troy – her actions too problematic to leave unquestioned – so it is with Sita, the heavenly wife, 'the jewel of womanhood, daughter of Earth' (as Kamban, the great Tamil poet, calls her). Further whispers about her virtue lead to her banishment by Rama, and Sita brings up their children on her own in the ashram of the sage Valmiki (who will later write down the story). Then, in the final meeting with her doubting husband, the ground opens up and swallows Sita, who is taken back by Mother Earth, just as Medea is taken back by the gods in the Greek myth. In both great mythic traditions the storytellers just couldn't leave things with a happy ending; a warning, perhaps, that golden ages exist only in fairy tales.

The Guptas and the Rama legend

But where and when was the legendary Ayodhia? And how and why did the story become, along with the *Mahabharata*, a national epic? Here in today's Ayodhia the tale about the discovery of the site of the million-year-old lost city is part of the repertoire of the pundits, the pilgrim guides, who can be hired anywhere along the bathing ghats by the Gogra bridge, as noted for example by the Elizabethan visitor Ralph Fitch, among 'certain Brahmins who record the names of all such Indians as wash themselves in the river running thereby'.

Our guide is a small, bird-like man sitting by the riverbank under a great old tree, a big yellow Vaishnavite mark on his forehead. In front of him is a cloth bag with his list of clients, and an old lithographed book of sacred texts. The tale of the founding myth of the city is first told in a text of the fourteenth century, and much the same tale is still the oral tradition, as our guide reveals:

> Once upon a time, long, long ago, there was a great king called Vikramaditya. One day Vikramaditya came hunting along the Sarayu river. Then his horse suddenly pulled to a halt, hearing strange voices, and would go no further. The king picked his way through the jungle on the hill there and found ruins of an ancient city. He cleared the ruins and then a rishi (a holy man or renouncer) appeared before him, who told him this was none other than Ayodhia, the sacred city of Lord Rama, which had existed in the Treta Yuga. Then the rishi

disappeared. So it was Vikramaditya who announced the discovery of Ayodhia, and he ordered its restoration for our time – to rebuild the city and bring back the rule of Rama.

Vikramaditya is a great figure in the medieval legends of India, such as the still popular cycle of tales called *Vikram and the Ghost*. The name was attached to many historical figures, but two ancient kings in particular used the name. The most famous of these was a ruler of the Gupta age in the fifth century AD, Skandagupta, who fought battles against the invading Huns and assumed the title Vikramaditya (sun of valour) after his victory. There is, though, an intriguing subplot to Skandagupta's 'restoring' of the town. At that time Chinese pilgrims described it as a thriving place, with twenty Buddhist monasteries and 5000 monks. However, it was not then called Ayodhia, but Saketa, the name by which it had been known to the ancient Greeks. So in the fifth century the earthly manifestation of the mythic Ayodhia, 'city invincible' was Saketa, until then a Buddhist centre.

The fifth century, the peak of the Gupta age, was a time of conscious revival of the old glories of India harking back to the *Mahabharata* and the *Ramayana*. The old Brahminical religion had suffered eclipse when Buddhism was the chief religion of India and under ecumenical rulers, such as the Kushans, who sponsored all religions. Now, in the changing world of the fourth and fifth centuries under the Guptas, began the evolution of the old, sacrificial Brahminical religion into what can be recognized as the precursor of modern Hinduism. Kings were most admired as battle winners, and a new doctrine arose that the king was 'a god in human form'. On Ashoka's great pillar at Allahabad (see page 89) a new inscription was cut, describing Samudragupta, son of Chandragupta I, as a divine king: 'a god dwelling on Earth, being a mortal only in the sense that he celebrates the rites of the observances of mankind.' And along with deification of the king came the theory of God's avatars on Earth, not as mythical creatures, but as historical human beings. Of these avatars the most popular was Rama. The beautiful gold coins of the Guptas underline this identification by showing their kings with crowned helmet and bow, the iconography of Rama ever since.

In this climate of politicized myth-making, the way was paved for recognition of the old town of Saketa as the epic Ayodhia. The first inscriptional evidence for Saketa as the city of legend comes from the year 436. Later Chinese sources say that it was Skandagupta who moved the Gupta court to the region of Ayodhia (in Kosala), and according to Paramartha's life of the Buddhist monk Vasubhandu, it was specifically to Saketa itself, which was then still a famous Buddhist centre. Epigraphical evidence from the town also shows that Saketa began to be called Ayodhia in the Gupta age. Curiously, though, excavation in the old city of Ayodhia

BELOW

The Gupta gold coinage often stresses the kings' attachment to Vishnu, of whom Rama is one avatar.

has not yet revealed any significant Gupta remains, even on the claimed birthplace site under the mosque destroyed in 1992. Maybe, like the Tudors in Britain using the myths of Arthur, the Round Table and Camelot, the Guptas were interested in the epic as part of their imperial ideology, just as the poets of Augustus in the Roman Empire used foundation myths of Troy. They perhaps refurbished the city, while still keeping their main capitals at Patna and Ujain.

Strangely enough, very little is known about the Guptas themselves. They were a local clan, perhaps coming from somewhere in the plain between the Ganges and the Gogra in the region of Benares and Ghazipur. Their age, the fifth century AD, was a time of invasions, especially by the dreaded Huns, and the attractions of an imperial epic were obvious to the kings of the Ganges plain, who saw themselves as the saviours of India, in the mould of the mythic kings of Ayodhia. From then on the story of Rama would be indissolubly associated with the rule of the native kings of India, and used as an example whenever their kingdoms were threatened by outsiders, demonic or otherwise: Turks, Afghans, Mongols and Mughals, and even – as in the nineteenth-century Rama plays at Benares – the British.

Hindu kingship

We are on the road from Ghazipur to Benares, travelling up the Ganges plain, which we seem to have crossed and recrossed many times during this year, through the heat and the rains. We are just coming into Bhitra, a little town where a crucial discovery was made in the 1890s, of which I am keen to know more. At that time a rare copper alloy seal was handed in to the British district magistrate by an old landed family, who seem to have kept it as an heirloom. The seal gave the sequence of Gupta kings, each of whom was named with his royal mother. The discovery was as crucial to early medieval Indian history as the recent Kanishka inscription is to the Kushans (see page 123), for it gave scholars the key to the Gupta kings. It is very tempting to think that this area was their home place, and if their family root was indeed near here, had the seal come down through an important family lineage from ancient times? A phone call to Lucknow Museum draws a blank: the find place was not recorded, nor was the name of the family. I am tempted to stop to try to discover more, but we must move on. As Bhitra recedes in the rear-view mirror, I can only reflect that the riches of Indian history are a subject that needs several lifetimes to unravel. For the historian the Hindu cycle of rebirths is a sine qua non!

But even for one lifetime, the search for the Guptas is perplexing. For most of the great dynasties of Indian history we can see monuments around us: the Sultanate and the British in Delhi, the Mughals in Agra, even Ashoka's pillars and rock edicts. The Guptas, contemporaries of the later Roman Empire (c.AD 300–550), claim to have ruled from the Bay of Bengal to the Indus. From their time there is a super-lative but disparate series of creations: play texts and poems revealing the sophisti-cation of courtly society; remarkable scientific findings; sculpture of wonderful quality (the sandstone Buddha of Sarnath surely has few rivals in the arts of the world). In the National Museum in Delhi there are terracottas so expressive that they might be from *fin de siècle* Paris – maquettes from the studio of Auguste Rodin, say – and in the coin gallery there is an astonishingly vivacious and technically brilliant series of gold coins. And what of the ethereal, crumbling beauty of the paintings in the Buddhist caves at Ajanta, some of which may be from this period? Or the 6-ton, forge-welded iron pillar plundered from its wooded hill at Vidisha and now in the grounds of the Qutab Minar complex in Delhi? Not to mention the world's first sex manual (something the Western world did not achieve until the 1960s). But where is the material dimension of Gupta power? Nowhere except in a few small temples can one stand and say 'Here is the Guptas' legacy'. No palaces, no public buildings, no grand shrines, only caves and ruined stupas. Virtually nothing is known about their day-to-day life, about the administration of their empire, about the execution of justice, about national and international commerce. Their kings' personalities are a mystery, but for a few high-flown eulogies. Their apparent greatness, then, presents us with a conundrum.

A golden age?

The idea of the Gupta golden age arose, curiously enough, not among Indians, but among the British. Vincent Smith was a civil servant and a brilliant historian, but fundamentally unsympathetic to many aspects of Indian civilization. His was a colonial viewpoint that helped shape British views of India. For Smith the Indians were never so happy as when held in good order under firm but benevolent authoritarian empires, such as that of the Mauryans, the Guptas, the Mughals – and the British. (And, after all, weren't the British – albeit distantly – Aryans too?) The Guptas, then, were the kind of imperialists the British empire-builders could admire as models.

The empire began with Chandragupta I (reigned 320–35), a member of a local landed family, who fought his way to power in the region. He married a princess of the Licchavi, an important clan in the northern Bihar-Patna region, with lands stretching up to Nepal. The alliance was so important to him that his son Samudragupta called himself 'son of the daughter of the Licchavi'. So where the Kushans celebrated the father's line, for the Guptas it was the uterine descent that made them. Like the Kushans, their accession was the start of a new era, beginning with Chandragupta's coronation in 320. With that, the time was renewed.

Chandragupta showed himself to be the restorer of ancient Vedic kingship by renewing the great Vedic horse sacrifice (see page 40), the roots of which are traced back to central Asia, and this act was commemorated on his gold coins. Decades later his grandson praised him as the great renewer of the horse sacrifice 'which had been forgotten for a long time'. So the Guptas were consciously trying to renew the old Vedic institutions of kingship, as a native dynasty that traced its descent, male and female, to the old clans of the Ganges plain.

The next king, Samudragupta (died 380), was (if we can believe his press) one of the greatest conquerors in Indian history. To Ashoka's Allahabad pillar he added a fulsome account of his deeds, including a long list of kings and realms conquered: fourteen border kings, eighteen jungle rajas and even thirteen southern kings. After that he proclaimed himself a *chakravartin* (universal ruler), and a new tone appears in Indian kingship: 'He was a mortal only in celebrating the rites of the observances of mankind, but otherwise a god dwelling on Earth.'

ABOVE

Vishnu on his seven-headed serpent: an exquisite piece of Gupta sculpture depicting the god favoured by the Gupta kings.

His son, Chandragupta II (reigned 380–413), extended the empire to its furthest extent, its greatest glory and cultural excellence. By then the empire stretched from the Khyber to Bengal. A poetic eulogy to him is carved on the Delhi Iron Pillar: touched with a smouldering evanescence, 'his face as beautiful as the moon … he has gone now to heaven but left behind his glory in the world, in the way that the earth still glows hot after a raging forest fire. He smashed the King of Bengal and crossed the seven mouths of the Indus to rout his enemies, so the southern ocean is still perfumed by the breeze of his bravery … '

The great kings of the line end with Skandagupta in *c.*467, though scions of the dynasty still ruled until the middle of the sixth century.

As regards real historical narrative, that would have been the lot were it not for a vivid picture of the Gupta realm written by a foreign visitor. Around 401, the same year that the iron pillar inscription was carved, a Chinese monk called Fa Xien travelled down the Karakorum into the Punjab to visit the sacred places of Buddhism. He was an eye-witness to the Gupta world at the end of the reign of Chandragupta II. At that time Buddhism was still thriving, he tells us: 'Everywhere in all the countries of India the kings had been firm believers in that law.' Intriguingly, he tells how the Gupta kings (who were not Buddhists, but followers of Vishnu) by long tradition visited Buddhist monasteries 'to make offerings to the monks with uncovered heads, and gave food with their own hands, sitting with them on the floor: for the laws and ways according to which kings rendered charity in the days when the Buddha was alive have been handed down to the present day'.

South of Mathura the Chinese visitor travelled between the Ganges and Jumna, in the 'beautiful and fruitful' landscape that impressed foreigners, from Megasthenes to Ralph Fitch, for 2000 years. Then comes this passage:

> All south from here is known as the Middle Land or Kingdom. In it the cold and heat are finely tempered, and there is neither hoar frost nor snow. The people are numerous and happy; they have not to register their households, nor to be ruled by magistrates; only those who cultivated the royal land have to pay a tax on the gain from it. If they want to go [leave their land], they can go; if they want to stay on, they stay. The king governs without decapitation or corporal punishments. Criminals are simply fined lightly or heavily according to the circumstances of the case … The king's bodyguards and staff all have salaries. Throughout the country the people do not kill any living creature, nor drink intoxicating liquor, nor eat onions, nor garlic … the only exception is the chandalas. That is the name for those who are held to be polluted, and who live apart from the rest of the population …

One must take such a eulogy with a pinch of salt; some of the details seem improbable – the non-drinking of alcohol for one – and it is curious that Fa Xien does not mention the ruling king. But much of his information is true: that untouchables had to strike a wooden stick before entering towns, as he describes later, is known from other sources; likewise the use of cowrie shells along with coins as currency, and the prohibitions on certain kinds of food. His account of the administration strikingly recalls what we know of the Mauryans.

Fa Xien later reinforces these observations on his journey further south to Patna: 'The cities and towns of this country [Maghada],' he says, 'are the greatest of all in India. The inhabitants are rich and prosperous, and vie with one another in the practice of benevolence and righteousness.' Particularly eye-catching is his description of how the citizens of Gupta Patna (whether Buddhist, Jain or Brahmin) shared each other's festivals and revered each other's teachers. As discussed in Chapter 2, despite the many conflicts over religion in Indian history, this kind of pluralism has long existed, and still continues in Patna and in many other places. Fa Xien, then, opens a window on a well-organized kingdom that could not have been guessed at from the scanty and fragmentary material survivals, and behind it an Indian ruler who claimed to be a 'universal king'.

ABOVE

The gorgeous quality of this mural from the caves at Ajanta vividly suggests the sophisticated culture of the Gupta age.

Art, poetry and science in the Gupta age

Like other great epochs of Indian history, the Gupta age was a pluralist time. Although the kings were followers of Vishnu, they sponsored other religions, and Buddhism in particular, as the Chinese pilgrims' accounts show, enjoyed a great flowering with royal patronage. The monastery at Nalanda, with its university, was a Gupta-period foundation, the first residential university in the world. It became a global institution, drawing students from the Far East and Persia, and lasted until the twelfth century.

This was also a time of major scientific advances. Aryabhata, the astronomer and mathematician, defined the concept of zero and proved that the Earth revolves around the sun and that it turns on its own axis some 1000 years before Copernicus and Galileo expounded this idea in the West. A hallmark of the age, then, seems to have been curiosity about the world in all its manifestations. Artistic creation, especially of the human form, is another. Some of the wall paintings of the life of the Buddha at Ajanta are from this time, and some of the finest stone images in Indian art come from the Gupta period: chief among them are the sculptures made by Dinna, the first Indian artist for whom we have a name and a collection of works.

The Gupta court also sponsored literature and poetry. Later legend speaks of the 'nine jewels' in the royal court, one of whom, Kalidasa, seems to have been court poet to Kumaragupta, rather as Virgil was to Augustus Caesar. He was the author of poems, epics and plays, the most famous of which is *Sakuntala*, a charming comedy (tragedy seems to be unknown as a genre in Indian drama – perhaps the law of karma would preclude it?). The play has distant similarities to *A Midsummer Night's Dream*: the king's love for a forest nymph, the lovers' pursuit in the woods, the contrast between court and country, the fairy-tale ambience. But what is most revealing in the play is what it tells us about the courtly culture thriving in Gupta cities such as Ujain and Patna and its self-reflexive quality. The play starts in an almost Pirandellian fashion, with a prologue where the director and his leading lady discuss tonight's show:

'They are a very high-powered audience tonight, they are the intelligentsia … really discriminating … So we need to serve them up something really good …

'With your direction nothing can go wrong,' says the star, perhaps with a hint of irony.

'Unfortunately, my dear,' the director replies, 'however talented we may be, we still all crave the applause of the discerning …'

Kalidasa's three surviving plays and his lyric poems (such as the 'Birth of the War God' and his *Raghuvamsa*) flatter the Gupta line, as Shakespeare's history plays do the Tudor monarchs, and make specific homage to the current ruler. This was fitting in a time of historical consciousness, when court scholars collected and edited the texts of the Puranas, compendia of the myths, history and genealogies of the northern dynasties. The fourth book of the *Raghuvamsa* glorifies the mythical dynasty of King Rama in a eulogy to the heroic deeds of his current representative on Earth. In this way the real world battles recorded on the Allahabad pillar are turned into literary art.

So the transformation of history into myth was part of the programme of the Gupta rulers. Whereas earlier rulers in the ancient Indian tradition saw their job as being to keep the cosmic order going, performing Vedic sacrifices advised by their Brahmin priests, or, like Ashoka, propounding a moral order articulated by Buddhist or Jain gurus, now kingship itself was central to the discourse: the Gupta kings were thought to be gods on Earth, bringing about a new golden age by means of their heroic deeds in battle, but also sponsors of a court culture where arts could flourish. In style and substance it would be the template of all later rulership in India.

The Kama Sutra: sex and life

The most remarkable of all the products of Gupta culture – and, for obvious reasons, the most interesting to our sex-obsessed time – is *The Kama Sutra*, the treatise or exposition on delight, love, pleasure or sex, though as Kama is also the personified god of love, the title could simply be translated as 'The Book of Cupid'. The oldest surviving Hindu textbook on erotic love, it was composed in Sanskrit perhaps between 300 and 400. The author, Vatsayana Mallanaga, was probably writing in Patna, the old Ashokan capital, still an imperial city under the Kushans and Guptas. The cultural context of the text is urban and cosmopolitan; the target readership is the *nagaraka*, the man about town, and it gives us a fascinating glimpse (echoed in the sensuous and pleasure-loving sculpture of the age) of what India was like in the age of the Guptas.

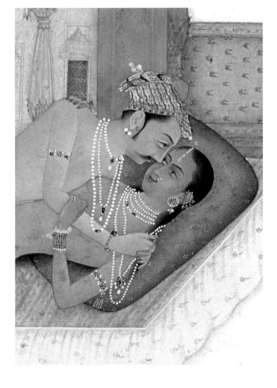

BELOW

Eroticism played a central role in Indian art, sacred and secular: the earliest great text, The Kama Sutra *was probably composed in the 4th century AD.*

The author of *The Kama Sutra* says his work follows many other writers in the past – earlier sexologists – but his is the first to survive. It became a landmark, being quoted as early as 400, and influenced many other Indian writers on sex and love through the Middle Ages, and came to be seen as a foundational authority on sexuality. It also had a deep impact on Indian literature: on Sanskrit and vernacular erotic poetry, as in the fabulous eroticism of Kalidasa's *Kumarasambhava*, which devotes the whole of its eighth book to the love-making of Shiva and Parvati as a paradigm of the way lovers grow in knowledge of each other through sex. As a text that was very aware of theorists on psychology and sex, this book echoes some of the concerns of *The Kama Sutra*, and was criticized by some Indians in later ages for its too overt sexuality.

The cataloguing of behaviour, acts, moods and traits is a cultural obsession in India, and the way the book is organized reflects that numbers game: the sixty-four sexual positions, for example, echo the sixty-four diseases in medical texts, the sixty-four arts, and even the sixty-four 'playful games' of Shiva. The book itself is wrapped in a further numerical conceit – that it is only a distilled essence, a boiled-down account of human behaviour, which has been drawn from an original text (rather like those lost encyclopedias in the mirrored world of Jorge Luis Borges), a text claimed to comprise 100,000 chapters– so various are the ways of human sexuality.

It is, on the face of it, incredible that the first true manual on sexual love in the West was that of Alex Comfort in the 1960s. But *The Kama Sutra* is not, as is usually thought, a text only about the positions of the sex act. It is a book about the art of living: a book concerned with a central aspect of human psychology. In it we see a fundamental difference between Indian and Western culture. *Kama* is a third pillar of human behaviour, alongside religious custom (in the law of Manu) and social law in the Arthashastra (which, as discussed in Chapter 2, was originally a Mauryan compilation expanded in later times down to the Guptas). All three of these texts are representative of what seems to have been a Gupta-period tendency to codify and regularize aspects of human, that is to say, Indian, knowledge. For them the science of pleasure was one of the principal sciences, along with dharma (virtue) and *artha* (prosperity), one of the three aims of human life.

Like all lasting works of literature, *The Kama Sutra* is brimming with perennial concerns. Its discussion of the sex act itself talks about the variety of regional customs, about violence in sex, about dangerous sex – 'acts outside this book', which also heighten passion but are only to be used with care, 'For the territory of the textbooks,' says Vatsayana, 'extends only so far as the limits of men's appetites. But when the wheel of ecstasy is in full motion, there is no textbook, and no order.' In our own time, which has so many issues about safe sex and the danger of HIV, this is still true; indeed, in present-day India, which has a growing Aids problem, these ancient writings are now being used as educational texts for prostitutes.

The monotheistic religions, of course, have a different emphasis. Early Christianity, for example, problematized sexual love, and surrounded the act itself with guilt. Consequently, Christian visitors to India saw erotic temple sculptures as disgusting and inexplicable on a sacred building – still quite a common judgement among tour groups visiting Khajuraho today. But as it says in the law of Manu, 'There is no sin or fault in eating meat, drinking alcohol or having sex because they are natural human inclinations, even though one attains happiness in being free of them.' The key in Indian thought is not constraint: rather, by including the physiology and psychology of sex and relationships within the totality of human behaviour, *The Kama Sutra* remains thoroughly modern in its concerns.

That brings us to one last observation. Alain Danielou, the great French Indologist who lived for many years with Saivite sects before the Second World War, saw *The Kama Sutra* as a characteristic product of an intellectually open society, a free society by the standards of the age. Vatsayana says that anyone, not just a 'man about town', can live a life of pleasure. Of course, the ideas in the book were not for the mass of society. But were there also other readers or hearers less privileged? Or was the text just for the rich, for city dwellers and merchants? A fantasy book, like men's magazines today (and a male fantasy at that)? Homosexual sex is not a major feature of the text, as one might expect in an ancient society where there were punishments, if mild ones, for gay sex. A bigger issue is that from the feminist point of view much of it is male-orientated, to which one would counter again that this is, after all, a fourth-century text. The author, moreover, does quote women in direct speech saying things that men were advised to take seriously, and he is often very realistic about women's sexual desires. Women readers are implied too. Indeed, Book Six in the textual tradition is said to have been commissioned by the most talented and literate, high-class courtesans of Pataliputra, a city evidently still redolent of grandeur in the Gupta age. All in all, then, *The Kama Sutra* is a remarkably revealing text about Indian society. Its realism, and its sexual fantasy, are the culmination, no doubt, of centuries of erotic meditations every bit as complex as the parallel ascetic speculations of the spiritual gurus. *The Kama Sutra*, one might say, is as typical of India as the *Bhagavadgita* and the eightfold noble path.

Harsha the Great and the end of the ancient world

The Gupta age ended with succession crises, weak kings and foreign invasion. Renewed attacks by the Huns destroyed many monasteries in Gandhara and northwest India, but the monarchy was restored under a *chakravartin* (universal ruler) in the seventh century. This was King Harsha, who revived the Gupta style of kingship both as warrior and patron. Another Chinese account of India survives from this time by the famous Buddhist monk Hsuan Tsang, who knew Harsha and praised him. He spent seventeen years in India during the 630s and 640s, which gives his observations unmatched authority. At that time the chief city of the north was Kannauj, an ancient city on the Ganges, which had been known to Greek and Roman geographers. Kannauj is now a forgotten field of ruins 4 miles across, dotted with villages, its chief landmark being the giant mosque built by Shah Ibrahim out of the ruins of earlier temples and buildings. But after Delhi and Patna, Kannauj is the third of northern India's great imperial cities. Until the tenth century, as a Persian geographer reported, it was the seat of a raja 'who is a great king obeyed by most of the kings of India, and said to be able to muster a huge army, 150,000 cavalry with 800 war elephants'. All of this, perhaps, gives an idea of Harsha's power.

Just as Chandragupta II is praised for his musicianship and his compositional skills, Harsha was a poet and wrote plays that have survived. Hsuan Tsang describes him (with pardonable enthusiasm, as he benefited greatly from the king's patronage) as 'virtuous and patriotic; all people celebrate his praises in song'. The king's life story is told by his chief minister, Bhanna, in the first full-scale Indian secular biography, which begins with the drama of his accession, the younger brother of the murdered king 'whose royal appearance and demeanour', as the Chinese monk also says, 'were recognized in conjunction with his great military talents. His qualifications moved heaven and earth; his sense of justice was admired by gods and men.' After Harsha 'made himself master of India, his renown spread abroad everywhere, and all his subjects reverenced his virtues. The empire having gained stability, the people were at peace.'

What followed immediately taps into old themes in Indian history, suggesting no one more than Ashoka himself. Once peace was established, says Hsuan Tsang, 'Harsha put an end to offensive military expeditions, and began to put into storage all his weaponry. He gave himself up to religious duties and prohibited the slaughter of animals … he founded *sangharamas* (Buddhist monasteries) wherever there were sacred traces of religion.' But as with earlier epochs, the king's role in religion was ecumenical, and there was no state religion. Instead religious festivals embraced all faiths in great acts of royal charity. 'Every fifth year,' says Hsuan Tsang, 'Harsha convoked a grand assembly and distributed the surplus of his royal stores as an act of charity.' In 642 Hsuan Tsang witnessed a great gathering of this kind on the sands at the confluence of the Ganges and the Jumna, where 'from ancient times until now, royal and noble personages endowed with virtue and love, for distribution of their charitable offerings, have all come to this place for that purpose. At the present time King Harsha, following this custom, has distributed here the accumulated wealth of five years, over a period of seventy-five days.' This, as we saw in Chapter 2, may be the 'great assembly' mentioned by the Greeks in 300 BC, and the predecessor perhaps of the medieval and modern festival at the same place, the *Kumbh Mela*, the biggest religious gathering on Earth. However, like a number of other present-day traditions – including the *ramlilas* in Benares and the *durga puja* in Calcutta – the *kumbh* reached its present form during the British period.

Harsha would be remembered among Buddhists as the fourth and last pillar of Buddhism, after Ashoka, the Greek king Menander and Kanishka, and the intellectual exchanges in his day between India and China are part of the history of the whole of humanity. Hsuan Tsang returned to China in 646. The Wild Goose Pagoda built to store his manuscripts still stands in Xian, and the small monastery that is his final resting place survives in a delectable wooded valley outside the city. Spared at the express command of the communist leader Chou En-lai (or so its abbot told me many years back), its library still holds palm-leaf manuscripts in the Pali language of Sri Lanka.

A stele in the library shows Hsuan Tsang, rucksack on his back, a lamp to light his way, braving the elements to bring home his precious cargo of manuscripts. Only fairly recently, copies of his letters have come to light, written nearly twenty years on to his old friends in India: they are among the most arresting texts in the history of civilization. To the master of Maghagda he sends news from China: 'the great king of the Tang, with the compassion of a chakravarti-raja, rules in tranquillity and spreads the teachings of the Buddha: he has even penned with his own hand a preface to a translation he ordered copied and circulated, and it is being studied too by neighbouring countries.' To the abbot of Mahbodhi in Bodhgaya the tone is even more touching, for they belonged to opposed schools:

> It has been a long time now since we parted, which has only increased
> my admiration for you … Now there is a messenger returning to India,
> I send you my sincere regards and a little memento as a token of my
> gratitude. It is too inadequate to express my deep feelings for you.
> I hope you appreciate that. When I was returning from India I lost a
> horse-load of manuscripts in the river Indus. I attach herewith my list
> and request that copies be sent to me. This much for the present.
> Yours, the monk Hsuan Tsang

The coming of Islam

The synchronicities of history are sometimes striking. In the summer of 632 Hsuan Tsang, on the last stage of his journey to seek the wisdom of India, was staying in Kashmir, then a land of hundreds of Buddhist monasteries. At that point Buddhism, having spread to China, the Far East and Southeast Asia, may well have had the largest number of followers of any organized religion in the world. That June, far away to the west in Medina, the Prophet Muhammad died, having enjoined his followers to 'seek knowledge as far as China'. An amazing new epoch in the history of the world was about to open up – one that would see within a single century the establishment of an Islamic caliphate and the spread of Islam over a vast area from Spain to the Indus valley.

The coming of Islam is fraught with difficulty in Indian historiography, and all the more so in light of the confrontational rhetoric of international politics at this moment in the twenty-first century. It is the subject of two great and conflicting narratives that have long been articulated in Indian politics, culture and education. On the one hand there is the secular interpretation fostered, for example, by the Congress Party, the main force in the Independence movement, which is supported by many secular Indians, by many Muslims, and by many liberal progressive

One of the great shrines at Uchch near Multan in Pakistan: a great centre of Muslim culture in the Middle Ages, and still a favourite haunt of wandering Sufis and musicians, especially at mela *time.*

Hindus. On the other hand there is the religious interpretation, broadly espoused by Hindu nationalists of various persuasions, from hardline fundamentalists to many in the middle of the road, such as those who resented the partial communal politics bequeathed by the British. The first admits a tale of conquest, but one in which the foreign invaders adapted, changed and became Indian; in which conversion, more often than not, happened through dialogue, and out of which an extraordinary exchange and interaction developed over many centuries, during which northern India became an Indo-Islamic civilization in which most Hindus and Muslims coexisted peacefully: in other words, another phase of India's unity in diversity. The Hindu nationalist view, however, says that the coming of Islam marked a break, an alien intrusion; it insists that foreign dynasties came bearing a form of monotheism fundamentally irreconcilable with Hindu religion, and that their intolerance towards Indian religions began centuries of hostility exacerbated in the modern era by British 'divide and rule' tactics.

As always in history, both narratives are to an extent true; yet both are distortions of much more complex realities that differed on the ground in every region. But both these narratives coexist in the minds of most Indian people, and one or other tends to come to the fore in times of peace or times of stress, especially when fomented by unscrupulous politicians for electoral gain. Certain historical facts, though, are insurmountable, the foremost being the Partition of the subcontinent on religious lines in 1947, which, however we argue, was a fundamental break with India's past. The roots of these events lay far back in history.

At the centre of the Old World, India had long had cultural and linguistic connections with the West and central Asia. Now Arabs, Turks, Afghans and Mongols enter the story in a new age of migrations. Islam seems to have first reached the coast of Kerala with Arab traders in the seventh century, and the earliest mosque on the subcontinent is said to be the one at Cranganore, the successor to the old Roman settlement of Muziris. In the south the migrants came peacefully, and over time became thoroughly acculturized. A military attack on Sind from the Indus delta in 711 led to Muslim settlement in parts of what is now southern Pakistan; but as late as the 980s a Persian geographer using first-hand merchants' reports could describe, for example, Lahore, in the heart of the Pakistani Punjab, as a purely Hindu city 'full of bazaars and idol temples', a city whose people were 'entirely infidels, with no Muslims'. It was not until the early eleventh century that Turkic and Afghan armies bearing the faith of Islam began to make headway against the Hindu kingdoms of northern India. These military incursions of Islamic conquerors in the Middle Ages influenced the cultures of the north forever, an intensely dramatic tale that brought about one of the biggest stories of cultural cross-over in history. One concomitant, for example, was the conversion of huge numbers of Indians to Islam. This phenomenon is not yet satisfactorily explained by historians; no doubt it was partly through coercion, but in part too a reaction to the hierarchical and oppressive nature of Brahminical religion in many places towards the lower castes, and, a response to the democratic bent of Islam. But this great historical movement began with violence.

Mahmud of Ghazni

Ghazni, eastern Afghanistan. Clouds of dust swirl around the crumbling citadel and the scorching blast of summer rises from the arid Afghan plateau. 'A truly miserable place,' the Mughal Babur wrote. 'Why kings who hold Hindustan and Khurasan [Persia] would ever make such a wretched place their capital has always been a source of amazement to me.' A few hours south of Kabul on the road to Kandahar, this was the capital of a vast Muslim empire in the eleventh century. The security advice these days is to stay only a short time. At the tomb of Sultan Mahmud, a plain stone slab with swirls of Kufic lettering, a knot of old, turbaned Afghans are at prayer. Mahmud is still remembered here as presiding over a high tide of Islam.

In the sectarian struggles of recent years his name has appeared on anti-Indian and jihadist banners, and even on a Pakistani rocket. Mahmud set the pattern of foreign conquests and the spread of Islam in medieval India. On fifteen expeditions he sacked cities and temples across the north. No character in Indian history today evokes more hostility: in Afghanistan he is regarded as a philosopher prince, the conqueror of infidels; in India he has left a bitter legacy for his violent conquests. His combination of brutality and high civilization was as characteristic of medieval Islam as it was of Renaissance and Enlightenment Europe.

A great deal of nonsense is talked these days about Mahmud's activities. The violent energies of eleventh-century India were no different on one level from the dynastic wars of contemporary Western Europe – the murderous feuds of the Normans, Franks and Ottonians, for example. Rulers of Afghans and Turks invaded northern India, sacked cities and plundered temples to sustain, feed and reward their armies. In southern India the Cholans did the same against their Chera and Chalukya neighbours, their fellow Hindus. The motive, as in most of these wars, was loot, and the seizure of images of their enemies' gods was both booty and humiliation. But these northern wars were also waged in the name of Islam. Although the Koran says that there should be no compulsion in religion, medieval Muslim kings nevertheless found in it ample justification for war against the infidel, just as Europeans did in the Bible, and thus it was used by Mahmud. But there were still high-ranking Hindus in his entourage, such as his general Tilak; he was still content to enter into client relations with Hindu kings; and it was still possible for Hindu, Buddhist and Jain temples to exist in his kingdom. So Mahmud's was by no means a thoroughgoing iconoclasm. The chief aim was not conversion or iconoclasm, but plunder. However, by crushing infidels, Mahmud could also advertise himself as a man risen from slave ancestry to become a caliph, a companion of the faithful, a successor of the Prophet.

Out of such disparate motives, then, his career was built. From two great bases in the Punjab – the old Hindu cities of Multan and Lahore – he launched a series of winter raids into the plains of northern India, marking the beginning of a historical process that would lead to profound changes in culture, language and allegiance on the subcontinent. 'This may sound an exaggeration,' one old Multani said to me, 'but you could see Mahmud as the first mover behind the idea of Pakistan.'

Mahmud in Multan

Multan, in the southern Punjab, Pakistan. The old city is being lashed by unseasonal December rains, which are falling in torrents over the citadel, running over the floors of the blue-domed Sufi shrines that loom impressively out of the grey mist. Auto-rickshaws gingerly navigate a lake in the street outside the Haram Gate, where the shop awnings in the narrow alleys are sagging with water. The city has had Muslim rulers since the ninth century, though in those early years it remained a famous Hindu city. Ali al-Masudi, one of my favourite historians, visited the place in 912, when it lay in the frontier zone of Islam, and described the riches of the pilgrim trade protected by its Muslim governor. In 982, only a few years before Mahmud's day, it was a 'large town with a famous idol and people come on pilgrimage from all over Hindustan to visit it: the large cantonment of the Muslim ruler lies outside the Hindu city'. Although Mahmud made his capital at Ghazni, up in the Afghan hills, Multan would be his main base in the Punjab, from which he would make his forays into India as far as Mathura, Benares and Kannauj.

My hosts, the Gardezi family, trace their ancestry to the very beginnings of Islam in the north of the subcontinent. I stayed with them on my journeys through Pakistan in the 1990s when I was travelling in the footsteps of Alexander. They have a wonderful manuscript library of ancient Korans and texts of poetry and history: indeed, the history of Islamic humanism is told in precious manuscripts of the Sufi mystic Amir Khusro, in Dara Shikoh's Persian translation of the *Bhagavadgita*, in the epics of Nizami and Firdowsi … the latter being the Persian poet who wrote the *Shahnama*, the tale of Persian kings, for Mahmud himself, having been drawn to the glittering court of the Ghaznavids with the promise of New World wealth.

The Gardezis have new houses in the suburbs now; their old family mansions in the medieval city, towering over a narrow lane behind the gate, are crumbling inside their high-walled brick compounds, women's quarters on one side, men on the other. Through an archway in a wide courtyard open to the sky the family tombs cluster around the shrine of their Sufi ancestor Sheikh Yusef in the classic Multani blue tiled style.

Family tradition takes them back to the caliphate, a story that mirrors the expansion of Islam itself from the time of the Prophet to the founding of Pakistan, whose constitution of 1954 bears a Gardezi signature. Hur Gardezi fills me in further:

> Our ancestors had gone from Baghdad in the first expansion into
> central Asia to Bukhara. Then we came from Gardez to Multan in the
> late eleventh century to serve Masud, the son of Mahmud. But we still
> bear the family name of Gardezi, which was a little fortified town
> southeast of Ghazni, surrounded by mountains that were covered with
> snow in winter. Babur thought little of it because it had no gardens or
> orchards: as far as he was concerned, anywhere with no apples and
> apricots was a dead loss!

The Gardezi family was one of many swept along in the great migrations of the Middle Ages. India was one of the richest lands on Earth: 'the greatest country in the northern world,' says a tenth-century Persian writer, 'with all the amenities of civilization, a numerous population and many kings. Numerous towns lie in it. All the inhabitants are idolaters.' Read the pages of writers such as al-Masudi and you see the fascination it exerted on outsiders. Like the conquistadors in the New World, some of the invaders were seduced by the culture of India. Al-Masudi, for example, was fascinated by the religious differences: 'Scholars of discernment and judgement say that the ancient Indians were particularly endowed with righteousness and wisdom,' he writes. Others speak excitedly of Indian discoveries in mathematics and astronomy, naming Hindu sacred texts.

Still others, though, were as intolerant of the native religion as most of the Spanish were of Inca and Aztec religions: they regarded it as work-of-the-devil idolatry – a view that still survives in fundamentalist Christian and Muslim literature. Mahmud's most notorious attack took place in 1023 and was directed at the wealthy pilgrimage place of Somnath on the coast of Kathiawar in Gujarat, a sea-washed promontory lapped by the waves of the Indian Ocean. While Turkic-Persian historians claim that loot was his main objective, strange stories nonetheless circulated about another motivation or, at least, public justification, that would be dismissed out of hand were it not recorded by two contemporaries who knew Mahmud and his son. This tale says that the lingam (the phallic stone of Shiva) of Somnath was actually the image of Manaat, the last of the pagan idols that had existed in Mecca before the days of the Prophet, when it had been spirited away to India. It comes from the historian Farrukhi Sistani, who went with Mahmud on the expedition that 'emptied the land of India of fighting men and fearsome elephants', and it is repeated by the poet Gardezi, who was in court twenty years later and knew the participants. This tale, then, was in the air at the very time of the attack, or soon after.

Mahmud assembled 50,000 troops on the parade ground at Multan, with 1200 elephants, and 20,000 camels to carry water. He marched south during the winter season, through the desert of Thar, past Jaisalmer on the old caravan route down to Kathiawar. Somnath was sacked after a fierce battle, during which the famous temple was plundered and burnt. There are various stories about the fate of the idol, the Shiva lingam, though all may be inventions. Some said it was sent to the caliph in Baghdad with a letter acclaiming Mahmud as a fighter for Islam. Others say he took it to Ghazni, broke it to pieces and buried it in the ground at the threshold of the great mosque, to be walked over by worshippers on their way to prayers.

The 1023 expedition, then, at least as it was construed retrospectively in the Ghaznavid historiography of his own time, was for a higher purpose in the eschatology of Islam: to complete unfinished business of the Prophet; to destroy Manaat. This was claimed to be the true meaning of the expedition, though it was perhaps a post-hoc justification, given the Koran's injunction against aggressive war. As it says on Mahmud's coins, 'There is one God, Muhammad is his Prophet, and Mahmud is his companion.' From Turkic slaves he had risen high.

The first historian of India

These early conquests saw a flood of migrants into the Indus valley and the Punjab – entrepreneurs, Sufis, saints, mercenaries – and many old preconceptions were challenged and enriched. Among the migrants was Abu al-Rayhan al-Biruni, scientist, astronomer, philosopher and the greatest historian of India. Al-Biruni was a thoroughgoing orthodox Sunni Muslim, but India and its ideas had a tremendous impact on him – a pointer to the way that India would change Islamic civilization and become a heartland of the religion.

One interesting aspect of this dialogue concerns views of time. Al-Biruni had grown up with biblical and Koranic traditions of time, but when he travelled to India and took up the study of Sanskrit and the Indian sciences he realized that these ideas were culturally specific and historically related. Biblical and Koranic ideas about the length of history were clearly absurd. The cycles of time in Indian thought were unimaginably long – billions of years – and Indian thinkers did not even believe in the Creation as Christians and Muslims conceived it, for in their theories each new age of the cosmos was formed afresh out of the debris of the last. A change of timescale inevitably brought a change of philosophical content, which even led al-Biruni to what reads like an early exposition of Darwinist theories. His remarkable portrait of India's religions should also be mentioned. Earlier Muslim historians understood that religion in India was very different from that of the 'Peoples of the Book' (the Jews and Christians whose scriptures, according to the Koran, were revealed to them by God before the time of Muhammad), and that it formed a set of related belief systems unique to the subcontinent, even though there were sects such as the Vaishnavites and Shaivites, which each had tens of millions of followers, with different gods, sacred books and rituals. But al-Biruni, who learnt Sanskrit and consulted with Hindu holy men, asserted that the fundamental religious beliefs of the Indians were the same as those of Islam, and that idol worship was only a superficial issue, an aid to the poor and simple. This remarkable perception sets the pattern for future Muslim–Hindu dialogue, from the medieval Sufi saints and mystics such as Kabir and Dadu, to Dara Shikoh in the 1640s and to modern thinkers such as Swami Vivekananda, Rabindranath Tagore and Jiddu Krishnamurti.

Empires of the south

So the twin figures of Mahmud and his philosopher-scientist al-Biruni represent the opposite poles of the first meeting of Islam and India. But this is another moment to note the synchronicities of history. In the year 1010 Mahmud of Ghazni marched across the Punjab and attacked the Jumna valley, sacking Ghur, and in 1011 Thanesar, the great ancient city at the site of Kurukshetra. Those years loom large in northern historiography, but the great centres of civilization in the south and east were untouched by these predatory forays. Also in 1010, a great emperor in the tropical south marked his conquests in the Maldives and Sri Lanka by dedicating the greatest building in India. Two years after Mahmud's 1017 attack deep into the Ganges plain, the son of that ruler – a Hindu king and devotee of Shiva – led an expedition that marched, incredibly, 1000 miles or more as the crow flies up the coast of Andra and Orissa as far as the Ganges. The inhabitants of Bengal were no doubt as surprised to meet an invading army from the deep south, speaking an unintelligible southern tongue, as they were to meet Mahmud of Ghazni's Turkic conquistadors from the Indus valley.

In the deep south the late tenth century had seen the rise of a vast empire untouched by events in the West and central Asia. As discussed in Chapter 3, the Ashokan age knew of the Cholans, along with the other great dynasties of the south – the Pandyas of Madurai and the Pallavas of Kanchi. The Cholas grew to be the pre-eminent power in the south of the peninsula in the tenth century, and remained so until the late thirteenth century. In the eleventh century they captured the Andaman and Nicobar islands, off the shores of Burma, which remain Indian today; they also occupied parts of Java, and exchanged embassies with China, where they left merchant colonies. One of the great civilizations of the day, its heartland was the valley and delta of the Cavery, the sacred river of southern India. To get there you must head towards the southern tip of India down the Coromandel Coast: Chola mandalam, the land of the Cholans.

Journey to Tanjore

I arrive in Tanjore with the late autumn monsoon. From my hotel roof by the station, a great bank of indigo clouds hangs over the town, and a curtain of rain moves across the damp green landscape to distant rumbles of thunder.

Tanjore stands just below the apex of the Cavery delta. From here forty streams spread out to irrigate the rice fields, the foundation of the wealth of the dynasties who shaped southern Indian history. The British thought this the most fertile province of their empire; for Marco Polo, who came here at the very end of the Cholan golden age, it was the 'richest province on Earth'. Over the town rears the huge pyramid of the temple of Rajaraja the Great, finished in 1010, and symbol of the Cholan Empire that dominated southern India from the tenth to the thirteenth centuries, and sent its armies to Sri Lanka and the Ganges.

It was an age of brilliant artistic and cultural achievement, often compared with that of the ancient Athenians. The Tamil culture went back into the deep past and they produced music, dance, poetry and sculpture as expressive as any on the

planet. And despite the erosions of time, and the depredations of colonialism and modernity, the culture is still alive. If you hanker to know what it is like to belong to a traditional civilization, southern India is the place: the Cavery delta is its fertile heartland, and Tanjore its imperial city.

The founder of the Cholan Empire was Aditya, whose dynasty traced its ancestry to pre-Roman times (as we saw, the Cholans are mentioned in the edicts of Ashoka). Aditya, who ruled from 871 to 907, consolidated the kingdom and is described in the poetic words of the royal inscriptions as 'building a row of great stone temples to Shiva down the banks of the Cavery river, all the way from the elephant-haunted Sahya mountains down to the ocean, where the moon plays on the folds of its restless waves'. But up until the mid-tenth century the Cholan kingdom was still a local one, mired in conflicts with its peninsular neighbours. The architect of the expansion was Arulmoli, subsequently known as Rajaraja (king of kings), who acceded to the throne in 985. As he grew in self-assurance, he sent his navy to conquer new lands, including the Maldives and northern Sri Lanka, while his son Rajendra sent the army to the Ganges and actually occupied parts of Java and the Malacca straits to protect the sea trade route to Cambodia and Sung dynasty China. Rajaraja created a state with a strong administration and a powerful army, which allowed the Cholans to dominate the south for three centuries, and left a mark on the culture and religion of the Tamils that persists to this day.

Rajaraja's personal story has some of the disturbing hallucinations of a myth. His dynasty had been overthrown by enemies during his childhood; his great-uncle committed religious suicide by fasting to death, probably when he (Rajaraja) was a child; his elder brother was assassinated in palace infighting; following this, his father died mysteriously ('Of a broken heart?' speculates historian Nilakanta Sastri), and his mother committed ritual suicide on his father's funeral pyre. Father and mother were subsequently elevated almost to divine status in the inscriptions recorded on bronze images commissioned by Rajaraja's sister Kundavi. After all this, his uncle, rather than the boy-prince, succeeded to the throne (shades of *Hamlet* or *The Lion King*?), and is regarded by some Tamil historians, though not all, as a 'wicked uncle'. Although Rajaraja was 'begged by the people to become king and dispel the darkness of the Kali age', he refused to do so. 'He did not desire the kingdom for himself, even inwardly, so long as his uncle coveted the rule of the land …' The tale no doubt conceals infighting within the royal house, as seems to have happened with so many ancient and medieval Indian successions. But to placate court factions, and after 'certain marks were observed on his body … showing that he was the very Vishnu descended to Earth', (which has hints of the Rama story) his uncle named Rajaraja as his heir. So he was installed as crown prince, while the uncle himself 'bore the burden of ruling the Earth'.

With the self-possession of Rama in exile, the young prince did not fight, but waited for his time to come. When it finally did, the king displayed a practical genius, a ruthlessness and a knack for self-promotion that has left an enduring mark on the cultural, political and religious life of southern India.

Rajaraja's personal deity – his family god (*kulandeva*) as the Tamils put it – was Shiva, but as with all great Indian rulers he was an enthusiastic patron of other faiths, building a temple and a huge Buddhist monastery in Nagapattinam, the main seaport, to welcome Eastern pilgrims. (This, incidentally, continued to be used by Asian pilgrims into the sixteenth century, and was not demolished until the 1860s.) He even sanctioned Buddhist sculptures on the walls of his great Shiva temple in Tanjore, built to commemorate his rulership, his conquests and, above all, himself.

Rajaraja's temple at Tanjore is a World Heritage Site today, but still a living shrine. The weathered red sandstone *gopuras*, or gate towers, announce the ceremonial entrance, looking for all the world like exotic petrified vegetation with their sprouting ornaments and horned finials. The temple is named after the great king, Rajarajesvaram (Lord of Rajaraja), and has lengthy inscriptions about his victories and donations carved all around its walls. The royal family and courtiers emulated his generosity by making lavish gifts of bronzes, utensils, candelabra and furnishings. Most prominent among the donors, though, are not his ten queens, but his 'beloved elder sister' Kundavi, with whom he seems to have had an unusually intense relationship. She takes priority over her brother's queens in all the inscriptions, and he would later marry one of her daughters and name one of his own daughters after her.

The great gateways open on to a campus so elegant and spacious after the crowded hurly-burly of the town that the effect is eye-popping. It measures 1200 × 800 feet and is entirely surrounded by a pillared cloister, with a dado and pilasters, that runs along a magnificent granite wall 40 feet high. Its beautiful and austere classicism is enlivened by rows of little sculpted figures of Nandi, Shiva's bull, along the top. Peeping over the wall, the bending heads of cocoa palms are tousled beguilingly by the warm wind as knots of pilgrims make their way around the shrines in brilliant saris of lemon, crimson and gold.

The court was a great ritual space, a theatre for royal ceremonies. There are perhaps few places in the world where so old a building is still perfectly preserved, and still works as a living institution. In the centre of the courtyard the main shrine stands on a great platform, with a huge pyramidal vimana (tower) 216 feet high, which, when it was completed in 1010, was the tallest building in India. The completion was celebrated in a grand festival in which the top royal acting troupe performed a specially written musical play telling the story of the king and his temple. Sadly, the text is now lost, though sitting in the courtyard in brilliant sunshine, with today's festival tents flapping, it is pleasing to imagine Rajaraja as prince and script editor-in-chief – both Hal and Hamlet, solid and quicksilver, swordsman and poet-philosopher – giving his actors last-minute instructions on how to deliver their lines extolling him: '... his deeds such as to make the goddess of fortune his own wife, and the goddess of the great Earth, his mistress.'

ABOVE

One of the ornate, ceremonial gateways (gopuras) *which led to the sacred enclosure at the great temple of Tanjore.*

Around the base of the vimana are rows of sculpted figures of Shiva in his warlike form with shield and sword, the destroyer of cities. Inscriptions list thirty Cholan regiments with battle honours. By the doors are carved images of Rajaraja and his guru Karuvur Devar. Up the steps the inner sanctum is approached through a dimly lit and fabulously atmospheric hall supported by massive, squared granite columns. Finally, inside the shrine, set against a giant bronze seven-headed serpent, a 12-foot black lingam stands on a huge pedestal – the emblem of Shiva. The name of the lingam is 'Lord of Rajaraja'. Every dawn milk libations are poured over the polished granite before it is washed and decorated with long golden streamers of marigolds and wrapped in a gleaming white cotton skirt. As is the custom in Tamil Nadu, on the day of Rajaraja's birth special pujas are still performed in the king's memory. (And could it perhaps be – given the insistently personal nature of the foundation – that the shrine was planned also to mark the eventual burial place of the king's ashes?)

As the king intended, the scale and spaciousness of it all creates a feeling of tremendous grandeur. From the last gate the pilgrim walks across the vast sun-beaten courtyard on a progress from wide open sky to the dark 'womb-chamber'. But the most beautiful, intimate and evanescent traces of Rajaraja's age have for many years been hidden from public view. Inside the wall of the shrine, in a narrow ambulatory passage, are much earlier murals that were rescued in the 1930s from underneath rain-damaged paintings from the seventeenth century. Little Cholan painting has survived, and what has been exposed and conserved here is magical. The technique is true fresco – paint on wet lime plaster – and the images give an extraordinary glimpse into the lost world of the Cholan Empire. Most striking is the strange mingling of militarism with the most exquisite delicacy. This was an age that produced love poetry of almost postmodern awareness and sexual frankness, yet also enjoyed bloodthirsty battle eulogies in which enemies' temples are looted, the heads of rebels squashed like melons under elephants' feet and, most grisly of all, royal women of the defeated side are mutilated – in one case the defeated king's mother, in another the king's wife, a woman 'as lovely as a peacock'. In one war in the Mysore region women in the conquered countries have their 'girdles loosened' or are 'deprived of their caste' – in other words, raped. More bizarrely, one condemned ambassador is humiliated by being dressed in women's clothes and set afloat in a boat with no oars. Perhaps all this casts a different light on similar wars between Turkic sultans and Hindu rajas in the north during the Middle Ages, when temples were sacked as an act of religious iconoclasm. Muslim hostility towards Hindu image-making is no doubt part of it, but one should never underestimate the retributive impulses of the conqueror. As in the medieval West, to renounce one's overlord was to break a religious vow.

LEFT

*Rajaraja the Great and
his guru Karuvur Devar:
one of the Cholan
paintings hidden inside
the shrine ambulatory
of the great temple.*

So it was a time of blood and flowers, evoking strange parallels – feudal Japan,
perhaps, or even the Aztecs? In the lamplight inside the ambulatory of the great
temple you can gaze on the faces of that age and gradually make out soft, blurred
outlines as if through a smoky mist: lapis lazuli, terre verte, white lime, lamp black,
yellow and red ochre. There's an extraordinarily lifelike portrait of Rajaraja himself,
fleshy lipped and golden skinned, with the faint suggestion of puppy fat you might
see in any well-fed, rich Tamil politician or Bollywood star today. Head inclined, he
is deep in conversation with his white-bearded guru and poet laureate Karuvur
Devar. On the wall near them is Shiva, again in his military incarnation – the
destroyer of the cities of the demons, full of bulging-eyed rage, tracers of paint

swirling around him like time-lapse headlights. Here too is the royal family worshipping its family god: the shadowy image of dancing Shiva in his ring of fire, jewels shimmering faintly, as if on a photographic negative, and behind him the unmistakable bowed roof of the sanctum at Chidambaram, the 'hall of consciousness' where he performed his cosmic dance.

The dance, both divine and human, is a central image in the temple and in the culture – as God's dance and as an art form. On the frescoes there are girls dancing, curvaceous and naked but for a waistband, bangles, anklets and elaborate hairdo. Upstairs, in the upper ambulatory gallery, unfinished at the king's death in 1014, is a great sequence of sculpted panels of the 108 poses of the dance, the Bharat Natyam, in the exact sequence of the ancient text book, the *Natya Shastra*. Of 850 temple employees dedicated by Rajaraja to his new establishment – servants, dance masters, musicians, drummers, singers, accountants, parasol bearers, lamplighters, watermen, potters, washermen, barbers, astrologers, tailors, carpenters, goldsmith – there were 400 dancing girls brought from all over Chola Nadu for its dedication in 1010. They lived in streets adjacent to the shrine and are all named in inscriptions on the exterior walls, with the address of their house and the name of their native village. All were dedicated to a life of service to God and king, and the details are there for all to see: terms of employment, remuneration, duties, pension arrangements and rights upon death. Take this typical example: 'South Street, south row. House number 80, the girl Sengulam, from Tiru Merrali temple in Pachchil village.' Or what about young Solam at number 79? The detail is so immediate and alluring that it is hard for the historian to resist trying to trace them …

In imperial Tanjore

Evening is coming on, the rains have stopped, and warm sunlight is slanting across the bus stand. I take a rickshaw into the old town. Despite the riches of the epigraphy from this period, there is no description of this great Indian imperial city, and no information about its situation or layout. It first appears in the early eighth century as a new town, Tanjapuri, that was fortified in the mid-ninth century when it became the Cholan capital. That city lay to the north of today's town on the banks of the Vennar river, where a little temple, whose god is called the Lord of Tanjore, still survives. Then, in the late tenth century, Rajaraja laid out a new city, with wide streets and bazaars, and a hospital dedicated by his sister Kundavi. But the city layout as it stands today seems to be sixteenth to seventeenth century. And whether Rajaraja's capital stood on the same site has not yet been proved: many think it lay somewhere outside the present moated city, but I'm not so sure. It's time for another exploration on the ground.

I bring with me an eighteenth-century map made by British military observers, 'engraved from an exact survey' during the Carnatic wars (1746–63). This shows the place as it stood in the days of the British–French wars, when the armies of the imperialists went on destructive marches across the south, causing havoc and huge loss of life. The map is so detailed that it marks the sight-lines of the artillery, and the locations of French attacks; but it also shows the pre-modern streets, alleys and shrines. Inside the defences there were four great streets forming a square, and off them was a warren of narrow alleys. Could these be the four great streets of the Cholan inscriptions? I leave the rickshaw and plunge down a narrow alley under the palace walls, where I swiftly stumble on a derelict medieval shrine, now used as a bike shed. The columns used to support festival canopies are still sticking up out of a midden heap.

Further on the centre of the old town is a warren hidden from the world, reachable only on foot. In the middle of today's West Street is a big shrine with Cholan inscriptions; and close by is a series of stone-lined lanes, part of what looks like a deliberately planned layout of housing plots, each with its own alley entrance. I then turn into South Street, where the dancing girls perhaps lived. The tenth-century house numbers are no guide. 'Are you looking for an old number or a new number?' I am asked by a shopkeeper, pointing at his door frame, where both are painted. Needless to say, neither fits. I wander into a narrow lane off South Street by a new concrete shopping mall. It takes me through a small archway and ends in a little yard flanked by a printer's shop on one side and an old family temple on the other. In the printing shop the printer makes tea, his old trays of metal type gathering dust: 'We are now computerized,' he says. We sit on his steps while across the yard an old man in a loincloth lifts the puja flame and rings the bell.

'I can only tell you the oral tradition of the street,' says the printer, 'but we are a Tanjore family and the story here is that this was inside Rajaraja's city: the royal staff were accommodated on that side, the singers and dancing girls on this. See how old my neighbours' shrine is: at least 600 years old. This is typical of old Tanjore.'

RIGHT

Inside a traditional Tamil 'agraharam' house and a moment's relaxation in the old culture of the south.

I sit on the steps, sipping my tea, the last light touching the shrine roof while rush-hour traffic roars past the end of the alley and shoppers hurry home. Of course, what I am looking at is the product of many layers of time – Cholan, Nayak, Maratha, British – but in my mind's eye I see the scene described in a great Tamil text of the tenth century: 'The hum of people in the city is like the noise of the ocean … in the streets all the colours of the rainbow … banners fluttering, blue-painted water pots on terraces, tanks as deep as the hearts of courtesans. Men and women beautifully dressed like a city of the gods.' This is from a poem by a Jain writer, influenced by traditional Tamil descriptions of cities, but it has the feel of the tenth century, when 'the people of eighteen languages were congregated here as thick as birds on a tree ripe with fruit'. The poem, the *Civakacintamani*, goes on to describe the interior:

> [Inside] the city was filled with the merchandise of the islands …
> its bazaar streets long and wide, beautifully arranged, glinting with
> treasures, their warehouses crammed with precious luxuries …
> People of the seven castes so numerous, so close together that sandal
> paste rubbed on one shoulder came off on another, and voices were
> heard but language was not distinguishable … The smoke of a
> thousand cooking fires gusting through streets, darkens the sun, and
> when the festival is over the visitor must tread over heaps of garlands
> in the streets, through pools strewn with petals and reddened by
> coloured powders.

Such, one imagines, was Tanjore in the days of Rajaraja.

From ancient to medieval

So the cultures of India in the Middle Ages produced brilliant flowerings in many areas. Beyond what we have briefly glimpsed in this chapter, one might also mention the architecture of Khajuraho, Orissa and Gujarat; the cave shrines at Ajanta, Ellora and Karle; the Jain temples at Mount Abu; or the Buddhist architecture of Bengal, where the Pala kingdom between the eighth and thirteenth centuries left great monuments, such as the university at Somapura, now in Bangladesh. Although India was never united as a state, it is likely that through these centuries the subcontinent was the richest and most populous part of the world. Of course, these were all hierarchical and caste-ridden societies, where the tribal and untouchable peoples were often suppressed with violence, and where the elites spent vast resources on their own royal prestige and cults. The masses did not

generally share in the surplus they generated, but still their culture had many qualities, and one notable area was pluralism in religion. Intolerance, of course, is the monopoly of no civilization, and it is easy to find examples of Hindu kings showing fanatical intolerance to Buddhists and Jains in the Middle Ages, and even towards other Hindu sects. But if a broad tendency can be detected, it is perhaps that foreign dynasties eschewed state religion altogether, and though some native dynasties favoured one – the Mauryans with Jainism or Buddhism, for example, the Guptas with Vaishnavaism, the Cholas with Saivism – enlightened Indian rulers were still active supporters of other faiths. The key, if at all possible, was pluralism.

In the south the old native kingdoms went their own way until the early fourteenth century, untroubled by the wider world. In the north the great powers of the late antique period and early Middle Ages were buffeted by blows through the eleventh and twelfth centuries until the establishment of the Delhi sultanate in 1192 began the centuries-long domination of Afghan, Turkic and Mughal dynasties, some of whose kings aggressively propagated Islam. But, as we shall see, accommodation came. In a telling anecdote that could be multiplied over and over, the great traveller ibn Battuta tells how, in the 1330s, even the temples at Khajuraho, with their magically erotic sculpture illustrating the cosmic marriage of Shiva and Parvati, became a source for Muslim holy men as well as Hindus. All of them were united in that perennial Indian quest – seeking after wisdom.

As for the Rama story with which I began, in the Middle Ages it became a metaphor, a carrier of meaning for the Indian experience, a lens by which to see the shifting currents of Indian history. There are said to be more than 300 versions, some containing radical retellings, in Tamil, for example, in Marathi, Telugu and Bengali, and in the northern lingua franca, Hindi. There is a Muslim Rama story told by the Mopylas, the old boat-building caste of Kerala: a tale of 'Sultan Ram' set firmly in tropical southern India in a Muslim milieu. There is even a Tamil 'Life of the Prophet' modelled on the Tamil *Ramayana*. In such ways the tale became a vision of Indian history: another root of a shared past, available to all communities and even all religions. Like all great creations of India, it came to belong everywhere. As an eminent member of India's Supreme Court, a Muslim, puts it:

> The entire country is Ramjanmabhumi, the birth land of Rama. The
> Ramjanmasthan, the birthplace, lies, however, in the hearts and minds
> of all those who have, over the centuries, loved, respected and wor-
> shipped Shri Rama as Maryada Purshottram: an ideal of rectitude,
> integrity, decency and sheer humanity.

OPPOSITE

Tiruvannamalai: fabulous images from the Kartikai *festival. This ancient Tamil hill shrine is celebrated by the 7th-century saints, and was later enriched by Rajaraja himself.*

5
The Rule of Reason: The Great Mughals

AT THE GREAT FORT Bala Hissar the trees are shaken by the north wind that blows through spring and summer across the Kabul plain. Zigzagging over bare brown hills, the city walls of Kabul were first built to withstand the attacks of the Huns in the fifth century. Kabul has seen many attackers since then – Genghis Khan, Tamburlaine, Mughals, Persians, British – and they are still at war today, as the fighting spreads in Helmand province. But here in the early sixteenth century a new invasion of India was planned, which would have a profound effect on the history of the subcontinent.

When I was here in the mid-1990s, during the first war with the Taliban, the city had been devastated: there was no electricity, no street lighting; at night the occasional car's headlights swept through the jagged pinnacles and murky shadows of a broken city. Since the overthrow of the Taliban in 2001, international commerce has returned and new buildings are going up everywhere, despite the rumble of war in the south. But the incessant fighting over the last quarter century has also brought a vast expansion of the population, spreading shanties up the hillsides, draping dingy suburbs over what was in the late 1960s, as all old Afghan hands will tell you, a heavenly land: as the poet Peter Levi put it, 'the light garden of the angel king'.

Babur, the first Mughal

The tomb of Babur, founder of the Mughal dynasty that ruled northern India from 1526 to 1857, lies in a once-lovely valley a short walk from the city centre – a walk that opens up views of the diversity of Afghan history. It is easy today to think of Afghanistan as a hotbed of Islamic fundamentalism, but traces of another, richer history are all around us. This place is a witness to the waves of history on the subcontinent, for Afghanistan, as we have already seen, has always been part of that story. In the Late Bronze Age and after, the Kabul valley was one of the lands of the Rig-Veda. It was a great centre of Buddhist culture in the early centuries AD, and was ruled by Hindu shahs between 600 and the tenth century AD. Indeed, until the civil war of the 1980s and the Russian invasion it still had a big Hindu population, nearly a quarter of a million strong, mainly traders, craftsmen, practitioners of traditional 'Yunani' (Graeco-Roman) medicine. Now only a few hundred families are left, but the valley bears evidence of its multi-faith past, when Hindus, Buddhists and Muslims came here to worship. There are the remains of a Kushan stupa at the southern end of the valley; an old Muslim cemetery commemorates the first Islamic missionaries to Kabul in the seventh century AD; and there was a Hindu temple still in this area until the Russian invasion. Sadly, the old picnics in the groves of mulberries are a thing of the past – at least for now.

But the most evocative spot of all is the garden of Babur, burial place of the legendary Mughal leader. His was an amazing tale. Born in Fergana, proclaimed king in the Tajik city of Khodzent, he was a direct descendant of Genghis Khan and Tamburlaine. He conquered Kabul in 1504, and it was from here that he launched his final attack on India in 1525, which at that time was, paradoxically, ruled by the Lodi sultans who had originally come from Afghanistan. Babur's bold and risky adventure succeeded. He founded the Mughal dynasty, whose leaders would become among the greatest and most glamorous rulers in the world. But he never forgot Kabul. In his memoirs he complains about the hot, dusty climate of India ('a place with few attractions … and no good melons'). Kabul was the place he really loved, 'with its excellent climate, overlooking the great lake, and three meadows that look very beautiful when the plains are green'. He liked the valley in particular, his home for twenty years, its altitude giving it the perfect summer climate, a place where vines, olive trees and fruit orchards could thrive. The garden here was laid out between 1504 and 1528, and has been popular with the people of the city ever since. The inscription on the tomb is his: 'If there is a paradise on Earth, this is it, this is it, this is it!'

Babur tells us that he felt most at home in these rugged landscapes with their emerald green valleys and fruit orchards; their brown whalebacks of mountains streaked with snow; in the serais and bazaars of Bukhara Merv and Samarkand. He never mastered an Indian language, but spoke the Chaghtai dialect of Turkic from Mughalistan, the lands north of the Syr Darya river stretching towards Lake Balkash. And to the end, in the sweltering plains of India, he still hankered after the

wide skies of central Asia, the purple deserts of Samarkand dotted with flowers
after the spring rains.

ABOVE

*The tomb of Babur
today, outside Kabul.*

Forty years ago, in the days of the 'Hippy Trail', this was still a delightful spot,
with magnificent chinar trees and the scent of wild rose and jasmine in the air. Since
then the catastrophe for Afghanistan has also swept up even the greatest Muslim
monuments. Decades of neglect, twenty-five years of war, and several years of
drought have dried up watercourses and killed all the trees and plants, leaving it
derelict and engulfed by the urban sprawl of shanties. Now it is being restored: the
gardens are to be replanted with trees and flowers, so it may once again be the haven
it was in Mughal times. Like so much of the tragedy of Afghanistan over the last
three decades, from the destruction of the Bamiyan Buddhas to the wrecking of the
Kabul Museum, the battle is also against the loss of the past.

But the garden is not just a setting for this part of the story of India; it is also
a symbol of a civilization that we have come to view as quintessentially Indian. It
was the first of the Mughal gardens of the subcontinent, while the garden at
Dholpur, south of Agra, was almost Babur's first act of state in India. Others laid
out by his successors include the magnificent group of gardens at Srinagar,
overlooking the Dal Lake in Kashmir and now languishing unvisited under the
shadow of the jihadists; and the recently rediscovered Moonlit Garden over
the Jumna from the Taj Mahal. The Kabul garden was the first model. Babur laid

out the site in a series of square gardens on low terraces, with octagonal and circular fountains, shaded by chinar trees beloved of the Mughals. The sides are gone now, but there is still the lovely view across the plain to the mountains of central Afghanistan, whose long ridges are seamed with snow even during the summer. Walk up the hill path once lined with stately cypress trees and you come to a beautiful marble mosque built by Shah Jahan in 1646 to celebrate his capture of the ancient city of Balkh, the 'mother of cities', on the Oxus plain beyond the Hindu Kush. Babur's tomb lies on the terrace above the mosque. Although he died in Agra, he loved this garden so much that he asked to be brought here for burial. War and civil unrest delayed this until, nine years later, his loyal Afghan wife Bibi Mubarika Yusufzai finally brought him back.

Babur stipulated that nothing should cover his grave: he wanted rain and sun to beat upon it, for snow to blanket it, and maybe wild flowers to grow. This request was honoured: the small headstone was built by his great-grandson Jahangir in the seventeenth century. Only in the1930s was the present marble stone placed on top, under a small pavilion, but the current restoration project will remove it and expose Babur's tomb once more to the elements.

The northern Indian empire he created would, in the end, be an extraordinary Indo-Islamic synthesis that, albeit briefly, comprehended all religions. It was ruled by Muslim emperors who spoke to Buddhists rather than bombing their statues, had pictures of the Virgin Mary in their bedrooms, and translated Hindu sacred texts rather than dismissing them as the abominations of idolators. The Mughal age today is a defining image of North India, and its achievements remain a source of fascination, but this is not its only own interest. Within this tale are pointers to what the Islamic world could have been, and perhaps can still be.

The Battle of Panipat

In the spring of 1526, harnesses jangling, the Mughal army came down from Kabul, crossed the Indus at Attock, and marched down the Grand Trunk Road. Crossing the Punjab, it turned south along the river Jumna on the ancient road into the plains. The army's guns, pulled by trains of horses, were the first artillery to be used in battle in India. This was to be the last of Babur's five attempts to gain the riches of the subcontinent. Forty-three now, a grizzled veteran inured to war since childhood, he was descended on his mother's side from Genghis Khan and on his father's from Tamburlaine:

> Hindustan is a vast and populous kingdom and a productive realm, but it is a strange country. Compared to ours it is another world. Its mountains, rivers, forests and wildernesses, its villages and provinces, animals and plants, peoples and languages, even its rain and winds are altogether different. Once you cross the Indus, the land, water, trees, stones, peoples, tribes, manners and customs are all of the Hindustani fashion. There is no limit to the people … and most of the people of Hindustan are infidels …

However, his enemy was not Hindu, but Muslim – Sultan Ibrahim Lodi of Delhi. The decisive battle was fought on Friday, 20 April 1526, when the heat was building in the northern Indian plain, and temperatures can go up to 45°C (115°F) or even more. He was up against the numerically superior forces of Sultan Ibrahim, who, it was rumoured, could muster 100,000 men, almost ten times that of his own forces.

The scene of the battle was Panipat, an old town on the Grand Trunk Road, 55 miles north of Delhi. Lying in the narrow tract of country where many great battles of Indian history have been fought, it was a place of legend too, feuded over by the Pandavas and the Kurus in the *Mahabharata.* Babur chose a position with his right wing anchored on the walled town and its suburbs, his left wing on an old, dried-up course of the Jumna, strengthened with fallen trees and brushwood. Seven hundred carts were commandeered from his own baggage and from the local people, and roped together with cables, leaving gaps where his matchlock gunmen could shoot and reload behind mantlets (movable screens). Several larger openings, 50–100 yards wide, were left for the cavalry to mount forays, especially on the wings where Babur was looking to make a decisive turning movement.

The battle was won by Babur's toughness, his nerve and his artillery. The Afghan dead were set by Babur at up to 16,000, and the sultan himself fell on the battlefield among a great heap of the slain. When the Mughals found his body, they cut off his head and took it to Babur. 'Honour to your bravery,' he said grimly, lifting up the blood-matted head. Local tradition places the luckless Sultan Ibrahim's tomb in a little shrine behind the bus stand in the bustling heart of today's town.

Babur now marched on Delhi, but before he left Panipat he decreed the construction of a mosque on the battle site as a thanksgiving. It's still there – the earliest Mughal monument in India. Now engulfed by Panipat's modern industrial expansion, it stands on a low rise that once looked out over the battlefield. Not easy to find, you must ask the locals, and eventually someone will point you the way to the Kabuli Bagh Masjid (Mosque of the Kabul Garden). It's a lovely little building of warm brown brick and red sandstone veneer, set in what the Mughals called a *char bagh*, a four-quartered garden with an ornamental pool. With this, he introduced the concept of the central Asian garden into India, and you can perhaps sense his personality here more than in any other place. Additions by his son Humayun and a lovely gateway by his grandson Akbar testify to the family attachment to this place. The Tuesday after the battle Babur reached Delhi: 'we came to Nizamuddin, which I circumambulated, and then we camped beside the Jumna directly opposite the city'. Nizamuddin is still the favourite Sufi shrine of all Delhiites, approached through narrow lanes of butchers' shops, *chai* stalls and a covered tunnel of pilgrim stalls, opening into a marble courtyard full of people from dawn till dusk. In terms of communal tolerance, it is one of loveliest spots in Delhi. 'Afterwards,' says Babur, 'I went back to camp, got on a boat and drank some spirits.'

It was a moment for reflection, both on his own life and on wider history. 'From the year 910 [AD 1504–5] when I captured Kabul,' he wrote in his memoirs, 'I had coveted Hindustan.' That this was a turning point he was well aware. After four failed expeditions, he had finally done it:

From the time of the Prophet only three great Muslim shahs gained dominion over and ruled the realm of Hindustan [by which he means the north and Delhi: he was aware of great southern kings outside the orbit of the Islamic world]. I was the third great shah to conquer Hindustan: first was Mahmud of Ghazni; second was Sultan Shiabuddin Ghuri, who with his slaves and followers ruled this kingdom for many years. I am the third. My accomplishment, however, is beyond comparison with theirs. When that first time we went to Bhera [on the Indus] we were 1500 strong, 2000 at most. The fifth time, when we defeated Sultan Ibrahim and conquered the realm of Hindustan, I had the biggest army I ever had – and that was only 12,000 on the muster roll.

Those words come from Babur's memoirs, one of history's great autobiographies from the pen of one of its great movers. Frank, intimate and (one senses) unbiased, it is one of the first and, until recently, the only true autobiography in Islamic literature. Full of conversations, letters, poems, decrees and historical and geographical detail, it is marked by a profound curiosity about the natural world, full of rich observations on flora and fauna. For a man who lived such a tough life in the saddle, sleeping in camp, he appreciated the small things in life, especially fruit: Bukhara plums were 'without rival', Kabul rhubarb 'excellent', and its grapes 'superb'.

As for Nasukh melons, 'yellow skin soft as glove leather, they are amazingly delicious, there is nothing like them'. Babur records his own foibles, his illnesses, boils and abcesses, his excessive drinking; he is a human personality. As a leader and man of action, he was also peremptory in his cruelty. A typical passage reads: 'I ordered the cook to be flayed alive, the taster cut to pieces, one of the women trampled by elephants, the other shot.'

Babur describes a gripping scene at Delhi after the great victory. There were signs of disaffection in the army, reminiscent of Alexander the Great at the river Beas. Deaths through sickness and heat were increasing, and so was hatred of India and nostalgia for the Kabuli gardens. 'Many began to sicken and die, as if under a pestilential wind. That's why most of the great warriors and chiefs began to lose heart.' Unwilling to stay in Hindustan they began to leave. This was a key moment.

> … if aged and experienced leaders say such things, it is no fault, for such men have enough sense and intelligence to distinguish between prudence and imprudence and to discern good from evil after a decision has been made. Such a person considers everything for himself and he knows that when something has been decided there is no sense in endlessly repeating words that have already been spoken. But these were men that I expected if I went through fire or water, they would go in with me and emerge with me and be at my side wherever I went, not speak out against me.

So Babur speaks to the council just as his Spanish contemporary Francisco Pizarro did to his men in South America, both being conscious that a continent lay before them that would be won by those who were prepared to gamble all. His message to his commanders standing in the mid-May heat of the northern Indian plain was direct:

> I said rule and conquest do not come without tools and conquest. Kingship and princehood are not possible without liegemen and domains. For some years we have gone through hardships, traversed long distances, cast ourselves and our soldiers into the dangers of war and battle. Through God's grace we have defeated such numerous enemies and taken such vast realms. Why throw it all away now, after gaining it at such cost? Shall we go back to Kabul and stay poor?

They went on, most of them, though Babur never lost his longing for his old homeland. His descendants for a long time would nurse imperial dreams of their central Asian homeland: they even, unwisely, fought battles there. But eventually their ancestral lands around Fergana would become a distant memory; the orchards of Samarkand, the legendary Timurid capital, once so ardently desired, would become a forsaken passion. Babur's descendants became Indian.

The legacy of Babur

Babur, like Tamburlaine and the Tuqluqs, was an invader, and his career was driven by violence. In the sacred writings of the Sikhs, Guru Nanak says he was a messenger of death, who 'terrified Hindustan', and accuses his armies of the rape of Hindu women. Mughal sources, on the other hand, say he went out of his way to protect the civilian population in war, even compensating farmers if their crops were ruined. But he was a man of his time, and his was a time when striking fear was part of being a king. There is much argument about his legacy now, especially by Hindu nationalists, who see the Mughal as an enemy of India. And it is true that he could on occasion talk the language of jihad, though only perhaps when his army seemed to be losing its nerve.

Also, as the Koran enjoins, he could be merciless towards unbelievers when they resisted him. But did he destroy Hindu temples, as others had done in the past and would in the future? Whether the mosque in Ayodhia was built on top of a destroyed Hindu temple has never been shown, but conquerors did this sort of thing, and whether Babur was different we cannot say. His bloodthirsty description of the killing of infidels at the siege of Chanderi in 1528, with the mass suicide of hundreds more (who 'went to hell') is a case in point. He was hardly squeamish about killing unbelievers, just as Akbar the Great could kill 'idolaters' and leave pillars made of their skulls. Such things, I daresay, were typical of wars of the time; if a city resisted, punishment was often merciless. But Babur was an intelligent man and saw that conciliation of enemies was the path

BELOW

Babur and his son Humayun with their ancestor Tamburlaine, the 'world conqueror'. Small origins but pride in their lineage gave them a great sense of history.

to the future. That is something central to the history of India. Sikh texts also mention that before his death Babur was blessed by Guru Nanak. Had something in him changed? Had he understood something important about India in the three and a half years between Panipat and his death?

The story of Babur's death has a truly mythic quality. His son Humayun fell ill and the physicians lost all hope of his recovery. Babur was told that in India people sometimes offer their dearest possession to God and pray to Him to accept it as a substitute for the life of their dear one. He readily said that he would do so, and the nobles thought he would offer the Koh-i-noor diamond. But Babur said, 'I can't offer God a stone!' After consulting a mystic, Babur walked three times around the sickbed and offered his own life in exchange for that of his son. Humayun recovered miraculously and Babur grew ill day by day. He died on 26 December 1530.

There were stories that before he died, Babur left Humayun a secret will. The purported document is now lost, but a photograph taken in the 1920s survived in a library in central India. Was it real? If so, it would be crucial testimony in the cultural and political battles now taking place in India. According to the document, Babur, with his dying breath, urged Humayun not to harbour religious prejudice, nor to demolish or damage the places of worship of any faith, for 'Islam can better be preached by the sword of love and affection, rather than the sword of tyranny and persecution'. It was then, and still is, good advice. Alas, although this is still contested, the will is surely a nineteenth-century forgery. But it points us to the remarkable events that took place in the reign of one of the most extraordinary figures in Indian and world history – Babur's grandson, Akbar the Great.

Akbar's line of life

'Of course, his horoscope tells you everything.' The astrologer of the maharaja of Jodhpur shuffles his papers and extracts a beautifully penned chart that he has drawn up at my request for 'Mr Akbar'. He has even made a phone call to the family in Umarcot in Pakistan, who still live in the old house where Akbar was born, where his mother, the then-pregnant wife of Humayun, had taken refuge after her husband had been driven out of India. The family is still Hindu and retains links with the Jodhpur royal family. In fact, it still has private documents in Sindhi dialect pertaining to Akbar's birth.

In the 1530s Humayun had been overthrown by Afghans under Shah Sher. He then spent ten years in Iran as an embarrassed guest of the shah, and was still in exile when his son was born in 1542. At that moment there must have seemed little prospect that Babur's Mughal dynasty would go beyond Humayun; everything pointed to it being a brief and unlamented blip in Indian history. But in the conjunctions and ascendants of their almanacs the astrologers prophesied a great king in Indian history. In fact, there was later some suggestion that the actual date and time of Akbar's birth – Sunday, 15 October 1542 at 2 a.m. – was adjusted to make it fall on the most auspicious day: but the reading turned out to be spot on.

Indeed, some later said that it was more than the date and time of birth that were changed. Humayun's wife Haminda Banu Begum had, up until then, given birth only to daughters, and it was said that she swapped babies with the rana of Umarcot's wife, who gave birth at the same time. Akbar, therefore, was really born a Hindu! To Hindu and Muslim alike, perhaps, that could be the only rational explanation for the course his life would take. Those two religions believe in fate and the influence of the stars, and what followed, was too extraordinary not to have been preceded by omens.

Akbar wins his kingdom

Akbar was proclaimed king at thirteen years of age, after his father Humayun died of his injuries after a fall down the stairs of his library in Delhi. At that moment he was a king without a kingdom. The palace is at Kalanaur, on a delightful country road in the midst of lush green fields east of the river Ravi, just inside today's border between India and Pakistan, north of Amritsar. Akbar always remembered this moment, and visited the place in later years. The platform and throne dais are still there, in a small walled enclosure by a copse of trees and a cluster of farm buildings.

When I arrive, a group of boys is playing cricket; they're the same age as the little prince was – like him, full of energy, garrulous, curious and sparky. The difference is that he had grown up with Afghan tribesmen – hard-bitten warriors in Kabul, whose toughness was proverbial, whether then or in the nineteenth century when the British endured their Kabul catastrophe, or now for that matter. Travelling on foot over the Hindu Kush in the 1990s with traders and gunmen from the northern alliance, I had a brief chance to observe such men at first hand: their tolerance of discomfort; their pragmatic, practical streak; their religious sensibility, but dislike of clerical claptrap. In such company Akbar never learnt to read and write. He remained illiterate, playing truant from his teacher, but acquired more practical skills, with an ability to think laterally, to make connections. As his horoscope indicated (so the maharaja's astrologer said), he had a very unconventional intellectual capacity, a fantastic memory and a brilliant ability to think (as management-speak puts it today) 'outside the box'. When we see the disasters brought on by lack of flexible and imaginative thinking nowadays, it's clear that Akbar's leadership skills surpassed anything currently displayed by most modern world leaders. Akbar, of course, had been brought up to survive in the real world.

RIGHT

Akbar the Great: 'In the past, to our shame, we forced many Hindus to adopt the faith of our ancestors. Now it has become clear to me that in our troubled world, so full of contradictions, it cannot be wisdom to assert the unique truth of one faith over another. The wise person makes justice his guide and learns from all. Perhaps in this way the door may be opened again, whose key has been lost.'

OPPOSITE

The Golden Temple at Amritsar. Despite initial conflicts with the Sikhs, Akbar granted them land on which to build their great shrine.

The enthronement at Kalanaur was no more than registration of a claim. Akbar inherited no kingdom. Military leaders who remained loyal after his father's death held Kabul, Kandahar, part of the Punjab and the city of Delhi. Ranged against him were the Afghan armies fighting for the king Shah Muhammad Adil – the same forces that had ousted his father. Based at the great fort of Chunar on the Jumna below Delhi, their leader Hemu, a Hindu, had a powerful army with 1500 war elephants. Aiming to drive the Mughals out for good, he now seized Delhi. But Akbar staked all on attack, and on 5 November engaged Hemu in battle at Panipat, where Babur had won thirty years earlier. The fighting went against the Mughals, until a chance arrow in Hemu's eye. He was beheaded by Akbar himself. By the time he was fifteen Akbar had defeated his other enemies and established his rule over 'Hindustan'. Fortune favours the brave.

Seeking the truth of religion

We cannot, of course, look at all the events of Akbar's astonishing forty-year reign here: he expanded the empire over Gujarat and Bengal, and ruled Kabul – an empire wider than any since the Mauryans. The young man also showed a great aptitude for government and administration. The greatest problem, though, soon became apparent. As Akbar's biographer Abul Fazl noted with characteristic bluntness:

> The emperor was aware of the fanatical hatred between Hindus and
> Muslims. But he was convinced this arose out of mutual ignorance.
> So this enlightened ruler sought to dispel this ignorance by making the
> books of each religion accessible to the other. In this way he wished to
> show Hindus that some of their customs and superstitions had no basis
> in their sacred books, and also convince Muslims that [for example] it
> was absurd to ascribe a mere 7000 years of existence to the world.

Abul Fazl's description of fanatical hatred must be taken at face value: deep dissensions had been caused by the high-handed and intolerant ways of many Muslim rulers and nobles, their hostility towards the native religions, their inequitable taxing of non-Muslims, and their forced conversions. The danger Akbar saw was that religion would become, as Salman Rushdie later put it, a 'poison in India's blood'. Akbar's solution was to move towards reconciliation: to abolish the hated tax on Hindus, and then boldly to examine the very basis of religious belief in the different communities, especially their pretensions to universal validity.

The core concept was very simple. Many religions claim a unique vision: some claim absolute truth. But any experience of religion in India was enough to demonstrate that no religion could possibly possess absolute truth. Violence in the name of religion and forcible conversion were intolerable in a civilized society, and not only on moral grounds: in terms of statecraft, religious divisions threatened the stability and fabric of society and undermined a stable empire. 'Justice and reason should be our guide,' said Akbar. He had already held discussions with Sunni and Shia scholars, and had been shocked to see how quickly they got angry, contradicted each other and came to blows, failing to answer each other's arguments. Reading between the lines of his biographers, one might well wonder whether he came to doubt the claims of any religion. Indeed, there were those in his entourage who thought he had renounced Islam and become a kaffir (infidel). This is unlikely, but his enquiries no doubt changed his view of what Islam – and religion – should be.

He decided to talk to the representatives of all the religions in his empire: Hindus, Muslims, Christians, Jains, Zoroastrians (Parsees). At Thursday seminars they discussed the basic premise of religious faith. What is good in each? What is bad? They also pondered the simply incredible – such as the biblical and Muslim belief that the universe was created only a few thousand years ago, which Akbar concluded was laughable.

The case of Buddhism is interesting. Buddhism vanished in much of mainland India until the British recovered the story in the late eighteenth and early nineteenth centuries, identifying the sites of the Buddha's life. But, of course, there were regions of the Himalayan foothills – Ladakh, Nepal and Bhutan, for example – that were still Buddhist, as they are today. The religion never vanished from India completely, and it was a comparatively easy matter for Akbar's advisers to contact Buddhists. His biographer Abul Fazl was aware that Buddhism was an Indian religion that had diffused across the world, and in an interesting parallel with the European Renaissance rediscovery of the classical Greek world, scholars of the Mughal renaissance made some study of Buddhism, which they realized permeated the thought of India. Their impact may not have been great, but Abul Fazl says that Buddhists did come to the debates: that 'Sramanas' (Buddhists) as well as 'Brahmanas' (Hindu Brahmins) played their part. In India nothing is ever entirely lost.

The kingdom of light

These ideas didn't come out of the blue. Indian mystics in the fifteenth and sixteenth centuries, some of whom initiated faiths and sects still alive today, had already engaged in thoroughgoing speculations about the unity of religion: Kabir, Dadu, Mirabai and, most famously, the founder of the Sikh faith, Guru Nanak. Kabir, for example, was a Muslim weaver whose name for God was Ram, who preached

Muslim and Hindu brotherhood, and denounced all fetishes, in which he included the Hindu sacred thread, the Christian cross and the Muslim Kaaba (the sacred shrine at Mecca). But for Akbar's elite there were other, more significant influences from Muslim culture. During Akbar's childhood there had been a flood of Iranian influence into the Mughal court: great scholars and artists who would transform Indian ideas in philosophy, architecture, art and manuscript painting. Akbar, for example, had grown up without the orthodox Muslim dislike of paintings and images. 'There are many that hate painting,' he observed, 'but such men I dislike. It seems to me that if a painter thinks of God, the giver of life, then he will increase knowledge.' Although there were many influences, it was this Iranian influx, along with native Hindu art and thought, that makes the Mughal synthesis. In Akbar's day it manifested in eleven of his eighteen key ministers being of Iranian origin, three central Asian and four Indian, two Hindu and two Muslim.

Akbar's policy of religious tolerance and favour owed much to these Iranians. The greatest civilizations in the Muslim world – the Ottomans, Iranians and Mughals – were all teetering on the edge of Western-style Enlightenment in thought, science and technology. Iranian culture also was in an ideological ferment, of which one fascinating aspect was the rethinking of Islamic philosophy. In his late twenties (from *c.*1571) Akbar was strongly influenced by these ideas, and particularly by the school of Suhrawardi (d. 1191). In this so-called 'philosophy of light' the Koran was not expounded literally – as so widely happened then (and does now) – but in an esoteric and allegorical way, in which, for example, the sun was the symbol of the 'Light of Lights' (God). Suhrawardi's ideas were especially attractive to a pantheistic project. He says he was influenced by a wide range of earlier traditions: that 'there was a wisdom before Islam'. Empedocles, Pythagoras, Plato, Zoroaster and many others from the pre-Islamic traditions were members of the 'eternal heaven' that animated all true sages. This 'Illuminationist' project, which is still a living tradition in Iran today, created a great impression at Akbar's court, with its mysticism of light, which had many points of congruence with Sanskritic tradition: 'Whoever knows wisdom and is assiduous in praising and revering the Light of Lights, they give him the kingly light and bestow upon him the luminous ray and the lightning flashes of God, clothing him in the robe of authority and state.'

The conferences on religion

In the 1570s Akbar entered his thirties and began to experiment in his own search for spiritual truth. He had been brought up as an orthodox Sunni, and issued persecuting firmans (rulings) against Shiahs as late as 1572. But now he became interested in the Sufi ibn Arabi's ideas about the 'unity of being'. The doctrine claimed no rational basis, but was a strong challenge to orthodoxy in its proposal that all that is not part of divine reality is an illusion. This led Akbar to the notion that all religions are equally illusory and should be tolerated in a state that sought real peace. He came to see himself as a specially chosen individual marked out by spiritual qualities, the 'ruler of the age', and, crucially, the necessary arbiter of religious law. This is what led Akbar to hold his discussions with the leading men of all religions. By 1580 he was set on pursuing a policy in which not only were all religions tolerated, but all kinds of religious views had equal access to him. The idea horrified some Europeans: the Jesuit Antonio Monserrate, for example, was disgusted: 'He cared little in that allowing everyone to follow his own religion he was in reality violating all religions.'

For Akbar's inner circle, though, these theories offered a dazzling imperial symbolism: 'Kingship is a light emanating from God and a ray from the sun, the illuminator of the universe, the embodiment of the book of perfection, the receptacle of all virtues. In modern parlance we call it *farr-i-izidi*, the divine light; the ancients called it *kaihan-khurira*, the light that illuminates the world ...' When Akbar's son Jahangir recalled his father's beliefs he enjoined his own court

circle to 'honour the luminaries [sun and moon], the manifesters of God's light'. It was, needless to say, a long way from orthodox Islam; but its ancient Iranian roots made it close to Hindu belief and ritual, which begins every day with the *gyatri* mantra to the rising sun. Akbar would even travel to the Hindu sacred site of Prayag (which owes its present name of Allahabad to him) to do dawn puja at the sacred confluence of the Ganges and Jumna, the place of creation in Hindu myth. In all this Akbar went about as far as a ruler of East or West could possibly go in the sixteenth century in matters of religion. Indeed, one suspects it would be too far for any political or religious leader today.

The rule of reason

Although we think of the Mughals as the quintessential Indian culture, it is important to remember that they didn't rule all India, even though in the pages of Abul Fazl they had a vision of all India. Many parts of the subcontinent were not under their control, and there were many acts of resistance to them from the mid-sixteenth century onwards. This state of war is the wider context of Akbar's religious reforms. 'A conqueror should never stop,' he said: and, as good as his word, he campaigned until the year before he died. So his religious ideas, his planned syncretism was not a personal whim (as some British imperial historians sneered). It should be compared with his land tax reforms, his reorganization of the civil service, and his idea that Muslims and Hindus should be made equal before the law – an idea that has not quite yet been achieved even in independent India. These parallels with his administrative reforms suggest that his religious ideas were rationally conceived and justified in a similar way to the ideas of the Enlightenment in Europe. No Renaissance ruler in Europe, not even the brilliant Elizabeth I, tried so consistently as Akbar to bring in the rule of reason. And one has to say, given the extraordinary resurgence of religious fundamentalism in our own supposedly more enlightened age, it is an idea whose time has yet to come.

English overtures to Akbar

A fascinating footnote to Akbar's story is the 1585 embassy from Elizabeth I, the beginning of the British relationship with India. Her ambassador, a merchant called Ralph Fitch arrived with a personal letter to Akbar from 'Elizabeth by the Grace of God Defender of the Faith to the most invincible and most mighty prince Zelabdin Echebar King of Cambaya'.

Her letter continues in a most interesting way, which reads slightly differently from mere conventional flattery, suggesting that Elizabeth's court had already received some account of Akbar from traders to India: 'The singular report that is of your imperial majesty's humanity has reached these uttermost parts of the world …' She was right to speak of his humanity: that is what makes him so attractive a character, one of the most engaging in history, despite all his flaws, and one of the greatest rulers of his age. Elizabeth goes on to talk of the English love of travel: living on a small island, 'the affection which our subjects have to visit the most distant parts of the world …' which has led to her knocking on his door 'with a courteous and honest boldness' in the hope of 'mutual and friendly traffic of merchandise on both sides'. As it happened, Akbar was preparing an important military expedition and was too busy to meet the English – especially a mere merchant rather than a royal ambassador. He ruled over 100 million people, whereas the England of Elizabeth, with a population of 3 million, was the equivalent of a small principality in the Deccan … That, perhaps, is a measure of the time. In his nearly fifty-year reign Akbar established India as one of the great powers. England then lay on the very fringe of the world, as Elizabeth notes in her letter. But fate and history, of course, would combine to bring India and Britain together in a way that neither Akbar nor Elizabeth could have imagined in their wildest dreams.

The Mughal state

So what went wrong? After Akbar's death why did the Age of Reason not come? Of course, it would not be the first time in history – and nor would it be the last – that an empire lost its way because of incompetent rule, over-consumption and extravagance, and ill-judged foreign wars. (All this would eventually happen.) The personality of the ruler also played its part. All the Mughals had demons, and some were undermined by them: Jahangir's alcohol and opium; Jahan's gluttony and rampant sex drive (his inordinate pursuit of women led even to accusations of incest). Aurangzeb's demons lay the other way, in a hard-line brand of religious fundamentalism. The Mughals were also engaged in a perennial struggle against other powers within India. This had severe social and economic consequences through a period when India was still one of the two largest powers in the world. But it would come to a head in Aurangzeb's long reign, when there was continuous warfare against Indian rulers in the Deccan.

Until the mid-seventeenth century, though, the Mughal court was one of the most brilliant in the world. Cosmopolitan, tolerant in religion, it was a place where literature, music and painting flourished, and magnificent palaces and mosques were constructed in Agra, Delhi, Lahore and Fatepur. But the gulf between rich and poor was acute. The nobility lived in walled castles with harems, gardens and large retinues; grand country houses that still dot the landscape of northern India. It was, as one visitor put it, a world of 'great superfluity and absolute power'.

This pre-British economy of India has often been portrayed as a golden age, when late Mughal India was a great manufacturing nation as well as an agricultural one. But new studies suggest that the gross domestic product of India, possibly the largest in the world during the Middle Ages, declined dramatically and was probably lower than that of Europe by the eighteenth century. The Indian ruling class had an extravagant lifestyle that surpassed that of European aristocracies. The portion of the Indian industrial sector linked to the royal court produced luxury goods that Europe couldn't match. India's cities were often bigger than those in Europe: in Akbar's day London, for example, had a population of 200,000, while

Agra's was nearer 750,000. But the thriving Mughal economy was achieved by subjecting the population to a high degree of exploitation, with a land tax amounting to a third of gross crop production. The total revenue of the Mughal monarchy and nobility is estimated at 15–20 per cent of the entire national income – by European standards, a very high burden. The hierarchical nature of the caste system, with its control over village life from top to bottom, no doubt aided the acceptance of such crippling exactions. A visitor in the 1620s refers to 'the utter subjection and poverty of the common people, a condition of stark want. A workman's children can follow no other occupation than that of their father, nor can they intermarry with any other caste.'

That was the reality of seventeenth-century northern India – a pointer too, perhaps, as to why Europeans were able to colonize areas of India so easily during the eighteenth century. Yet, paradoxically, the Mughals oversaw an incredible flowering of Indian civilization, the like of which the world has rarely seen. In this Akbar's grandson Jahan was the greatest patron. In his time Mughal architecture reached its height in Delhi, Agra, the Shalimar Gardens and the great tomb of his father, Jahangir, in Lahore: but above all in the Taj Mahal.

Jahan and the Taj

'A dome of high foundation and a building of great magnificence was created,' wrote Muhammad Qazwini Padshahnama during the early 1630s. 'The eye of the Age has seen nothing like it under the nine vaults of the enamel blue sky, and the ear of Time has heard of nothing like it in any past age … It will be a masterpiece for ages to come, increasing the amazement of all humanity.'

Our lodging house is in the narrow lanes of the bazaar built by Jahan. From the roof terrace the familiar dome rises above the rooftops, its white marble skin still aglow in the pink twilight. From this unfamiliar angle – not the one seen in the tourist brochures, looming ethereally over the Jumna – the Taj appears in its urban setting. From our rooftop we can look down on the yards and enclosures of the early seventeenth-century town outside the Taj: bazaars, caravanserais, craft workshops and houses for the service staff. Part of the overall plan, this is the first of several rectangular enclosures through which one progresses from the secular world into the paradise garden of the tomb itself.

At dawn the creamy white marble of the dome appears cool, soft and translucent, and will change colour through the day. Mughal poets compared it to an early dawn or a cloud, 'a piece of heaven. The colour of dawn's bright face …

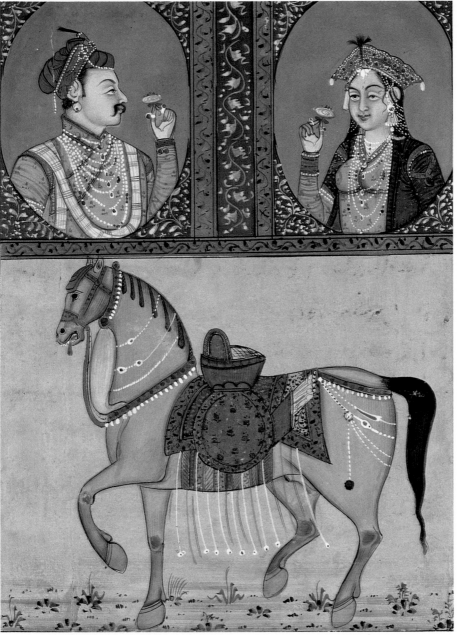

LEFT

Jahan and Mumtaz.

OVERLEAF

Jahan's eternal monument to the memory of Mumtaz: the Taj Mahal. New theories have elucidated the symbolic language of its architecture.

not marble at all, its translucence the eye can mistake it for a cloud.' This is no mere hyperbole. Marble transmits and refracts light, so it responds to atmospheric changes and alters from hour to hour. As a British visitor in 1836 noted 'the mind seemed to repose in the calm persuasion that there was an entire harmony of parts, a faultless congregation of architectural beauties'.

The tale of the Taj begins with the death of Shah Jahan's most beloved wife Mumtaz. In his grief he decided to create a wonderful and eternal monument to her, a tomb to represent on Earth the house of the queen in paradise. For the location Jahan went to some lengths to acquire a plot by the river Jumna from the Hindu rajah of Amber, to whom he gave four mansions in Agra as payment. We will see shortly why the specific landscape was so important to his plan. When work began in 1632 one of the builders' very first jobs was to plant trees so that they would have grown to some height by the time the building was ready more than ten years later.

One might think it hardly possible to say anything new about one of the best-known buildings in the world. But fascinating new theories about its conception have emerged only recently. The plan of the Taj was influenced in the first place by earlier Mughal ideas about gardens, especially the Eight Paradises Pavilion, which is the funerary form of a paradise garden. This had many ancient relatives in the Byzantine and classical Mediterranean world, and even in the ancient Near East. But the plan also drew on number symbolism in Hindu and Buddhist thought. These numerical schemes were assimilated by the architects into Islamic traditions about paradise. In medieval Muslim tradition paradise had at least seven levels, often eight. In particular, the famous mystic ibn Arabi in his *Meccan Revelations* of *c*.1230 described paradise as three gardens, of which the third is divided into eight sections with eight doors. These ideas of a paradise pavilion had long been present in Mughal art – they are used in the tomb of Humayun in Delhi – and, interestingly enough, Renaissance artists such as Bramante, Michelangelo and Palladio were also interested in this numerical symbolism.

To this architectural plan Jahan's architects added the largest scriptural inscriptional programme in the Islamic world: twenty-five quotations from the Koran, including fourteen complete suras (chapters), were depicted on the great gate, the mausoleum and the mosque in elegant black marble inlay on rectangular white marble plaques framed by red sandstone bands and enlivened by ornate floral patterns above the gate arches. The theme of the inscriptions connects with the function of the building as a tomb. It was eschatological, that is to say, concerned with the Day of Judgement. All the suras on the building speak about the Day of Judgement, divine mercy and the paradise promised to the faithful. Indeed, one new theory about the Taj sees the building as a symbolic replica of the throne of God on Judgement Day, specifically as expressed in a mystical diagram drawn by ibn Arabi and reproduced in the manuscripts of his *Meccan Revelations*. This may be too schematic: but, nevertheless, as a whole the programme of the Taj represents a highly intellectual conception of the tomb as the house prepared for Mumtaz (and eventually Jahan himself) in paradise.

The garden of paradise

Evening shadows fall over the platform of the mausoleum as the heat fades and the last visitors depart. Inside the mausoleum, in the still air, someone calls and we hear the famous echo: eerie, unearthly. Incredibly, the tomb holds a musical tone for almost half a minute. The architects omitted nothing, even using sound as an expression of eternity. As the British author William Sleeman observed in 1836: 'We feel as if the sound were from heaven, and breathed by angels; it is to the ear what the building itself is to the eye ... It was heavenly, and produced heavenly emotions.'

Upriver the sun is setting over Agra, smoke drifting through the trees from the funeral pyres at the burning ghat on the bank of the Jumna; flocks of birds rise, twittering.

We take a boat over the river to where a decayed Mughal turret with a cupola points to one more extraordinary discovery. Legend has it that Jahan planned a black Taj for his own tomb, as a mirror image on the other side of the river. We now know from archaeology that this myth is untrue. Jahan always intended to share his wife's tomb. What was on the other side of the river, though, was indeed a mirror of the rectangular enclosure of the Taj, but it was a paradise garden, and was always planned as such. To reach it you must go where Jahan's architects laid out the Moonlit Garden, full of delicate but sensuous pleasure in contrast to the more austere courtyard of the Taj. There the Great Mughal could sit in an ornamental pavilion with a huge octagonal pool in which moon and Taj were reflected as if in a dream. As is written in the Koranic texts displayed on the mausoleum itself, 'Their reward is with their lord: gardens of everlasting bliss graced with flowing streams.' (Sura 98) 'They will suit on couches feeling neither burning heat nor biting cold, with shady branches spread above them and clusters of fruit hanging close at hand.' (Sura 76)

Flooded within years of its construction, the paradise garden was forgotten for three centuries, though a drawing by the British artists William and Thomas Daniell, done in 1789, enabled the whole plan to be recovered in the 1990s. An archaeological dig has since revealed what was growing in the garden, and night-scented trees and flowers are now being replanted. Away from the polluted uproar of Agra and the tourist-choked courtyards of the Taj, the paradise garden is one of the few places where one may feel for a moment the original intentions of Shah Jahan and his architects.

The other element in this grand design is the river itself. Sadly, the Jumna today is a shadow of the sacred river beloved by Indians over the centuries. In the summer season it is reduced to a small trickle between stagnant pools, and after it passes Delhi nothing in it is said to remain of the source water from the ice fields of Jumnotri in the Himalayas. With global warming and the gradual reduction of all the glacier-fed rivers of India to seasonal flows, will it ever recover? Today one can only imagine the royal barge drifting on its broad flow from the fort to the garden, where the shah could climb the steps to sit in his pavilion and take in the view of his wife's tomb, at sunset and by moonlight, and enjoy its ethereal likeness shimmering in the great octagonal pool. As the Koran says, 'in a garden, by a river, in the presence of the Almighty'. One may censure Jahan for his vanity, vainglory and megalomania, but all the same, the effect is fantastically poignant. Especially when one recalls his end, imprisoned by his own son in a gilded cage in Agra looking downriver to the great tomb, always visible, but always beyond reach.

Dara Shikoh and the meeting of the two oceans

The growth of trade with Europe was still slow, the possibility of colonization not even a shadow on the horizon. Jahan issued the first firman, or permit, to the British only in 1657. But in that year fateful events were beginning to tear apart the Mughal state. These events would have the greatest significance in India, but also impinge on the wider world. Only fifty years or so after Akbar's death his great-grandsons fought a battle over his legacy, the effects of which are still with us today. The issue in the biggest Muslim civilization in the world was nothing less than the course Indian Islam should take. Akbar, Jahangir and Jahan had all revoked discriminatory laws against Hindus, employed eminent Sanskrit scholars, invited Hindu Brahmins and yogis to court, and commissioned a huge translating programme to make Indian religious texts accessible to Muslims in Persian. Jahan's eldest son, Dara Shiukoh, was drawn to go further. Impressed by radical figures in Islam, such as the Sufi ibn Arabi, he also immersed himself in the Hindu scriptures. His younger brother Aurangzeb, however, was educated by legalists and orthodox Sufis, the converting orders who had made much headway converting Hindus in Kashmir and Bengal, and viewed such experiments as un-Islamic. Their dissension would lead to civil war in the empire, in which (at the state level) orthodoxy would triumph.

Educated in the religious texts of both religions, Dara took his stand on the Koran's revelation (in Sura 56) that before the Prophet Muhammad, God had sent humanity messengers to all peoples – and given them scriptures. The Hindu sacred books too – for example, the *Bhagavadgita* – say that God had sent messengers throughout history 'whenever injustice thrived'. Was it not therefore the case that the core of all religions was divinely given? Dara argued that it was the moral duty of all Muslims to learn from other religions; and, indeed, that the 'concealed scriptures' of Sura 56 of the Koran were none other than the Upanishads, the

original core of monotheism. The wisdom of India, then, was just that: the earliest spiritual vision of humanity. So with the help of pundits from Benares, Dara translated the *Gita* and some of the Vedic hymns and Upanishads into Persian under the title 'The Great Secret'. He always insisted that his translation was intended to clarify the Koranic revelation, not to devalue it. His motive, he said, was personal rather than political, and 'not intended to be of relevance to common people of either community'. How he came to this is revealed in his preface to a treatise on Hindu mysticism, the *Yoga Vasistha*, translated at his behest after a dream in which the author Vasistha, one of India's legendary seven sages, and Rama himself, to whom the book is addressed, appeared to Dara in a dream:

> I was naturally attracted to them, and Vasistha was very kind to me and patted me on the back. He told Rama that I was his brother because we were both seekers after truth. He asked Rama to embrace me, which he did in an exuberance of love. Thereupon he gave some food to Rama, which I also took and ate. After this vision a desire to have the book newly translated intensified in me.

Manuscripts of Dara's translation can still be found preserved in the libraries of old humanistic Muslim families in Lucknow, and in Multan and Lahore in Pakistan. Put into Latin in Paris in 1801, Dara's translation of the Upanishads played a major role in the discovery of India in Europe in the early nineteenth century, part of the influx to the West of Hindu mysticism that inspired, among others, the poet William Blake and the philosopher Arthur Schopenhauer.

Of course, it was impossible that such enquiries in a great prince could be seen as non-political. At Lahore in October 1653, after a campaign in Kandahar, Dara held public meetings with Baba Lal, a great Hindu renouncer of the Vaishnavaite sect – meetings so famous that they were illustrated by Mughal miniature painters. They took place in seven main sessions over a period of nine days in various palaces, gardens and hunting lodges around Lahore. Their conversations ranged over the technical vocabulary of Hindu sacred texts, the works of Persian mysticism, the theory of the avatars of Vishnu, and a fascinating symbolic exegesis of the *Ramayana* in which, according to Baba Lal, 'Sita in reality is the dharma, pure justice'. These questings were not official in the sense that Akbar's seminars were, but as we look at it now, sixty years on from Independence and Partition, when the effort of mutual comprehension failed, this seed of reconciliation is worth pause. One of the most fascinating sources for the meeting of Islam and Hindu religion, these conversations in Hindi were interpreted and written up in Persian by Dara's Punjabi Brahmin secretary.

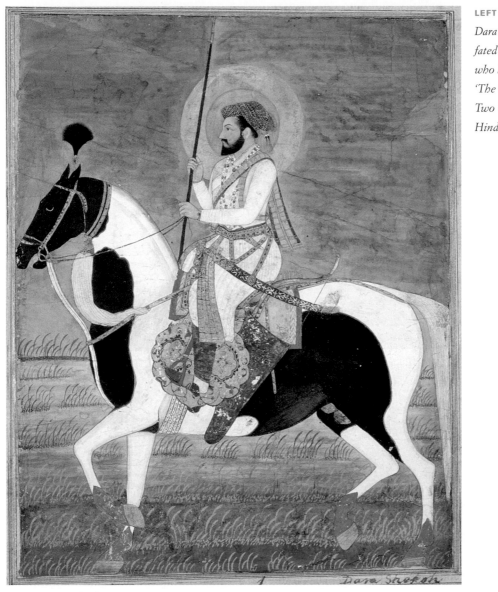

LEFT

Dara Shikoh, the ill-fated Renaissance prince who hoped to show 'The Confluence of the Two Oceans' of Hinduism and Islam.

'Tell me,' said Dara, 'about the cult of idols in the Hindu world: who prescribed this?'

'This form of observance began as a way of concentrating the mind,' Baba Lal replied. 'The person who understands the true reality of things has no need of such exterior forms. In the same way a little girl before her marriage plays with a doll, but once she is married she leaves that behind. It's the same with the cult of idols: when one does not know the core, one is attached to the exterior form; when one knows the core, one passes beyond the appearance.'

These researches led Dara to compose a treatise on comparative religion, in which he tried to prove the equivalence of Sufi and Hindu mysticism through their technical vocabulary. Although the two faiths were 'hairs on the same head,' he thought, they were, 'like two opposite poles, not working as they should to serve as a means for people to attain beauty and the divine'. However limited its audience, it was a ground-breaking book for its time, and in our time too, when interfaith dialogue and knowledge of other cultures are becoming matters of vital urgency. Here, in his own words, Dara's introduction to one of the most extraordinary attemps in history to bridge the gap between religious faiths:

> I discussed and talked openly with certain Hindu learned men, but saving a few differences in verbal usage, I found no difference between them as for their way of understanding and knowing God. Based on these exchanges, I set out to compare the tenets of the two faiths and to bring them back together, reunite those among them whose knowledge is of value and absolutely necessary to aspirants to the truth. Finally, I made an essay of that collection of the truths and esoteric sciences belonging to both communities, and I called it 'The Confluence of the Two Oceans'.

Dara's fall

This heroic but quixotic enterprise would cost Dara his crown and his life. Needless to say, such syncretistic leanings did not go down well with many in the royal family, the ruling class and the Muslim orthodoxy, for whom the Koranic message was complete, and could neither be added to nor taken away from. Dara's younger brorher Aurangzeb felt that Dara had become a 'kaffir' (infidel), and induced the lawyers to pronounce him an apostate for claiming, among other things, that Hinduism and Islam were 'twins'. The decree stated that Dara 'had apostatized from the law, and having vilified the religion of God, had joined himself to heresy and infidelity'. The dissension culminated in a succession crisis of a kind frequent in Indian history, where siblings battle for the throne with relentless savagery.

The story unfolded with all the inexorable momentum of a Shakespearean tragedy. Jahan had fallen ill in 1657, and with rumours of his death widespread, a struggle broke out between his four sons. The youngest, Murad, was captured and killed by Aurangzeb; the second son, Shuja, died mysteriously in exile. So Dara and Aurangzeb were left to fight for the crown. Defeated in battle near Agra in May 1658, Dara, who was now forty-three, fled up the Grand Trunk Road into the Punjab. After Hamlet-like vacillations, and gripped by fear of seeing his wife and children killed before him, he tried to rally support and raise another army. His desperate situation is revealed in letters in the Udaipur palace archive, including an agonizing message from his wife, Nadira Banu, who sent her breast milk to one former ally in a symbolic plea for support.

Dara's last stand was at Ajmer, his great-grandfather's beloved shrine, in a wide valley between rugged hills south of the town. The date was 15 March 1659. Although no soldier, Dara had taken up a good position, anchored on the hills, his artillery under a young European gunnery officer called Niccolao Manucci, who later wrote a dramatic and moving account of events. The battle went well until Dara was betrayed by one of his own side, who revealed the existence of a path over the mountains, like the pass of Thermopylae, which led to the rear of his position. His last hope gone, Dara fled back towards Sind, reduced to a core of supporters, including his now desperately sick wife, and a small mounted force.

'More dead than alive', Dara attempted to flee to Iran via Kandahar, with his wife in a carriage behind cloth screens. They crossed the wilderness of the Rann of Kutch through waterless, trackless salt marshes by moonlight with lighted torches, pursued by Aurangzeb's officers closing in exultantly on their prey with all the strung-out energy of hunters. He crossed the Indus, only to be robbed and abused by Baluchi tribemen, his wife's strength all the while ebbing away. Finally, on 6 June, they reached the castle of a former vassal, the Afghan Malik Jiwan, at Dadar, near Sibi, 9 miles below the entrance to the Bolan Pass. There Dara's wife

BELOW

Aurangzeb, an ultimately tragic figure whose intellect and talents were wasted in sectarian antagonisms.

died, and for him 'the bright world grew dark and the pillars of his judgement and prudence all at once shook and fell down'. Although he knew his enemies were closing in, he performed her funeral rites for two days before sending a captain and seventy horsemen to escort her body to the tomb of her favourite saint, Mian Mir, in Lahore, as she had requested. Dara's party was now sunk in gloom and foreboding. Next day, as he prepared to move on to Iran with his son and a handful of retainers, he was arrested by his host and delivered to his enemies.

There was some debate as to whether he should be killed or kept as a state prisoner. Escorted back to Delhi, on 29 August Dara was dressed in dirty clothes and a cheap turban and put on a 'mangy old female elephant' accompanied on the open howdah by a slave bearing a drawn sword. He was paraded down Chandni Chowk, the great commercial street of Delhi, under the walls of the Red Fort, accompanied by wails and tears from onlookers. Alarmed at this display of popular sorrow, that night Aurangzeb and his council resolved that Dara should be killed. In this they were supported by other members of the royal family: Dara's sister, Raushandra Begum, was among those who thought it 'unlawful to allow him to live any longer'. Lodged in a house close to Humayun's tomb, the murder scene was worthy of the greatest tragic drama. Dara was cooking lentils in his cell with his little boy when the murderers arrived. His child clinging to his knees, Dara tried to fight with a small knife he had concealed on himself. They killed him, cut off his head and sent it to his brother. 'Ah, I would not look on the apostate's face when he lived and I will not now,' said Aurangzeb. Next day the body was paraded on an elephant through the bazaar to show that Dara was dead. His head was sent to their father Jahan, imprisoned now by Aurangzeb in his gilded chamber overlooking the Taj Mahal. Jahan was shown his son's head at table and fainted, breaking his front teeth. Dara's son, the young prince Selim, was given a draught spiced with opium, then strangled.

Lost dream or continuing legacy?

It is unlikely, perhaps, that these great Mughals could have succeeded in putting their ideas into the service of the state. Indeed, both Akbar and Dara were driven by elite and esoteric forms of knowledge that could only ever be shared by the nobility. Dara tells us specifically that he was not concerned with the mass of the population. Nevertheless, then as now, it is elites who drive policy. Had they done so, other possible trajectories might have emerged, which are fascinating to contemplate in the light of the present so-called 'Clash of Civilizations' and the 'War on Terror'. First, the most powerful and populous Islamic civilization in the world might have developed from a great Renaissance state to an Islamic Enlightenment state, even using modern science and technology. (Although poorly explored by the Mughals in general, such things were a special interest of Akbar, and would be characteristic of, for example, the southern court in Tanjore during the eighteenth century, which imported Western texts on medicine, optics, anatomy and surgery.) Second, Hinduism among India's elites (as opposed to religion at the popular level) might have evolved on a path more in line with its monotheistic potential (as it did under the impact of the British and Christianity during the nineteenth century). Third, Indian Islam might even eventually have been absorbed into Indian religion more fully, rather as Buddhism had been. But this did not happen, and now, sixty years after Independence, as India is fast rising to become an economic giant, there are still battles being fought over this history – over mosques built by Babur or temples demolished by Aurangzeb. The great struggle for accommodation and understanding continues.

Aurangzeb

The sixth great ruler of the Mughals, Aurangzeb, became absolute ruler of the empire at the age of forty, and would rule for nearly fifty years. There are few more controversial and hated figures in Indian history today. In his long reign, from 1658 to 1707, he instated shariah law, reimposed the tax on non-Muslims stopped by Akbar back in 1562, rejected all crossover in cultural politics, and condoned many forced conversions. As a ruler, he had some formidable qualities: his long experience as governor in the Deccan, Gujarat and Balkh stood him in good stead, and he was a warrior, unlike Dara (to whom his father, he felt, had always shown preference). Austere, devout and self-denying, he was not a man for opium, wine and women. But his long reign was, in hindsight, a disaster for India: he overstretched the resources of the empire with campaigns in the Deccan and Afghanistan, and at home he undid what his predecessors had achieved through tact and conciliation. He faced many rebellions from Marathas, (led by their hero the great Shivagi), and from Rajputs and Sikhs, whose ninth guru he tortured to death, leaving a bitter memory among many Indians for his negative view of Hinduism. He even attempted to outlaw music and wine-making, and to ban Diwali. Needless to say, history could have told him that this was not the way to rule India.

Aurangzeb had, perhaps, ceased to understand the purpose of it all by the time he was nearing ninety: 'I came alone and I go as a stranger. I do not know who I am, nor what I have been doing,' the dying old man confessed to his son in February 1707. 'I have sinned terribly, and I do not know what punishment awaits me.' Whether he counted the persecution of other faiths as one of his sins is not clear. His simple tomb, open to the sky at Khuldabad, is still reverently maintained, and visited by wandering dervishes. Aurangzeb, more than most, paved the way for the problems of the modern period, leading to Partition. Piously weaving Haj caps in his few moments of spare time, and copying the Koran in a firm scholar's script, he had lost one of the greatest opportunities ever given to a ruler of India. As the Roman poet Lucretius put it, '*tantum religio potuit suadere malorum*' (such are the heights of wickedness to which men are driven by religion).

Enter the Honourable East India Company

On the Hooghly river below Calcutta, soon after dawn. The heat is already coming up as we glide past the forested banks dotted with boatyards, factories and warehouses. Back in 1585 Elizabeth I had written to Akbar hoping that 'mutual and friendly traffic of merchandise on both sides may come'. With that end in mind, the East India Company was given its charter in 1601. How that private company metamorphosed into the greatest empire the world had ever seen is an extraordinary story with many twists and turns; and, as we shall see, there is a grain of truth in the old joke that the empire was gained 'in a fit of absent-mindedness'. But the key was this. Other empires in northern India – Greeks, Sakas, Kushans, Turks, Mongols, Afghans, Mughals – had come by land from the northwest over the Khyber. The British came from a tiny country, but they were a trading nation, and with their navy would eventually control the sea. Their ports and factories around the shores of India grew into the great entrepôts of Bombay, Calcutta and Madras, and eventually became a 'ring of steel' around the subcontinent. In the crucial areas of conflict, in the south and in Bengal, violence would be used to tip the scale, but in the early days the system owed its existence to Indian permission, partnership and complicity in the business of making money. And, of course, the fact that India was not a single entity: it was many different states and regions. Mughal rule didn't cover much of the subcontinent, which made it easier for the British to divide and rule.

From 1657 the British began trading in Bengal under a permit from Shah Jahan, siting their main textile factories in villages on the Hooghly tributary of the Ganges. They processed stuffs from the village-based handloom industry, made by hundreds of thousands of highly skilled weavers, dyers and washers. They exported enormous quantities of different kinds of cloths, with different designs aimed at specific markets around Asia and at home. In surviving examples from the eighteenth century held in collections, and, of course, still in today's industry we can see the fabulous designs and colour combinations that can be created with hand-painting and wooden blocking. Eventually, the 1765 treaty with the Mughals gave the British the *diwan*, the rule of Bengal, and, above all, the right to collect taxes. It was the first step in the almost incredible tale of how a private company came to rule a vast empire, the forerunner of the modern multinationals, who exercise power of life and death over great swathes of the world.

Dawn of a new age

The Mughal dynasty in India began in war and ended in war. But it also started and ended with literature, music and poetry. Its best rulers had the most highly developed aesthetic sensibilities of any rulers in the world – superior even to the brilliant Elizabeth Tudor, who translated Boethius, conversed in Latin with the conquistador Sarmiento de Gamboa, and watched with critical interest the dramas of Shakespeare. Within a few decades Indian rulers and artists developed a wonderful style that tried to harmonize all human creation, from cities, shrines and gardens to the tiniest enamelled turban pin. The kings had to be practical rulers, stern and determined, but the culture allowed them also to be dreamers: think of Babur's imperial ambitions, Akbar's utopian aspirations, Jahan's mystic flights at the Taj, Dara's erudite translations from the Sanskrit. In the wings, waiting for their chance, practical, clear-sighted, ethics subordinated to the ruthless imperatives of profit, were the British, who had some very different ideas about what the Age of Reason could mean.

6
Freedom and Liberation

I'M SITTING OUT ON THE TERRACE of a little boarding house in Allahabad, one of the last of the British bungalows that once gave the city – alternatively known as the 'Oxford of India' or the 'Oven of India' – its low-rise charm. Tea and fruit cake are on the table. The owners of the hotel are Parsees (key people here during the Raj, the time of British rule: the first photographers; the first car dealers; some of the first native lawyers, dentists and doctors, were all Parsees). They are related to

Feroz Gandhi, who married Jawaharlal Nehru's daughter Indira, whose family were also Allahabad people. The hotel has a rather faded touch of the Old World, but I prefer it to the new, slick international-style hotels in the Civil Lines (the former European city), despite the attraction of air-conditioned rooms, plush bars and wireless Internet. The front garden, with its old well and spreading pipal tree, is a nice place to sit after a long day and watch the crowds of lawyers, with their starched collars and gowns, hurrying to their waiting auto-rickshaws.

Allahabad ('Godville' is Mark Twain's apt translation) has already appeared several times in this story. It got its present name from the emperor Akbar, who proclaimed his new religion here in 1575 (see page 198). At the *sangam*, the sacred confluence of the Ganges and the Jumna, he built a giant fortress, one of the four greatest Mughal forts, along with Delhi, Agra and

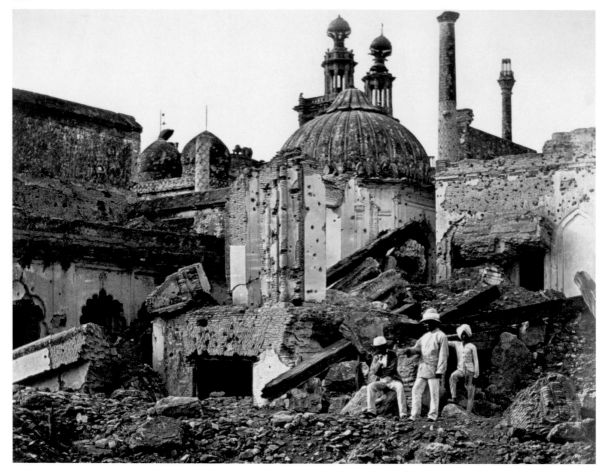

*Mumbai, Maximum
City: embodiment of
India's growth and a
scene from the first war
of Independence in
1857.*

Lahore. What a role the place has played in Indian history! As the ancient Hindu holy site of Prayag, it hosts the *Kumbh Mela* festival, which on one night in 2001 attracted 25 million pilgrims, dwarfing all the other gatherings there have ever been on Earth. It is also the final point in the circuit of India's holy sites in the *Mahabharata*, and still known among Hindus as the 'King of Holy Places'. Inside the Mughal fort is the famous stone pillar carrying the decrees of Ashoka and the inscriptions of Samudragupta and Jahangir. The mythological navel of the Earth, it is a place whose symbolic life is almost richer than its real history.

When they became the rulers of India in the bloody aftermath of the Mutiny of 1857, the chastened British were mindful of these great associations. It was a few yards away from Ashoka's pillar, on the outer bastion, that Lord Canning proclaimed the end of the East India Company's rule and the beginning of Victoria's Raj (an event commemorated in the little garden of Minto Park as 'India's Magna Carta'). But that came after savagery. The Civil Lines, with their neat, tree-lined avenues, their parks, gymkhana clubs and orderly cantonments, were laid out over eight Indian villages that were razed to the ground in revenge, and where 'nigger' women and children perished along with the 'vilest malefactors'.

In the next three decades the city fittingly became a centre of the nascent freedom movement. The site of British India's most important High Court, Allahabad was a city of lawyers, and the men who made India free, including Jawaharlal Nehru, the first prime minister, would all be British-educated lawyers. The Nehrus, old Kashmiri Brahmins, were Allahabad people, and the house owned by Nehru's father, Motilal, still stands in the European town: a spacious estate, fitting for a rich advocate who became a London QC. Around it there are still many places with British associations: the university with its Gothic cloisters; the beautiful Anglican cathedral, all flying buttresses and stained glass; the Civil Lines shopping arcade, with Wheelers Bookshop and the neoclassical Picture Palace; not forgetting Barnetts House of Confectionery (now the Harsh Hotel), which serviced the Imperial Airways stopover from Croydon to Calcutta. In Motilal's day a soon-to-be iconic Raj figure, the writer Rudyard Kipling, worked here for the local English-language newspaper, the *Pioneer*, which 'ably opposed Indian aspirations', as John Murray's *Guidebook* blithely put it. The *Pioneer* has long since moved to Lucknow, and the old newspaper building, another red-brick bungalow only yards from the Nehru residence, has been demolished since I was here in the summer of 2006, a victim of Allahabad's building boom. But the house where Kipling lodged is still here, in an overgrown garden inhabited by a bony cow and a mongoose. It is now

OPPOSITE

Above: One of Felix Beato's photographs of the devastation wrought in the Mutiny and its aftermath. Below: Outside Government House in 1858 as the East India Company's rule came to an end.

lived in by a sprightly eighty-year-old journalist called Durga, who started with All India Radio in 1943, and covered the last phase of the freedom struggle. 'I was glad to see the back of the British,' she told me with a clear eye. 'Which people doesn't want to be free?'

Sitting here in Allahabad (a town I feel I know better than many in England), I am painfully conscious of my own ancestry. I am a child of post-war Britain, and though I could not see it at the time, colonialism shaped me too. In the 1950s and 1960s we were brought up at home and school with rose-tinted spectacles about the British Empire. Scented with saddle soap and railway steam, and orchestrated by Edward Elgar, we were given a Raj drenched in nostalgia in novels, on television and in the cinema. But, however we dress it up, imperialism is still imperialism. India was turned into a classic colonial economy, exporting raw materials and importing finished goods. The natural resources of India were plundered, and her people treated like children by those who saw themselves as the superior race. These days some British historians put forward the argument that colonialism was a good thing, lighting the world's path to progress. I have to say that I am not, by and large, of that persuasion. Over thirty-five years travelling in Asia, Africa and the Americas, seeing things on the ground, has given me a different perspective, and has left me with the conviction that its impact has been largely destructive. The age of European empires unleashed tremendous historical forces, many of them no doubt creative, but for much of the population of the globe this was a cataclysmic epoch that left few native cultures intact. Only great and resilient civilizations, such as India, were able to hold their own, take what was useful, and emerge still themselves.

The period of the British Raj – from the East India Company's rise to power in the eighteenth century to Independence in 1947 – lasted roughly 200 years, a time comparable to the Kushan era, but shorter than the Mughals'. It is a long and tortured story, full of splendours and miseries, of pride and greed, and of fantastic cultural crossovers, as remarkable (I am tempted to say more so) than even under the Mughals. In the open-minded atmosphere of the eighteenth century there were many meetings of minds. General Charles 'Hindoo' Stuart in Calcutta bathed daily in the Ganges, recommended English ladies to wear the sari, and made the first collection of Indian art. With striking foresight, Stuart also argued for native customs to be allowed in sepoy army regiments. In his *Vindication of the Hindoos* he scathingly deprecated European missionaries and praised Hinduism as a religion that 'little needs the meliorating hand of Christianity to render its votaries a sufficiently correct and moral people for all the useful purposes of a civilized society'.

Such 'White Mughals' had their counter-parts in the intellectual sciences. William Jones (see page 37), James Prinsep and Francis Buchanan, for example, were leading lights in the rediscovery of ancient Indian history; nor should one forget the remarkable Warren Hastings, the troubled first governor general of British India, who knew native languages and played an instrumental role in the cultivation of scholarship in Bengal. This meeting of cultures led to a prodigious multilingual flowering of Bengali civilization that would eventually bring the Bengali reformer and polymath Ram Roy sailing into Liverpool in 1833 on his own version of the search for the 'meeting place of the oceans.' Orientalism these days has become an overused and overstated catch-all. Colonial forms of knowledge could indeed be instruments of oppression, but between the late eighteenth and early twentieth centuries England and Bengal would engage in one of history's great cross-cultural exchanges, and one that is by no means exhausted yet.

But the British relationship with India did not develop further on those lines. In the end, the ideologies and exigencies of empire proved too strong. If one by-product of the eighteenth century was a love affair, the nineteenth century saw the falling apart, and the twentieth century the tragic and costly divorce. Thankfully, in our own time the children and grandchildren are friends and are building a new relationship.

Warren Hastings, first governor general of British India. A major figure in the British 'discovery' of the Indian past, Hastings is a problematical figure due a re-evaluation.

The East India Company and the 1857 rebellion

The story of the East India Company uncannily echoes that of modern multi-national companies, who trade in natural resources and gain new spheres of influence through economic intervention, private armies and proxy war. The British triumphed because of India's own internal divisions, the decline of Mughal power in the north and because they controlled the sea. Where earlier

ABOVE

Clive receiving the diwan *of Bengal in 1765, the moment the British moved from trade to real power.*

conquerors had entered India through the Khyber and the Northwest Frontier, the British extended their influence along her coasts, founding fortified trading ports in Calcutta, Madras and Bombay as the first bases of their rule. They were backed by armed force, though at first the numbers were small: 2200 Europeans and a similar number of native troops won the decisive battle at Plassey in Bengal in 1757 against the last independent nawab of Bengal, who also had a tiny force from the French East India Company. A similarly sized army gained victory at Wandiwash in the south, where, between the 1740s and 1760s, the British and the French fought out another part of their global confrontation. Then, in 1765, the Mughal Shah Alam in Delhi formally awarded the British the *diwan* of Bengal – that is, the right to raise revenues. What had begun as a speculative piece of Elizabethan merchant-venturing had entered a new phase.

In the south too the struggle with the French soon reached its climax. Between the 1760s and 1799 the British fought four wars with the Muslim

The coming-on of the MONSOONS;—or—The Retreat from SERINGAPATAM.

LEFT

Political cartoon of the day by Gillray showing the British in retreat from Seringapatam in 1791. The British would come back with a vengeance.

rulers of Mysore, who were French allies, ending in the siege of the island fortress of Seringapatam in 1799, in which Sultan Tipu was killed. At that battle the armed forces at the disposal of the Company were 50,000 strong, the size of a big European army. Investment now grew, and in the next few years Company profits rose astronomically: accounts registered with the British parliament show that revenues rose from over £8 million in 1794 to £13.5 million in 1803 – the equivalent of three-quarters of a billion today. The changing perspective is revealed in the vast archive of the Company now preserved in the British Library. In the aftermath of the victory over Tipu the governor general, Richard Wellesley (brother of the future victor of Waterloo), wrote:

> Seringapatam I shall retain full sovereignty for the Company as being a Tower of Strength from which we may at any time shake Hindostan to its centre, if any combination should ever be formed against our interests. I shall not at present enlarge upon the advantages which are likely to be derived to the British interests from this settlement, they are too obvious to require any detailed explanation.

Soon India could be depicted in British art as a naked black female, submissively offering her riches to Britannia. The conquest had happened piecemeal and opportunistically, with no thought-out, long-term goal. It was effected at no expense to the British taxpayer, by mercenaries picking off regional threats one by one. By the 1830s the Company archives reveal a shift from trade in textiles to ownership of land, and at this point the colonial project acquires a new ideological tone that is exemplified in Lord Macaulay's 1835 edict on Indian education, which announced the replacement of Persian by English as the new language of government. With this there also came a new emphasis on the desirability of spreading the Christian religion. From now on British dominion in India was not only to be about making money, but about changing India.

These interventionist attitudes, with their increasingly strident Christian tone, form the background to the 1857 Mutiny, the greatest rising against any colonial power in the Age of Empire. The rising began as a protest in the army ranks against British insensitivity to Hindu religious custom, but rapidly spread as a rebellion against foreign rule in which even Muslim jihadists for the moment made common cause with Hindus. As rebellion spread like wildfire up and down the Grand Trunk Road from Bengal to the Punjab, the presence of Britain in India hung in the balance. But in the end, by luck and grit and ruthlessness, the British gained the upper hand. The war was conducted with horrific violence and savage reprisals by both sides. Both Hindu and Muslim rebels expressed their loyalty to the ageing Mughal in Delhi, Shah Bahadur, who, after the defeat, was exiled to Burma. His sons were killed in cold blood by the British, who were merciless in their revenge.

In their many colourful histories of the war the British retrospectively painted the rising as if it had come out of the blue, but there had in fact been many revolts against them over the previous fifty years, notably the Vellore Mutiny of 1806, in which southern rebels had proclaimed a son of Sultan Tipu as king. The rising of 1857 wrecked Mughal Delhi and its refined cultural life, and brought devastation on its population, many of whose adult males were summarily massacred. But the rising was a terrible shock to the British establishment, and it put an end to the 258-year existence of the Company. In the aftermath the British parliament decided to take direct control of its Indian possessions. Ever mindful of tradition, the first viceroy, Lord Canning, read Queen Victoria's proclamation on 1 November 1858 from the outer rampart of Akbar's fort at Allahabad, overlooking the sacred confluence. India was now to be taught the new secular dharma of the West.

LEFT

Shah Bahadur, the last Mughal. Focus of the rebels' patriotism in the Mutiny of 1857, he was banished to Burma where his tomb is now a place of prayer.

British rule and colonial knowledge

At the heart of the British colonial project was the exploitation of India as the centre of Britain's world trade system. But to rule such an immense and diverse country the British needed an educated Indian class who would join with them in their imperial enterprise, by assimilating British cultural ideals.

To achieve this they set about the ideological and practical construction of modernity in India. Time, space, geography, caste, religion – all would be redefined by the supposedly superior knowledge, science and ethics of the imperialists. This meant both physical and mental mapping. Sir George Everest, for example, after whom the world's highest mountain is named, made a great survey to measure the subcontinent down to the last foot, lugging cumbersome theodolites up Tamil temple *gopuras*, and traipsing with huge segmented metal measuring rods on ox-carts across the Punjab. The imposition of the British legal system was another crucial introduction, along with the codifying of Hindu and Muslim law, and the detailed categorizing of caste in Indian society, as customary law was caste-based. Like the Kushans and the Mughals, the British wanted to know what made their subjects tick.

Attitudes to traditional Indian religious customs and practices also became much more defined. For example, the British saw it as their Christian duty to wage war against 'superstition', and clamped down hard on archaic customs such as child marriage, blood sacrifice and suttee. Sometimes, no doubt, they were justified; but sometimes, as exemplified in their attack on the ancient Gond culture in Orissa, all they managed to do was undermine a people's identity and cohesion

As for Hindu religion itself, from having been a source of fascinated admiration in the eighteenth century to the likes of 'Hindoo' Stuart, in some quarters it now became an object of disparagement, dismissed as superstition and 'debased fetishism'. Indeed, the evangelical element in British society actively crusaded against it. It was at this time that the somewhat misleading term 'Hinduism' came into common parlance as a description of India's religious systems. This connects with the growth in the nineteenth century of the idea that Indian religion was one world religion, like Christianity and Islam. Texts such as the *Bhagavadgita* or the Tamil *Tiruvasagam* were given Christianizing interpretations by missionary scholars, quarrying the monotheistic or monist strand in Hindu thought. There was and still is some truth in such ideas, though the great medieval teaching texts of the Saivas and Vaishnavas could equally well be used to demonstrate that these were separate religious systems, with different supreme deities and different sacred texts, rituals and eschatologies. The creation of modern Hinduism was therefore to some extent both a colonial construct and a reaction to colonialism. In the hands of Hindu reformers the Christianizing aspect came to the fore, and offered a congenial bridge to the colonisers for the educated Indian elite. When the great Bengali philosopher and nationalist Swami Vivekananda was hailed as the star of the World Parliament of Religions in Chicago in 1893, Hinduism in its modern sense had arrived.

The British project also involved giving a British education to the native ruling class, who would interpret their own culture to the Indian masses in British terms. One curious aspect of this was that the study of English literature became the canon in India before it was institutionalized in England. The choice of exemplary texts, though, was of its time, replete with colonial ideas about ideal manhood. Shakespeare, however, with his pronounced scepticism about power, was not included. Ironically, he ended up being gratefully received by Indian radicals as a liberating tool, as Michael Madshudan Dutt argued in his brilliant essay on the Hindu and the Anglo-Saxon in 1865: the British must go, but they can leave us Shakespeare!

The idea of India

For the future of independent India one critical area of the British imperial project lay in the very idea of India itself. As we have seen throughout this book, India had never existed as one unified state at any time in its history, although Ashoka, for example, had claimed to rule as far south as the Krishna river, and the Kushans, Guptas and Mughals had all wielded power across a great area of northern India between Afghanistan and Bengal. But it was the British who first conceived of India as a political unity; a country rather than a state of mind. Winston Churchill (who counted daredevil adventures among the Pathans in his youthful experiences) famously said, 'There is no such thing as India'. But that opinion was not shared by the great observers of India over many centuries, for whom India – for all its diversity of peoples, languages and religions – was a unitary civilization. In the tenth century al-Biruni equated Indian civilization with all the lands between the Himalayas and Cape Comorin. The fourteenth-century poet Amir Khusro (an Indian Muslim of Turkish descent) speaks movingly of his love of his country, India, which he says includes people who speak Sindhi, Punjabi and Bengali, but also Tamil, Telugu and Kannada: all inhabit this 'paradise on Earth'. A similar idea of India can be found in the writings of Akbar's biographer Abul Fazl, even though the Mughals never extended their rule over the south of the subcontinent.

The British Empire on which the sun proverbially never set. But the British trade network stood or fell by their possession of India.

The strong perception far back in time, then, is of a broad cultural unity. The British would make their own vital contribution to this. Look at any map of India in the British handbooks of the Raj, and you will see pink covering the lands from Burma to Baluchistan and from Bhutan to Kerala, bounded by the natural frontiers of the sea, the Khyber, the Himalayas and the eastern jungles. Within the map, though, is the image of one of the most ingenious and adaptive empires in history, an immense patchwork loosely embracing almost a quarter of the population of the planet. In different colours are an amazing 675 feudatory and independent princely states (of whom seventy-three were ruled by rajas 'entitled to salutes of eleven guns or more'). Two of them, Hyderabad and Kashmir, are each the size of a large European country. This was the British solution to the diversity of India: an incredible political sleight of hand. An arrangement so extraordinary that it is hard to believe that it actually existed on the ground rather than just in the mind. But it was India.

Jewel in the Crown

Astonishingly, even at the peak of their empire, the British were able to rule the most populous region on Earth with just 50,000 troops and a quarter of a million administrators. Most of the day-to-day working of the empire was done by Indians, so they depended entirely on Indian cooperation; and as soon as that was withdrawn, the story was over for an empire acquired, as it was said in a disingenuous British understatement, 'in a fit of absent-mindedness'. That moment came with Indian disillusionment after the First World War, in which a million Indians fought for the king emperor and 50,000 died, and was confirmed by the massacre of Sikh demonstrators at Amritsar in 1919, from which the Indian perception of British fair play, goodwill and justice never quite recovered.

This is not to deny the complex and profound legacy of the British: above all, the English language, but also English ideas of secular law, education and constitutional government, the first attempt comprehensively to solve one of

ABOVE

Cavalry of the Queens Own Regiment alongside native sepoy troups of an Indian prince. The regiment went out to India in 1857 to crush the so-called mutiny.

the great issues of Indian history – the source of secular authority. For all the political struggles since 1947, Indian democracy has been a remarkable success in sustaining an open society and making astonishing inroads in such a short time into the deep-seated injustices of the caste system. In sixty years the idea of secular democracy has powerfully taken root.

Another legacy was practical: the communications network. India is a huge country; it is a 1000-mile journey by rail from Delhi to Calcutta, and the same distance from Calcutta down to Madras. Such developments also helped shape the political and psychological unity of India: indeed, perhaps the very possibility of a single Indian state only arose as a workable idea because the British made it so. But perhaps the most fateful legacy of the British was to open India irrevocably to a wider world: to force Indians to redefine their age-long civilization in terms of the secular ideals of the West.

The freedom movement

In Calcutta in 1835, as we saw earlier, Lord Macaulay published his far-reaching edict on education. A black name among Hindu nationalists, Macaulay believed in the 'immeasurable superiority' of the British and their culture. His famous remark that 'a single shelf of a good European library is worth the whole native literature of India' was the product of profound ignorance, but his recommendations on the need for a Western education for the Indian elite were pointedly designed to facilitate more thoroughgoing social transformation in India. English, not Persian, would now be the language of government. But from that moment, of course, it was inevitable that the self-professed ideals of European Enlightenment should be applied by Indian intellectuals to their own country, mediated by the rich teachings of their own tradition. The Indian freedom movement was the result: the greatest anti-colonial movement in history. The driving force, the Indian National Congress, was founded in 1885 with the initial, limited object of gaining a greater share in government for educated Indians. In the almost thirty years since the Mutiny they had seen for themselves the failure of British government in many key areas, but especially in the basic one of providing food and security to the population.

In the National Library in Delhi are stored the day-to-day administrative records of this period. In the basement, miles of shelving are stacked with yellowing files of telegrams, reports and memoranda from revenue inspectors and district collectors; and walking along them, the most striking and shocking fact is how many of these files are about one topic: 'famine'. These were very hard times for the ordinary Indian people. The last four decades of the Victorian

*The first session of
the Congress Party in
Bombay, 1885. In the
middle is the lone Briton,
A. O. Hume, the rebel
in the Raj.*

era coincided with a disastrous phase in the world climate: what happened was
nothing less than a series of late Victorian holocausts. From Bengal down to the
south, India was caught up in a cycle of global famine that began with the
failure of the El Niño world climate system. It started in 1866 in Orissa, a
disaster remembered with painful immediacy in the great autobiography of
Fakir Mohan Senapati, who was a mission teacher at the time: 'To this day,' he
wrote later, 'people in Orissa have never forgotten this terrible catastrophe:
3 million people died in one year, and there were 6 million homeless. The roads,
the bathing ghats, the fields, the jungles, wherever you went you saw dead
bodies. Fifty years have passed and it remains engraved on my mind.'

The Congress Party was founded in the midst of all this, after the great
drought and famine in the south in the late 1870s, in which 8 million died, and
during the series of famines that ravaged Bengal in the 1870s and 1880s. The
initial impetus came from a Briton, the remarkable Allan Octavian Hume. In
the view of one of today's leading Indian historians, after Gandhi, Hume is one
of most important influences in the freedom movement. Forgotten now in
Britain, this great figure in modern Indian history was recently the subject of
a question on the Indian version of the TV quiz show *Who Wants to be
Millionaire?* Hume was the son of a Scottish radical. During the Mutiny he was
a young district administrator at Etawah on the Jumna, where he subsequently
undertook many social projects and is still remembered as something of a local
legend (the town square is still known as Hume Ganj). In later years he rose to
high office in the Raj as revenue inspector for agriculture. In that capacity he

Mahatma Gandhi's freedom march to the sea: his espousal of non-violent resistance would inspire many freedom fighters of the modern era.

saw something of the famines at first hand, and was horrified not only by the terrible suffering, but by the often callous disregard of the British government in its reluctance or slowness to shift surplus from one part of the country to another; in some regions not touched by famine grain was even shipped abroad. In his government role Hume had had the chance talk to many prominent Indians, and he was the initial connecting link between some of them. For this he would be attacked by Tories in London, one of whom suggested he should be hanged as a traitor.

The Congress Party held its first meeting in Bombay in 1885, in the middle of a crucial decade for the mobilization of Indian public opinion, when the British lifted press restrictions and hundreds of new newspapers appeared, most of them in the vernacular languages. A very broad church of radicals, socialists Hindus, Muslims and secularists, Congress did not at first set itself overtly against British rule, but initially pushed for greater representation, and only gradually was transformed into a more radical movement with the ultimate goal of self-rule.

The story of the Indian freedom movement from 1885 to 1947 has generally been told to the outside world through the powerful and seductive narrative of the Congress. Even Hollywood has turned the myth into a worldwide cinema epic (Nehru and Gandhi are, after all, among the greatest and most interesting figures in modern history). But, as always in history, there were other trajectories that could have taken India, and perhaps could still, on a different path. Representation of the different religious communities would become a particularly thorny issue. In 1906 some Muslim members split from Congress to form the Muslim League (see page 237). Then, in 1907, Congress split into two halves: Gandhi's mentor Gopal Krishna Gokhale's 'moderate faction' and the 'hot or hardline faction' of Bal Gangadhar Tilak, who supported direct action to overthrow the British and went to prison for it. Extremists, nationalists, secularists, Hindus and Muslims: the effort of keeping all on one track in the end proved too much for the Congress leadership. But after the First World War Mohandas Gandhi (another British-educated lawyer) became the dominant figure, with his appeal to Hindu popular discourse and his espousal of the key idea of *ahimsa*, non-violence. Under Gandhi's influence, Congress became the first integrated mass organization in the country, bringing together millions of people by specifically working against caste differences, untouchability, poverty and religious and ethnic boundaries. Although predominantly Hindu, it had members from virtually every religion, ethnic group, economic class and linguistic group. By the 1930s Congress could claim to be the true representative of the Indian people, and under Nehru's presidency formally declared as its goal *poorna swaraj* – complete independence.

Partition: freedom but division

By the early 1930s it was obvious to most observers in Britain too that there was no way India could remain British, despite Churchill's blusterings and the rabid and racist polemics of the likes of Lord Rothermere and the right-wing British press. The issue then at stake was not whether India would be free, but what that India would be. The India beloved of Amir Khusro? The India made patchwork reality by the British? An Indian federation of semi-autonomous states? Or a divided India? In the 1930s the united India that was the Congress dream was threatened by new developments that would have the greatest significance for India, but also impinge upon a wider world in the modern era.

Muslims made up nearly a quarter of British India. Their coreligionists, as we have seen, had been the rulers in the north for several centuries. But the British deposition of the last Mughal in 1858 had left them disinherited and fearful of the political power of a Hindu majority who had not always been well treated by their Muslim overlords. A new Islamic consciousness had already shown itself in the 1857 rebellion, and the future of Islam in a post-British India was already being canvassed in the radical *madrasahs* of Deoband. Back in 1900 the British had chosen to make the official language of India's most populous region, United Provinces, Hindi rather than Urdu, written in Devanagari, not Arabic, script. With this, many Muslims grew more and more concerned that in a future time they might be dominated by the Hindus who would 'suppress Muslim culture and religion'. One British official at the time reported to his masters that many Muslims saw their destinies as completely separate and thought that 'no fusion of the two communities was possible'. The great issue that had preoccupied Akbar had returned to haunt India.

In response to these events, the Muslim League was founded in Dhaka in 1906, to represent Muslim interests in the forthcoming liberation struggle. Among those who left Congress to join it was yet another British-educated lawyer, Mohammed Ali Jinnah, a secular Shia who was destined to play a central role in the history of modern India. Congress had always worked to draw Muslims to its cause, but was often accused of being 'too Hindu', though some eminent Muslims remained committed throughout to its secular goals, including the philosopher, poet and educationalist Maulana Abul Kalam Azad, who remained all his life a supporter of Hindu–Muslim unity and who was the first minister of education in free India. In the end, events unfolded, as they often do in history, partly by accident rather than design. The idea of Muslim separatism was pushed first of all as a bargaining counter for seats in parliament, then as a negotiation for autonomous Muslim states within a federation; only later still did it become a serious demand for an independent country.

ABOVE

Nehru (standing) and Maulana Azad (seated far left) in April 1942.

It is a little-known paradox, though, that the idea of a separate country for Muslims was first mooted by a Hindu nationalist in 1924. At that time Jinnah and the Muslim League were still fighting for an Indian federation, with Muslims guaranteed a third of parliamentary seats. The fateful moment came in 1928, when Congress offered the League only a quarter of the seats. Compromise then would perhaps have changed the course of Indian history. For Jinnah, though, it was a 'parting of the ways'.

Whether Partition could or should have been avoided is a moot point that has been agonized over by many Indians and Pakistanis ever since. Indeed, from time to time one still reads articles in Indian newspapers that canvas the possibility of reunification. This is especially strongly argued by those who believe that Partition came about because of British realpolitik. Did the British tacitly approve it because it would help them divide and rule in the post-war, cold war world? Full publication of the papers in the last forty years at least absolves the British of that. Partition was really the result of multiple failures: the failure of Congress and the Muslim League to make concessions, and the failure of the British to act up to their historic responsibilities. The historical parallels are instructive. When the American states debated in 1776, the powerful ones conceded rights and powers to the small in order to achieve the Union. The goal of Congress was a united India, but in the end they were unable to make the concessions that would perhaps have got it. Jinnah, the brilliant but intractable Muslim leader, formerly a convinced nationalist, argued himself into a corner. The British, their power and sense of destiny broken by the Second World War, wearily gave up responsibility for their legacy and agreed to the Partition of India, separating the Muslim majority areas around the fringes of the subcontinent, including Sind and western Punjab, heartland of India's first civilization.

The British deadline for Independence was originally set for June 1948, but already Hindus and Muslims had clashed violently and bloodily in the northwest and Bengal. Beset by the growing threat of disorder, the British rushed the date forward to 14/15 August 1947. Fearing the reaction on the ground, the British didn't reveal the exact line of demarcation until the next day. In the Punjab the Sikhs who were divided by the line immediately took up arms to defend their own community. Meanwhile, Hindus and Muslims, often former neighbours, turned against each other amid rumour and hysteria. The result was terrible bloodshed and the largest migration in history, as 11 million people quit their ancestral villages and fled for their lives across the invisible border drawn up by a foreign power that was no longer present. The exact death toll will never be known; often estimated at one or two million, it may well have run into hundreds of thousands.

So the Muslim League got their independent country. Pakistan formally became an Islamic republic in the constitution of 1956, though this was not quite what Jinnah had planned: he kept his palatial 1930s' bungalow on Malabar Hill in Bombay (it is still owned by his family), fondly imagining that he might spend part of his retirement there, which only shows how badly he misread the outcome. Pakistan began as two parts, the eastern one, East Bengal, having nothing in common except religion with the lands to the west that

Nehru and Gandhi are blessed by Rama in a painting from the period of the freedom movement. To Nehru's discomfort Gandhi had promised to bring back the 'rule of Rama'.

comprised Baluchis, Punjabis, Pathans and Sindhis. Separated by 2000 miles, East and West Pakistan were never a plausible state, and the East went its own way in the war of 1974, supported by Indira Gandhi's government, becoming Bangladesh, the seventh largest country in the world (Pakistan is the sixth). Meanwhile, a large portion of the Muslim population of British India remained in independent India, though the bitter aftermath of Partition has left many of them an increasingly disadvantaged part of the population. India today is the second largest Muslim country in the world, with around 180 million Muslims. Not surprisingly, many have since wondered what all the suffering was for.

Independent India

Just before midnight on 14 August 1947, Nehru made his long-awaited speech, shot through with pride and regret: 'Long years ago we made a tryst with destiny, and now the time comes when we shall redeem our pledge, not wholly or in full measure, but very substantially. At the stroke of the midnight hour, when the world sleeps, India will awake to life and freedom ...'

Initially, hard times followed Independence. The fiscal balance sheet of the British had seen India, one of the two greatest world economies in the sixteenth century, slump to 3 per cent of world GDP by the early 1900s. The austerities of the early years were exacerbated by the Congress government's self-imposed socialist economic model and Gandhian ethic of self-sufficiency. Famine struck as late as the 1960s. The modernizing of India's 'great tradition' made slow progress until the opening up to foreign investment in the early 1990s. Since then there has been a dramatic rise in India's standard of living and economic power, which is predicted to overtake even the USA by the late 2030s. The twenty-first century, then, will see the old Asian giants returning to their place in history.

An important issue since Independence has been the battle over India's identity. The narrative of Indian history shaped by Congress during the freedom movement was created by Western-educated, English-speaking lawyers and emphasized secularism and Hindu–Muslim unity. Since Independence, and especially in the last two decades, this narrative has been contested, often bitterly. In Nehru's great book *The Discovery of India* (1956) the heroes are enlightened leaders like Akbar, whose idea of India was pluralist and tolerant – hence the importance attached to the Buddhist emperor Ashoka (rediscovered only after 1919), whose lion capital became the emblem of India, and whose wheel of dharma replaced Gandhi's spinning wheel (to the mahatma's displeasure) on the national flag.

But, as always, there are other histories. The majority of India's people are Hindu, and already in the nineteenth century a nascent Hindu nationalist movement saw the British occupation as the catalyst for the end of Muslim power in India and the coming of Hindu rule once the British had gone. The partial failure of the secular ideal in Partition was now to problematize Islam within India for the first time. For if Partition had been on religious grounds, and if Pakistan was an Islamic state, then was India, as Congress asserted, a secular state, or was it really a Hindu country? For Hindu nationalists the answer was obvious. These questions were already insistent at the moment of freedom. Gandhi, who (to Nehru's disquiet) had promised to restore the Ramraj, the golden age of Rama, was assassinated by a Hindu for pandering to Muslims. And this sectarian divide has continued to influence Indian politics

ABOVE

In the shadow of the mahatma: Indira Gandhi and her son Rajiv. Nehru's daughter, Mrs Gandhi suspended democracy in the emergency of 1974, but in a signal display of its resilience Indian demo-cracy was strong enough to throw her out.

over the last twenty years, during which even the terms of India's secular constitution have been called into question.

The main opponent of Congress became a Hindu nationalist party, the BJP, which was founded in 1980 but grew out of earlier 'Hindutva' parties, such as the Hindu Mahasabha (which began in 1915 as a response to the Muslim League), and more hardline organizations, such as the militant RSS (founded 1925) and the VHP (1966). The BJP's rapid rise in the late 1980s was predicated on historical arguments about Hindu–Muslim history (supported and contested by opposing groups of professional historians and archaeologists). They mobilized support around the issue of the destruction of Hindu temples by Muslim rulers in the Middle Ages, focusing in particular on a mosque in Ayodhia alleged to have been built on top of a demolished Hindu temple by Babur, the founder of the Mughal dynasty. Dangerously tapping into communal tensions, the leader of the BJP rode a Toyota truck converted into Rama's chariot on a rabble-rousing pilgrimage across northern India to 'liberate' the birthplace of Ram at Ayodhia. This issue, which, as it turned out, was based on a fantasy of the past, was to threaten the very fabric of the body politic, as Nehru himself had accurately foreseen in 1950. The destruction of the mosque by a mob in 1992 generated an atmosphere of fear and violence that intermittently spilt over into horrific killings, as in Gujarat in 2002. When they became the leaders of the government in the late 1990s the BJP sponsored an archaeological dig on the site of the destroyed mosque to prove the truth of the myth, but, ironically, the dig proved that there had been no significant structure on the site before the Middle Ages: it had not been an early location of the Rama cult. A salutary lesson for those who mix myth and politics.

India Inc.

Unexpectedly, given the increasingly favourable economic climate, the BJP Hindu nationalists were defeated in the 2003 national elections, and the old Congress consensus returned to office to preside over India's economic 'miracle'. These dramatic economic changes had begun in the same year as the Ayodhia disaster, but their long-term effects will reshape our world. To avoid national bankruptcy the then prime minister, Narasimha Rao, dropped Nehru's socialist protectionist economics and opened India up to foreign investment, reformed its capital markets, and deregulated domestic business. Soon Pepsi and Coke could be found on stalls even in India's remotest villages. The final rejection of Gandhi's self-sufficiency ideas has caused some introspection; the biggest Bollywood hit of 2006 even brought the mahatma back to offer guidance

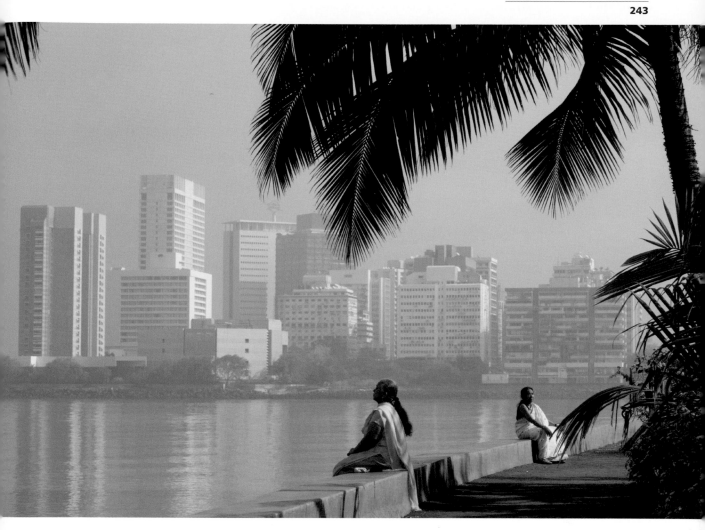

to India's new 'It' generation! Tremendous problems no doubt remain, especially in caste inequalities, rural poverty, environmental degradation and overpopulation. But the world's largest democracy is now firmly set on the path of growth and change, and will go about it in the way that Indian people have always done – adopting what is useful from the outside and holding on tenaciously to the old goals of life inherited from their past.

Unity and diversity

'You have to remember that "India" is your name for us,' says my journalist friend Ravi, expansive and jovial in an extravagantly patterned weekend *kurta*. We are sitting on the steps below the Great Mosque in Delhi: good-natured

ABOVE

Eternal India and its modern incarnation. With population boom and environmental problems, the country's exraordinary growth is not without its dangers, but India has always had an uncanny ability to let the old coexist with the new.

ABOVE

*India's headlong rush
into consummerism has
provoked much
introspection. Will the
old values survive?*

crowds are pouring out after Friday prayers; shoppers are milling around the clothes stalls and *dharbas* (roadside restaurants); boys are selling cheap watches and laminated posters of the Kaaba, the Taj and London's Big Ben. Around us are smoky fires heaped with sizzling kebabs.

Our name for us is Bharat, which has a very different meaning from India. In India time is linear. In Bharat it is circular, mythic. They stand for two different mindsets; and Indian people, even the lowliest, move comfortably between the two. Multiple identities have been part of our history for thousands of years. And these identities are perfectly comfortable with both the ancient and the modern. There is no stigma for a nuclear scientist to worship Ganesh, the elephant-headed god – in fact, we all love him. India has gone through many ups and downs. We have known terrible poverty, but we have great riches from our past. We are comfortable with our culture.

Ravi gestures to the crowds around him:

> India is a modern construct – a creation of the British that was made political reality by the freedom movement. Essentially, India was a fantastic, supremely aesthetic and ethical idea dreamt up by a handful of outstanding nationalists, chief among them Nehru, a child of modernism and rationality. He saw the future of India as a grand fusion of West and East. He wanted to cut across ancient allegiances, those encoded memories built up over thousands of years. That past to him was a bar to progress: the iniquities of ignorance, superstition, the caste system and untouchability were all gross inequalities. Democracy and secularism, he thought, would free people from the weight of the past. And despite Partition and secession wars, they did it: they created an allegiance. And about religion surely Nehru was right. In a land of so many religions and 33 million gods, secularism is the only protection for human rights. In any case, is religion the way we should be defined? You know, in the 1991 census, for the first time, they asked a series of questions about religious belief. The interesting thing was, whether Hindus Muslims, Christians, Jains or Parsees, people agreed on most things. In fact, more than 90 per cent of people agreed on what they did and what they believed. Whatever you believe, if your allegiance is to India then you are Indian.

'But there have been scary moments,' I reply. 'The emergency of Indira Gandhi, the Sikh rebellion, Ayodhia. Look at Gujarat in 2002.'

> But still it worked. Democracy has taken real root. And perhaps India's economic isolation till the 1990s – Nehru's socialist experiment – played its part. It may have held back the material and social advancement of the Indian people, but it preserved the older ways longer than otherwise could have taken place had there been a headlong rush to modernity and consumerism. When India joined the global market in the 1990s they didn't throw the baby out with the bath water.

'And after all, in the 2004 election,' I say, 'didn't the Indian people go back to a version of Nehru's model?'

Ravi laughs:

> Look, when Sonia Gandhi, the widow of Rajiv Gandhi, Nehru's grandson, who like his mother and grandfather had been prime minister, stood down as PM-in-waiting after the 2004 election, you saw the unlikely situation of an Italian Catholic woman as prime minister-elect, giving way to a Sikh swearing the oath to a Muslim president, in a majority Hindu nation. Now I ask you, where else on Earth could that happen?

By way of an ending

Our last shooting day is in Delhi. At sunset, as the May heat slackens, I climb the minaret at the great congregational mosque, the Jama Masjid, to look down over the teeming streets of the old city. Our journey has taken us tens of thousands of miles and we have seen the marks of waves of Indian history over tens of thousands of years. Great civilizations, it seems to me, develop responses over time, rather like a cultural immune system that enables them to absorb the shocks and wounds of history, and to utilize its gifts. The history of India is a tale of incredible drama, of great inventions and phenomenal creativity, and of the biggest ideas. To observe the story of India is to see the story of the human race itself in our imperfect efforts, as the Hindu scriptures put it, to gain worldly wealth, virtue and love, and eventually, if we are lucky, to achieve enlightenment.

From the top of the minaret, looking towards the sunset, I can clearly see the darkening profile of The Ridge, where the British, in the steaming summer of 1857, hung on grimly before exacting their terrible revenge on the city. To the east, lit up by the last light, is the Red Fort, where Independence was declared. Below us evening crowds stream down Chandni Chowk, the great bazaar street, after Friday prayers. Seeing this seething, exhilerating vision of humanity, a last thought comes to mind. The subcontinent is the most populous area of the world, the most rich and complex linguistically and genetically. Nowhere else can you see so clearly, as we approach what may be the most challenging decades humanity has ever faced, what the big story of human history really is. How we all started off as brothers and sisters, spread out across the world, created societies, achieved power and domination, erected our fences of imagined difference – language, ethnicity and religion – but now, in the end, must – and surely shall? – come back together again.

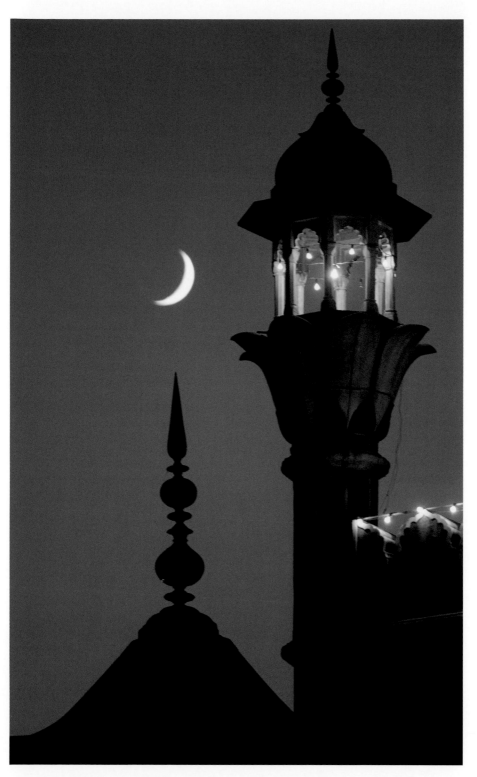

A crescent moon over the Jama Masjid mosque, Delhi. For all the upheavals during and since Independence, Indian democracy has shown a remarkable ability to hold its many communities together.

With love to
Jyoti and Minakshi
Nagaratinam, 'Tatta', Punnidah, Shanti,
Chitra, Akila, Kartik and Sivakumar,
Lakshmi Vishwanathan and Sushila Ravindranath

Acknowledgements

For a project long in the making I have many debts. First I would like to thank the Government of India, the staff of the Ministry of External Affairs, and the Archaeological Survey of India for their great help in facilitating the filming. In London I must especially thank the High Commissioner of India Kamalesh Sharma and Mrs Babli Sharma who went out of their way to help and encourage us; also the then Indian Minister of Culture and Director of the Nehru Centre in London, Dr Atul Khare. At Air India, staff were unfailingly helpful over all our journeys. Thanks also to the staff at the National Museum in Delhi, and at the museums of Patna, Sarnath, Mathura, Calcutta, Allahabad, Chennai and Tanjore, and to the Asiatic Society in Calcutta and the National Archive in Delhi. The Vice-Chancellor of the University of Madurai kindly facilitated our shooting their genetics programme. Saregama generously allowed us to use some of A.R. Rahman's compositions in the films. In Pakistan, I am grateful to the Archaeological Survey of Pakistan, to Orya Maqbool Jaan, to Raees Abbas Zaidi, to Jalil Abbas the then Minster of Culture, and to the staff of the Museums at Taxila and Peshawar, and the sites at Harappa and Takht-i-Bai.

At home, at the British Library Catriona Finlayson and her colleagues opened that wonderful resource for shooting and provided much research material; at Imperial College London Dr Sanjiv Gupta showed us the long view; at the British Museum Richard Blurton, Joe Cribb, and Liz Errington generously answered queries and lead us into new directions. Professor Nick Sims-Williams shared the excitement of his Kushan discoveries. In India, I would like to thank Prof R. Pitchappan, Irfan Habib, D.N. Jha, A. Prasad, S.P. Gupta, and S. Mehrotra, for their help and insight; Prof Ihsan Ali was our guide to the archaeology of the North West Pakistan; and Zahoor

Durrani, again our host in Peshawar, enthused us with his knowledge and passion. Thanks, too, to Shereen Ratnagar and Nayanjot Lahiri for talking on the phone about their work; Lolita Nehru at a dinner in London, Indira Peterson in a Tanjore garden; and Romila Thapar for kind words of advice to a young beginner many years back. It cannot be too strongly stressed that none of the above bear any responsibility for any errors of fact or interpretation that may be in this book: there are many contentious topics, such as the 'Aryan' invasion, or the interpretation of Islam and Hinduism in the Middle Ages to name but two, and the conclusions drawn are mine alone; one hopes that a work of popularization has not fallen too far short of their high standards. On location, my thanks to Sandhya Mulchanani and Rakshander Jalil; Prof Dhiditi Biswas; Prof R. Balasubrahmaniam; Prof B.B. Lal; Shashi Tharoor; Dr Ajit Prasad at Patna; Prof Harbans Mukhia at Panipat; Aggamaha Bhadanta Gyaneshwar at Kushinanaghr; William Dalrymple and Mahmood Farooqi; Prof Mridula Muckerjee; Profs Sathyabama and Pandian in Chennai; Dr A Sivakkolundu; Dr S. Suresh; Dr Pradhan and his colleagues in Orissa; R. Krishnamurthy; Drs Selvakumar and Shajan in Kerala; Ambika Shukla in Delhi; Ranjeet Choudary and his family in Benares; Bhikku Bodhipala at Bodhgaya; Mahathero Wathai in Sarmath; Kunwar Rani Kulsum Begum and her husband Rajkumar Amir Nakheer Khan in Lucknow and their family and friends with whom we spent a memorable Eid; Dr Liladhar Gupta and his family who showed us the ancient traditions of Ayurveda in Mathura. In Kerala, Vinod Bhattathiripad and Namudiri community; in Allahabad Rustom Gandhi and family, Shantum Seth in Rajgir and Bodgaya for his wisdom and his good company; Pankaj Mishra in Simla; Prof Sriram

Mehrotra at Etawah Simla and Bareh: Ed Moulton in Calgary.

It is a pleasure also to thank the Maharajas of Jodhpur, Tanjore and Benares, their staff and secretaries for whom no trouble was too great. In Rajisthan, Munnu Kasliwal at the Gem Palace in Jaipur was incredibly obliging and knowledgeable. In the South I am grateful for their many kindnesses, and for the extraordinary access they gave us, to the priests of the Minakshi temple at Madurai and to the shrines at Tiruvannamalai and Tanjore; and the priests, oduvars and devotees at the lovely temple of Tiruvengadu.

To my many friends at Chidambaram, thanks yet again to the community of Dikshithars, to the Shiva-Shakti dance school, and to M. Nagaratinam and family for their loving kindness and for first initiating an outsider into the ancient traditions of the pathways of the Tamil saints. Lakshmi Vishwanathan in Chennai, as always, was a much valued sounding board!

In Benares thanks to the staff of the Rashmi Guesthouse which has been a home from home: it is hard to think of a nicer place to stay. The same goes for the Hotel Finaro in Allahabad, a haven for twenty years.

In Pakistan, my thanks to Umer Mumtaz for all his hard work and good humour, to J. Mark Kenoyer, and to Dr Muhammad Hassan at Harappa. It is a great pleasure to thank Zahoor Durrani once more and a real delight to be back in Multan again and see the Gardezis: Sultan, Hur and all the family. Thanks too to Imam Bukhari and family at the Jama Masjid Delhi; and the Devanasthapathy family at Swamimalai who showed us the ancient art of the bronze casters. Further afield, in Iraq, my thanks to Lt General Sir Rob Fry, and to Captains Harry Sherwood and Tony Aguilar from the US Army. In Turkmenistan Prof Tim Williams led us to Prof Victor Sarianidi and his wonderful team out at Gunur Tepe.

Last of all, I must express my thanks and deep respect to HH the Dalai Lama for sparing the time to talk to us about the historical legacy of Buddhism and to give us his unique insights into the life of the greatest Indian.

On the film making side, our great production team in Delhi who fixed and enabled the whole project on the ground were Earthcare Films, and I cannot praise them enough: thanks to Madhurima and Krishnendu Sen Bose, Rahul Pal, Mohit Rastogi and Carolyn Syangbo and also to Jamyang Thinley and Kelsang Gyari from Middle Path who were unstintingly kind and supportive. Special thanks too to Sakeeb Ahmed, our second camera and camera assistant; a key and unflappable member of our team throughout. In Chennai our friend Sentharamarai Kannan organized our southern shoots with his customary phenomenal energy and flexibility; Koushik Chatterjee set up things in West Bengal and Rajasthan.

At the British end, Jeremy Jeffs did an incredible job both directing and shooting the series for which he deserves much thanks and great praise; and Rebecca Dobbs produced and oversaw the series, as ever our insightful and always enabling *guru*. Callum Bulmer recorded the sound and took many of the stills in the book; Gerry Branigan the editor did a wonderful job making sense of everything while adding his own lyrical perspective, ably assisted by Aleks Nikolic; while Sally Thomas, as always, did a stirling job managing the production. Howard Davidson wrote the beautiful and haunting music, sung by Jatinil Banerjee and recorded by the Royal Philharmonic Orchestra. On the team over the eighteen months of shooting and editing were Sonali Chaudhury, Kevin Rowan, Stefania Buonajuti, Sheila Marshall, Amber Tufail, Jonathan Page, Fatima Rizvi Tamsin Ranger, Claire Cluskey, Genevieve Harrison, Aaron Young, Aleks Nicoli and Ed Radford. Post production all took place at 'Envy' managed by the incomparable Jannine Martin – special thanks to Bob Jackson for the stunning surround sound. Our office computer maestro John Cranmer also did the great maps for the films. Brendan McGinty did the stunning time lapses, Chris Krupa the terrific graphics and Paddy Mark directed the extra sequences; Jatinder Verma, Sasha Behar, Robert Mountford and Claudia Mayer at Tara Arts performed some of the legendary texts. Thanks to all, and to all friends of Mayavision, past and present, around the world in the 25th year of its life as a small and eccentric independent film company still producing quality programmes in a world where the big corporates rule. And farewell, too, to Bhaskar Bhattacharyya, a founder member of our company who died in India during the period of making this series.

At BBC2, a special thanks to Martin Davidson for his wise advice, his enthusiasm and his encouraging guidance, and to Emma Swain, Krishan Arora, Roly Keating and Jana Bennett for their support. In the States CPB saw the point, and were an invaluable support in starting the project off; and at PBS we relied on our old friends Leo Eaton, John Wilson and Sandy Heberer – thanks to them and all our colleagues in the US, including, Jennifer Lawson and Kathy Quattrone with whom we first talked over this series. On the book: my agent Lavinia Trevor, and Pru Cave, Lara Heimert at Basic Books, and at BBC Books, Linda Blakemore and Eleanor Maxfield achieved the almost impossible guided by Martin Redfern who held his nerve to see the whole project through from start to finish in six months while we were still filming in India!

Finally, I must once more thank my family who have supported and enriched me through this demanding but exhilarating time: fortunately they all love India as much as I do. My wife Rebecca and I first travelled together in India twenty years ago and I cannot imagine a better travelling companion. Without her love, energy, insight and comradeship, none of this would have been possible. My daughters Jyoti and Mina, always sources of realism and good humour, kept things down to earth. To them my thanks go beyond words.

Further Reading

There's a last ritual at the end of a long filming project – emptying the rucksack for that very last time when you get back home. Spread over the floor is all the traveller's clutter: the mosquito net, the old copies of *India Today*, pilgrim guidebooks, framed pictures and postcards of Hindu gods, chewed-up maps, and cheap dhotis. But with me the biggest pile is always books: all those irresistible purchases from Wheelers of Allahabad, Motilal Banarsidas in the Chowk in Varanasi, or the unmissable bookshops in Delhi's Khan Market. These books (for research but most of all for pleasure), lying on the floor amid the train tickets and cheap posters, and the brown paper packet of cloth from the Madurai tailors' bazaar, draw the eye like familiar friends and recall the delight with which one turned to them on distant shores or mountain tops, in crowded pilgrims lodges, or on late night station platforms. Reflecting on that, it seems to me that not only is there no need in a book of this kind to provide an academic bibliography, it is even undesirable. It is perhaps more helpful to list some books that gave me pleasure and insight, books that I carried with me in my rucksack, and which the reader might wish to carry in his or her own.

First, for a read on the road: *The Picador Book of Modern Indian literature* (ed Amit Chaudhuri, 2002). This is a brilliant idea brilliantly executed, an indispensable introduction to modern Indian literature – and more. It includes a selection of translations from modern vernacular Indian literature, about which most of us, I daresay, are shamefully ignorant.

Other sets of essays: Salman Rushdie and Elizabeth West, *The Vintage Book of Indian Writing 1947–1997* (1997), *India in Mind* (ed Pankaj Mishra, 2005) and that author's *Temptations of the West* (2006). Amartya Sen's *The Argumentative Indian* (2005) and his *Identity and Violence* (2006) are challenging and humane overviews of India's Great Tradition and its modern dilemmas. Another great pleasure on these travels has been traditional poetry: pride of place goes to the late A.K. Ramanujan's path-breaking translations of early Tamil poetry: *The Interior Landscape* (1967) and *Poems of Love and War* (1985). *The Purananuru*, a wonderful collection of ancient Tamil poems is now out in Penguin (ed G. Hart and H. Heifetz, 2002). The two most famous ancient Tamil epics are also available in Penguin: *Manimekhalai* (tr Alain Danielous, 1996) and *The Cilappatikaram the Tale of an Anklet* (tr R. Parthasarathy 1993). *The Civakacintamani* is untranslated: I used the edition of Book One by James Burgess (1865).

Of the later Tamil devotional poetry (still alive in Tamil Nadu) an old favourite is *Hymns of the Tamil Saivite Saints*, by F. Kingsbury and G. Phillips (1921); see too *Poems to Shiva* by Indira Peterson (1991) and *Songs of the Harsh Devotee* by David Shulman (1990), a guru to all who discover Tamil through translation.

A great Telugu collection of the 16th-century poet Dhurjati is *For the Lord of Animals* (ed H. Heifetz and V. Rao, 1987); wonderful Telugu courtesan songs are in *When God is a Custom* (tr A.K. Ramanujan, V. Rao and D. Shulman, 1994). A Kannada anthology *Speaking of Siva* by A.K. Ramanujan (1973) and his *Songs for the Drowning* (1993) is a great selection of the ninth-century hymns to Vishnu by Nammalvar. These devotional poems are still a living tradition all over India: the works of Kabir, Dadu, Mirabai, Guru Nanak and many others are easily available. In Bengal, Jayadeva's *Gitagovinda* is memorably translated by B. Miller, *Love Song of the Dark Lord* (1977).

On the southern oral tradition try *A Poem at the Right Moment* by V. Rao and D. Shulman (1997), and on oral folktales, *Folktales of India* by A.K. Ramanujan (Penguin, 1994). Many of the great texts of Indian history are easily available in translation: the *Rig Veda* for example by Wendy Doniger (Penguin, 1981), the *Ramayana* in *Rama the Steadfast* by J. and M. Brockington (Penguin, 2006). A fascinating series of essays on the diversity of the tradition is P. Richmann's *Many Ramayanas* (1991).

Modern retellings of the old stories are legion, but *Gods Demons and Others* by the novelist R.K. Narayan (1965 and later eds) is a good railway journey read, along with his longer retellings of the *Ramayana* and *Mahabharata*. The *Kamasutra* is published in Oxford World's Classics by Wendy Doniger and Sudhir Kakar (2002). Babur's Autobiography is published by Penguin (ed Dilip Hero, 2007). Among recent reflections on Indian history is Pankaj Mishra's brilliant *An End to Suffering* (2004) about the Buddha, and the rediscovery, Charles Allen's engaging *The Buddha and the Sahibs* (2002).

General questions of the psychology of Indian culture are treated in many works of Sudhir Kakar, on healing traditions, political and religious violence, and sexuality. His most recent came to my hands too late to use: S. Kakar *The Indians* (2006). The British story too is too vast to go into here: for a judicious recent overview, Lawrence James *The Rise and Fall of the British Empire* (1997), and for the British in the wider context, John Keay *A History of India* (2000). On the Freedom Struggle and Partition there is a vast literature, but a good start is Stanley Wolpert's biographies of Jinnah (1984), Nehru (1996) and Gandhi (2001) and his recent book on Partition *Shameful Flight* (2006), as well as H. Seervai's *Partition of India* (1994). See too Shashi Tharoor's *Nehru*, (2003)

For a broad sweep view of post Independence India, R. Guha's *India After Gandhi* (2007), and for the idea itself, Sunil Khilnani, *The Idea of India* (2003), and Irfan Habib *India – Studies in the History of an Idea* (2004).

Lastly, a few guidebooks and travellers' tales. My old copy of Diana Eck's *Benaras: City of Light* (1983) is falling apart after a dozen visits to that great city and still its pleasures are nowhere near exhausted. *The Last Bungalow* by A.K. Mehrotra (Penguin 2007) is a new anthology on Allahabad's rich modern and mythic history. There are many books on the seven cities of Delhi; Wiliam Dalrymple's *City of Djinns* follows wittily and effortlessly in that great tradition. On Agra and the Taj, Ebba Koch's *The Complete Taj Mahal* (2006) is indispensable and authoritative along with her *Mughal Architecture* (2002). On Mumbai: *Maximum City* by

Suketu Mehta (2004). On Lucknow, among many books by Rosie Llewellyn-Jones are *Lucknow Then and Now* (2003) and *A Fatal Friendship: The Nawabs, The British, and the City of Lucknow* (1985), to be found with other works in her *Lucknow Omnibus* (2001). There is a growing interest in the South now: for example, see *Temple Towns of Tamil Nadu* (ed George Michell, Marg, 1993). I have contributed to a recent study of one great southern religious centre: *Chidambaram* (ed V. Nanda, Marg, 2004) and my *Smile of Murugan* is reissued as *South Indian Journey* (Penguin, 2007). Lastly, Mark Tully *No Full Stops in India* (1994) is the view of a supremely knowledgable outsider and William Dalrymple's *Age of Kali* is an engaging read by the doyen of modern British writers on India.

Index

Copyright © Michael Wood 2007; First published in 2007 by Woodlands Books Limited, one of the publishers in The Random House Group Ltd.

Published by Basic Books,
A Member of the Perseus Books Group

Library of Congress Cataloging-in-Publication Data is available
ISBN–13: 978–0–465–00359–4
ISBN–10: 0–465–00359–1

10 9 8 7 6 5 4 3 2 1